Cherry Smiley is a radical feminist artist from the Nlaka'pamux and Diné Nations. She has worked on the issue of Missing and Murdered Indigenous Women and with survivors of the prostitution industry. She has written for *Globe & Mail*, *Policy Options*, and *Herizons*.

https://cherrysmiley.com/

NOT SACRED, NOT SQUAWS

Indigenous Feminism Redefined

Cherry Smiley

PINIFEX

We respectfully acknowledge the wisdom of Aboriginal and
Torres Strait Islander peoples and their custodianship of the
lands and waterways. Spinifex offices are located on Djiru,
Bunurong, Wadawurrung, Eora, and Noongar Country.

First published by Spinifex Press, 2023
Spinifex Press Pty Ltd
PO Box 5270, North Geelong, VIC 3215, Australia
PO Box 105, Mission Beach, QLD 4852, Australia
women@spinifexpress.com.au
www.spinifexpress.com.au

Edited by Susan Hawthorne, Pauline Hopkins and Renate Klein
Cover design by Deb Snibson, MAPG
Typesetting by Helen Christie, Blue Wren Books
Typeset in Minion Pro
Printed in the USA

A catalogue record for this
book is available from the
National Library of Australia

ISBN: 9781925950649 (paperback)
ISBN: 9781925950656 (ebook)

Acknowledgments

I'd like to acknowledge myself for not ever giving up on myself, even though sometimes I wanted to.

I'd also like to acknowledge my cats, Big Al and Lumiere, who also never gave up on me even though they judged me consistently and harshly; my partner/hiboux, Alexandre, who made sure I was loved and fed; my sister Sunny, my backbone and my Space Mountain co-pilot; my cousin and Sharknado connoisseur, Jared; my grandparents who were my parents, Nellie Blankinship and Victor Rettenbacher, who both passed away while I completed my PhD dissertation that became this book; Ane M., who changed my life by helping me learn how not to draw another face on top of my own face; all the incredible women I met and worked with on this project and all the incredible women I've met and worked with over the years; my co-conspirators at Women's Studies Online; my friends who are family: T.B., L.F., K.M. who reminded me not to give a fuck about you (them), J.L., A.F., R.V., and so many other incredible women.

I'd also like to acknowledge my former supervisors, Dr Monika Gagnon and Dr Yasmin Jiwani, who convinced me to come to Concordia University in the first place; My committee members Dr Amy Swiffen, Dr Elizabeth Fast, and Dr Elizabeth Miller; Dr Michael Markwick for his support during my defense; My women's advisory committee members Trisha Baptie, Jackie Lynne, Fay

Blaney, and Eden Green; And my sheroes Dr Susan Hawthorne and Dr Renate Klein.

This is for Taanis and for all women, everywhere.

Contents

List of Figures

KICK ASS GRANDMA:
a poem by cherry smiley

My grandma:

Threw rocks every year at the woodpecker who was pecking on her chimney because he was being too noisy too early in the morning.

Went after a young bald eagle with a broom because he was staring at her grandchildren through the window at night.

Threw grass snakes as far as she could by the tail so they couldn't eat little birds. Frogs, ok.

Threw rocks into the water to shut the frogs up because they were being too noisy too late at night.

Would shoot a .22 in the air to stop the owls from hooting at her.

Said no way she wasn't going to go into the woods by herself for days and fast.

Dug a hole with her brothers and sisters at the old home place to make sure they had a place to go and hide in a squatch emergency.

Asked why Elders don't just go sit in a corner then if they don't want menstruating women walking behind them.

Wouldn't let grandpa forget that half of everything belonged to her.

Gave advice like don't ever get married and always have money that he doesn't know about and I find all menfolk are problems somehow or another and why is he being stupid grandma because men are stupid hun.

Can never remember the Nlaka'pamux word for 'muskrat'.

Came first in her class to become a military policewoman during World War Two.

Would smuggle money she earned from fruit picking across the border in hair rollers on her head.

Never learned to drive a car but would drunk drive her walker on Christmas.

At 95 said she didn't want to go to activities at the senior's centre because she doesn't like old people.

Likes her old mill let's go to the beer parlour.

Is quiet and loud and small and big.

Is not afraid of anyone. Except ghosts, sometimes she's afraid of ghosts. Makes sense.

Introduction

This book is an action. It was conceived, written, edited, copy-edited, proofread, designed, and illustrated by women (Morgan, 1970, p. xiii).

This book is an action, a political action where revolution is the goal. It has no other purpose. It is not cerebral wisdom, or academic horseshit, or ideas carved in granite or destined for immortality. It is part of a process and its context is change (Dworkin, 1974, p. 1).

This book is an action and it was born from the rage I collected completing a PhD dissertation on prostitution. It's not a thought-experiment or postmodern intellectual exercise or another boring man-centred man-study. This research refuses the woman-hating status quo (i.e. patriarchy) in content and in structure and its primary goal is to contribute to feminist theorizing within the Women's Liberation Movement. Initially, however, this wasn't how I would've described what I was doing; it took a few years of doing it to realize what it was I was actually doing and then another year or two to find the courage to say it without fear or apology. The initial scope of my doctoral research project was much narrower than how it turned out: I started out researching prostitution and Indigenous women in Canada and New Zealand. As my research moved forward, however, the project became more broad, holistic, and interconnected as I learned how important bias, context, and purpose is when it comes to doing, analyzing, and communicating research—honesty and courage are so important in this process.

My research question reflects what I've learned and the ways my research has grown over the years: how does feminist knowledge of prostitution and responses to male violence against Indigenous women contribute to the construction of a decolonizing feminist methodology, theory, and practice? Building on the ground-breaking work of feminist theorists, activists, and Women's Studies practitioners[1] such as Renate Klein, Gloria Bowles, Maria Mies, Robin Morgan, Anne Stoler, Kathleen Barry, Andrea Dworkin, Janice Raymond, Melissa Farley, Jackie Lynne, and others, I develop a decolonizing feminist methodology and theory that prioritizes women's sex-based oppression and resistance—even Indigenous women's. Although I started in a different place with somewhat different intentions, this work has ended up being about the production of knowledge, academia, and the patriarchal world we live in; it's about honesty and courage and asking why and why not of others and most importantly, of myself. This work is joyfully and defiantly feminist and expressly political. The goal of this research is to contribute to furthering the aims of the Women's Liberation Movement—the most difficult, revolutionary and transformative purpose one can have.

The Beginnings of the Beginning

I began a PhD program in Communication Studies at Concordia University in 2015. I came to academia through feminist front-line anti-violence work. I worked as a collective member at Vancouver Rape Relief and Women's Shelter (VRRWS) in their rape crisis centre and transition house for battered women and their children where I

---

1   Women's Studies Practitioners are feminist women who are part of Women's Studies, as either students or teachers, and who work to also improve the conditions of women's lives as part of their research practice (Bowles and Klein, 1983). Women's studies practitioners are accountable to the Women's Liberation Movement outside of academia (Bowles and Klein, 1983).

gave support, information, and advocacy to women who had been assaulted by men. While at VRRWS, I learned to organize and advocate with Indigenous and non-Indigenous feminist women and groups to end prostitution and other forms of male violence against women, eventually becoming a collective member of the Aboriginal Women's Action Network (AWAN) and co-founding Indigenous Women Against the Sex Industry (IWASI). This important work provided a feminist foundation for my research, although I had started developing my research questions much earlier without knowing it. My research actually began when I was very small and continued, very messily and painfully, with my own direct and indirect experiences with the statistical horror stories told about Indigenous women in Canada. Although I didn't have a frame to make sense of, or words to explain, what I was experiencing at the time, this is when I began asking questions about the world around me. I kept asking questions and it wasn't until I was introduced to feminist theory as an undergraduate student that I began to find and imagine some answers to my questions that made sense; and it wasn't until I became active in the Women's Liberation Movement as a front-line anti-violence worker and activist that I was able to apply and build feminist theory in action.

When I began this PhD journey, I knew it wasn't going to be easy but I also knew ground had already been broken for feminist research in academia by the courageous feminists who had come before; I firmly believed that I could maintain, maybe even expand, the little bit of wiggle-room that radical feminists had created in academia with the development of Women's Studies programs in the 1960s and 1970s. This wiggle-room had given me confidence in the validity and usefulness of feminist methodology and theory in the manstitution of university; it allowed me to imagine pursuing a research project that I felt was important in a way that made sense to me. In 2015, I set about this PhD journey with the intention of using Indigenous feminist theory to examine the prostitution of Indigenous women in Canada as a process of ongoing colonization. Given Canada had just come through a constitutional challenge to prostitution laws that resulted in the 2014 *Protection of Communities and Exploited Persons Act* (PCEPA) and that the long-awaited National Inquiry into Missing and Murdered Indigenous Women and Girls ('the Inquiry') began in 2016, looking at connections between prostitution and Indigenous women was urgent and timely and Canadian governments and the Canadian public were paying attention. I began this PhD program aware of the difficulties of doing feminist research but excited and hopeful at the revolutionary possibilities feminism offered to academia, research, and to communities of women everywhere. At the other end of this PhD journey I have concluded that academia is terrible and I hate it. The general consensus is that the feeling is mutual—academia, as it stands, and I, are not a good fit for each other; actually, we're incompatible. How the heck did this happen? And why? And isn't this document that I'm reading right now born from a dissertation, also known as a giant-flaming-hoop you jumped through on your way to the academic stamp of approval known as doctorhood? To answer the second question: yes, shitty isn't it, oh the contradictions we live with.

The first question—how and why this happened—will be answered in this story of my dissertation, a process that almost killed me but a process that I survived in which I learned a lot of amazing things and that changed me in ways I'm still discovering. Now, including thoughts like these are probably not common practice in an academic dissertation, but I also know that some women aren't commonly found—alive, anyways—in academic settings, but here we are. To be extra clear, just in case there was any doubt, my dissertation was not a traditional document. I've never been good at doing things a certain way just because that's how they're supposed to be done and it turns out that it was important that not only the content, but also the structure of this work, reflect what I've learned as a formerly award-winning, once 'promising scholar' now 'SWERF' and 'TERF' whose "... views are literally killing our trans indigikin,"[2] "... an insult to the community"[3] who actually has the nerve to say and do things without apologizing at all,[4] let alone profusely. I should be ashamed of myself [5] but don't worry, I'm not.

Figure 1: "It's called garbage can."

Now That We're in the Middle Let's Start at the Beginning

Men disproportionately target Indigenous women for violence. For example, Statistics Canada found that 48% of Indigenous women who reported being assaulted by a current or former domestic partner, "... reported the most severe forms of violence, such as being sexually assaulted, beaten, choked, or threatened with a gun or a knife" (Brennan, 2011, p.10). As Indigenous women, the male violence we experience is

> ... not experienced as single incidents. It is cyclical. All too often, violence describes most of our lives. Even when we manage to create a safe environment in which to live our individual lives, the violence still surrounds us. Our friends, sisters, aunties, and nieces still suffer. The violence is inescapable (Monture-Angus, 1999, p. 69).

---

2   See Appendix A, Twitter grab 1.
3   See Appendix A, Twitter grab 2.
4   See Appendix A, Twitter grab 3.
5   See Appendix A, Twitter grab 4.

The male violence directed toward us as Indigenous women has a particular history and serves particular interests that are linked to not only patriarchy, but also to racism and capitalism in a process of colonization.

One face of the disproportionate amount of male violence committed against Indigenous women shows itself in the overrepresentation of Indigenous women in prostitution in Canada (Farley et al., 2005; Kingsley et al., 2000; Cler-Cunningham and Christenson, 2001; Conseil du Statut de la Femme, 2002; Krüsi et al., 2012). While men disproportionately harm Indigenous women through the inherent violence of prostitution itself, Indigenous women in prostitution are also disproportionately targeted by men for additional forms of violence such as beatings, stabbings, kidnapping or burnings. Given that the sex industry categorizes women according to a race- and class-based hierarchy (van der Muelen, 2013) and assigns women more-or-less value depending on their location within the hierarchy, this makes sense that men, who already disrespect women enough to pay them to engage in sex acts with them, would further exploit the inherent inequality of prostitution. This happens outside prostitution as well, as this is the same hierarchy that impacts all women—it's just encouraged, sexualized, and marketed within prostitution and pornography, making it easier to see and (one would think) harder to deny.

Original Documentary Research Plan

My original plan for my dissertation project consisted of making a feature-length documentary film with facilitation guide and written thesis that considered the prostitution of Indigenous women a key site in the historical and present-day examination of the links between colonization, patriarchy, and male violence against women in Canada. Initially, my plan was to use film as a method to disrupt representations and self-representations of Indigenous women to critically examine prostitution and international policy responses to this issue; investigate the connections between prostitution, colonization, and other forms of male violence within Canada and internationally; and gather potential solutions to the issues. I planned to interview prostitution survivors, prostitution survivor researchers, academics, and feminist advocates in Canada, New Zealand, and Australia to feature in the documentary. My project was to be guided by an academic supervisor and committee, as well as a women's advisory committee (WAC) that consisted of prostitution survivor researchers, advocates, and Indigenous leaders. The film and facilitation guide would be made available to organizations working on the issue of male violence against women for public screening and discussion. It all sounded really good and it was really good, until it wasn't.

I followed my research plan: I travelled in Canada and to New Zealand and Australia; I filmed interviews with prostitution survivors, prostitution survivor researchers, academics, and feminist advocates in each of these countries; and I was guided by an academic supervisory committee and a women's advisory committee. When it came time to put everything together into a documentary film, or even a series of short films, or any other version of video I could think of, *I didn't*. I chose not to, and it was a tough decision, especially considering I had all the footage I needed, all the recordings of the interviews I did, I had everything ready to go and all I needed to do was put the story together into a documentary film—and instead I stopped and changed direction. Over the course of this research project, I had already changed directions a few times, so it wasn't exactly a new process, but it was a decision fraught with all kinds of new anxieties and doubts and questions. I felt badly for asking women to share their stories with me and then making the decision not to share these stories as I had initially intended to, but presenting the interviews and footage I took in a nice little documentary package for evaluation of my doctoral worthiness just didn't sit right with me. As much as I worked with the footage and had a million false starts, I just couldn't feel ok with it. At this point in my research project, I was so disillusioned and so angry at academia. I took time to think and to reflect on my anger and to reevaluate my process, and I made the decision not to include the interviews I had filmed for this project, either as individual interviews or as part of a documentary film. I made the decision that these incredible stories I had on video wouldn't be presented to academia for academic evaluation; that this academic evaluation is not fair or good or appropriate to apply to the interviews I had; and that presenting my research as a video, or even as a series of videos, left out many important parts of the work I had done and didn't communicate everything that I had learned and that I wanted to share. I decided that academia does not deserve to evaluate the video interviews I'd filmed and had I gone ahead and made the documentary or a series of short films or any other kind of research-creation project with the footage, that's what I would be doing: submitting these women to be evaluated by academia—a manstitution—on academia's terms. I refused to do that. I decided that the interviews needed to be presented as part of the feminist relationship they reside in and contextualized as part of the Women's Liberation Movement. During the process of my research, I founded the online platform Women's Studies Online (WMST) in 2019:

> Based in Canada with global impact, Women's Studies Online is a platform for decolonizing feminist research, education, action, and community building. WMST is informed and inspired by the radical feminist politics that initially guided the creation of Women's Studies programs in universities across Canada and elsewhere. WMST builds on feminist theory to help women make sense of our lives and takes action by organizing with women for our collective liberation. We provide women with theoretical tools, practical skills, and a political network where we can further our feminist thinking, organizing, and action. We currently offer by-donation online short-courses for women who don't have time to take courses, lectures, and workshops and continue to grow (Women's Studies Online, n.d.).

I founded WMST because of increasing anger and frustration with the current anti-feminist and misogynist state of academia that disguises itself as 'progressive' and 'inclusive' and promotes itself as concerned with social justice which may well be the case, but social justice for whom? And what does social justice even mean? What I do know is that social justice is not feminist because women are not centred and feminist theory is not used in social justice discourse and action. So I guess in this sense, academia is being honest about its intentions—although I have to admit, it's a contradictory and confusing position to champion 'inclusion' when inclusion means everyone but women and everything but feminism. WMST is, unintentionally, what this dissertation looks like when its activated and it's in this explicitly feminist forum where the videos about prostitution that I create will eventually live. I will, with the permission of the women I interviewed, use the footage I have of their interviews to create short videos that I will use as part of Women's Studies Online when teaching about prostitution. This way, the footage will be used for the benefit of women and on women's terms.

I did, however, include stories and reflections about the time I spent in New Zealand and quotes from various filmed interviews throughout my dissertation and I have also included, in full, the anonymized transcript of a group interview I did with seven Indigenous women who had been in prostitution. Parts of this group interview were only audio-recorded as I didn't want a camera watching a process that I felt could be emotionally intense and transformative for the women involved. These women are, and were, absolutely incredible and their words are powerful. Together, their stories and analyzes indisputably describe the realities of the prostitution of Indigenous women in Canada.

The Women's Advisory Committee

I convened the WAC to provide overarching guidance, direction, and feedback for my doctoral project. The WAC is comprised of Indigenous and non-Indigenous prostitution survivor researchers, prostitution survivors, and feminist and Indigenous leaders. It was important for this project that the WAC was involved from the beginning to ensure their input helped to guide the project from its foundation up. The WAC functioned similarly to the academic advisory committee convened for this work in that women provided guidance and feedback to assist in the completion of the doctoral project; however, the WAC also provided community oversight and accountability. Some members of the WAC were also interviewed as part of this project and in that sense, 'wore two hats'. The role of the WAC wasn't to comment on individual interviews with themselves or others or the technical aspects of the work, but to provide overall direction for the project; that is, to provide feedback on the overarching methodology, themes, messages, and representations throughout the project. The roles of the WAC was clearly communicated to its members and this minimized the risk of WAC members attempting to influence individual aspects of the film, including (potentially) their own or others' contributions. The WAC's oversight of the project, including providing feedback on the scope of the research, on issues related to the representation of women on film and in research, and on the written components of the project ensured that participants are being portrayed in a respectful manner that recognized their experiences and knowledge.

The structure of the WAC changed over time. We had an in-person meeting at the very beginning of my PhD journey where we decided, as a group, on no set meeting schedule and that I would convene meetings when I found them to be necessary and keep WAC members updated on the progress of the work. We also decided at that first meeting to engage in negotiations with each other should a disagreement occur as to the direction of the work and to use a process of constructive criticism (Lyons, 1988) that focuses on behaviour, behaviour changes, and political reasoning in order to deal with any conflicts that may occur. In exchange for their expertise and participation for the duration of this project, I compensated each woman on the WAC monetarily. The WAC members are:

Trisha Baptie is trying to reframe the questions, assumptions, and analysis surrounding the world's oldest oppression, the commercial sexual exploitation (CSE) of women and girls or as it's more colloquially known, prostitution. She believes we must shift the focus, conversation and responsibility off the women and onto the mostly invisible side of the conversation: the men, or purchasers of sex. Having a 15-year history in CSE she uses her lived experience and analysis to implement real change. In 2014, Trisha was invited to help create this change by testifying at both senate and justice senate subcommittees on Canada's new prostitution laws that were passed December 2014, with her group formerly Exploited Voices now Educating (EVE) that she founded in 2009. She is now working and sitting on coalitions of like-minded groups to get the police to take the new laws seriously and get funding to help women and girls successfully leave CSE. In trying to end CSE, she also realizes we need to address the issues that drive women into prostitution poverty, sexism, racism, colonialism, mental health, addiction, the pornified culture we live in and other factors all of which she is well versed in.

Fay Blaney is a Homalco woman with over 40 years of experience as a community organizer and advocate for Indigenous women and girls.

Eden Green is an Anishinaabe woman with many years of experience as a front-line anti-violence worker.

Jackie Lynne, a Métis prostitution survivor, scholar, social worker and co-founder of Indigenous Women Against Prostitution, laid the groundwork for understanding the historical imposition of the European institution of prostitution in the lives of First Nations women in Canada. Her analysis examined how the church, state and early capitalism worked in tandem to create a sub-class of brown women to meet the white male demand of our bodies.

How I imagined the WAC to function as part of my research project wasn't how the WAC ended up working. I wasn't in contact with the WAC as a group or with some individual members as much as I intended to be. As I reflect on this process, I can see the very real impacts of patriarchy, racism, and capitalism and how these systems worked to disrupt our ability to come together regularly as a group. Historical and ongoing personal, family, or community crises, health and mental health issues, and a whole host of other issues impact our lives on a daily basis. This means sometimes the desire to reach out with a WAC update is there, but the energy to do so isn't—or maybe the very deeply-held belief that I don't matter and I'm actually wasting the time of these incredible women with my project update stops me from checking in—even when I know these women as sisters and as allies. These very real systemic consequences—the same ones we fight against—impact our ability to come together as women and as Indigenous women.

However, the WAC was, and continues to be, a foundationally important part of this research project in terms of accountability. Although I wasn't in as much contact with the WAC as a group as I intended to be, I was in contact with individual WAC members at different points throughout the project. I think this speaks to the strength of the relationships I have with these women and that I will continue to have. In that sense, creating a formal structure to ensure my accountability was actually unnecessary—not because I didn't need to be held accountable for my decisions and actions but because the relationships I have within and as part of the Women's Liberation Movement ensure that ongoing informal accountability measures are in place. When I met with the WAC for the first time, the first thing I said was something like "Ok. I'm getting a PhD out of this and you women aren't. Let's talk about this." We bounced around ideas including, for example, co-authoring academic papers and presenting together at academic conferences. Fay said that she was looking forward to seeing my reference list when my research was complete. This confirmed for me that the work would benefit others outside myself and outside of academia and also confirmed the importance of an intentionally feminist research process.

Outline of a Shapeshifting Thesis

My PhD journey meant stopping and starting; sometimes sprinting, sometimes crawling, sometimes falling on my face, and sometimes crying and screaming from anger and frustration as I navigated all manner of roadblocks and detours. This book feels as alive as I am at times (and sometimes that's not very), but to meet the requirements of doctorhood and to provide some structure and organization so this writing makes sense, here is an outline of what you're about to get yourself into:

In Chapter 1, I describe the historical and contemporary landscape as it relates to male violence against Indigenous women in Canada with a focus on 2007 onwards. This has, and continues to be, a period of heightened awareness and discussion about male violence against Indigenous women and prostitution. 2007 was the year in which lawyer Alan Young[6] launched a seven-year-long constitutional challenge to strike down Canada's prostitution laws and was also the year Robert Pickton was convicted of the murders of six women from Vancouver's downtown eastside (DTES), although he committed many more—Pickton himself claims to have murdered 49 women, some of whom he fed to the pigs on his farm in Coquitlam BC (House, 2016). The case gained global attention due to its horrific details and because many of the women murdered by Pickton were Indigenous and most were involved in prostitution. After the launch of *Bedford v. Canada* and Pickton's conviction, inquiries were held, research was done, reports were released, campaigns were launched, international human rights bodies intervened, rallies were held, laws were struck down, new laws were adopted, and Indigenous women called for a national inquiry into male violence against Indigenous women that finally came to fruition in 2016.

---

6   Many claim that the constitutional challenge was initiated by sex workers/former sex workers, but Young stated in the 2013 National Film Board of Canada documentary *Buying Sex* (Clarke et al., 2013) that the constitutional challenge to Canada's prostitution laws was his idea and that he simply had to find sex workers/former sex workers that he could list as applicants as in the case.

In Chapter 2, I discuss the limits of our current dominant definition of 'colonization' in Canada and examine the concept of 'colonization' from a sex-based perspective. This happened as a result of realizing about two-thirds of the way into my PhD that I had been doing my research upside-down. I had made a big mistake—what I'd done was too easily accept Indigenous theorizing about the concepts of 'colonization and 'Indigenous feminism' in Canada without considering that these concepts have been defined and theorized by men (Morgan, 1977) and what these sex-based 'blind spots' might mean for women. As my research continued, I realized there were significant contradictions I couldn't account for and so in order to use 'Indigenous feminist' theory to look at the prostitution of Indigenous women as a process of ongoing 'colonization', I had to take a few giant steps backwards and re-evaluate my work, my beliefs, what I knew, and what I thought I knew.

In Chapter 3, I describe the methodological foundations of my research, including what the heck happened and what I learned during the research process. I interviewed 16 women on-camera for this project across two different countries, conducted an online anonymous survey that sought participants from three different countries, and gave two public presentations about my research. I interviewed three groups of women: a) Indigenous women who had survived prostitution; b) Indigenous and non-Indigenous prostitution researchers, feminist advocates, front-line anti-violence workers, organizations working on the issue of prostitution, and women who had survived prostitution and other forms of male violence who were over the age of 18, were actively working on the issue of prostitution and/or other forms of male violence against women from a critical perspective, and agreed to have their names, images, affiliations, and analyzes shared publicly as part of the film, written components of the project, and any presentations or additional publications related to the research; and c) representatives of prostitution/sex work organizations and government and other institutions in their professional capacities.

All of the primary research participants were women. Two interviews were conducted in group settings and the rest of the interviews were done individually. All of the interviews, except for one of the groups, were filmed with the help of my soundperson and male partner of seven years, Alex. It was important for me that I had established close and trusting relationships with all the individuals helping me in the (turns out, non-) construction of the video documentary, from those assisting with sound to transcription to editing. A total of 217 people participated in the anonymous online survey that I conducted. In this chapter, I suggest a framework for a decolonizing feminist methodology.

In Chapter 4, I outline the basics of sex work politics and argue that this position is anti-feminist and anti-woman. Turns out, all these years of thinking and saying 'sex work doesn't work', I was wrong; well, partially wrong. Sex work *does* work—the problem is that it works for men and doesn't work for women. Sex work is a patriarchal practice that aligns perfectly with the patriarchal ideology that governs our world. In this chapter I outline the basics of sex work theory and argue that this position is anti-feminist and anti-woman. Sex work researchers reject feminist methodologies, analysis, and politics in their work. Not only that though, but they are also decidedly anti-feminist in that they actively misunderstand and misrepresent feminist arguments against prostitution and work to discredit feminist methodology, analysis, and politics.

In Chapter 5, I outline the basics of feminist politics that argue for the recognition of prostitution as a form of male violence against women and explain how this position is feminist and pro-woman. Prostitution abolitionists take the position that all prostitution, including indoor and outdoor prostitution, brothels, stripping, pornography, and other forms of paid sex acts include primarily men as buyers and women as sellers of sex acts and is therefore a sex-based practice of inequality that constitutes a form of male violence against women (Barry, 1979; Hill Collins, 1990; Barry, 1995; Whisnant and Stark, 2004; Raymond, 2013; Norma and Tankard Reist, 2016; Bindel, 2019).

In Chapter 6, I tell stories about the research trip I did to New Zealand including what happened there and what I learned there and after there. One of the things I learned from my trip to New Zealand was the very covert and sometimes very overt ways that the realities of prostitution are kept hidden inside Aotearoa. I go on to describe academic hostilities and barriers to decolonizing feminist research and analysis when researching prostitution and the ways in which feminist Indigenous and other women who engage in public scholarship are punished and/or silenced for their perspectives. Starting—and finishing—a PhD is tough work by itself. When a scholar takes a feminist position on controversial issues such as prostitution and gender, that task becomes almost insurmountable ... almost. It's important that I tell the story of my PhD as honestly as possible and this includes sharing the mental, emotional, and physical harm that has been done to me because of the feminist positions I take on political issues that disproportionately impact women—issues such as prostitution and gender and their corresponding legal and policy implications. When I think of my PhD adventure, the hostile territories in which I passed through and in which I continue to work immediately come to mind. The issue is not that most academics disagree with the feminist position that prostitution is a form of male violence against women (which they do)—it's that most academics and the culture of academia in Canada and elsewhere believe that it's entirely unacceptable and even harmful to question the idea that 'sex work is work' and that it's an act of violence to hold the feminist position that prostitution is a form of male violence against women. In academia, feminists who take this position shouldn't be challenged or debated—they shouldn't be heard *at all*. It's in this hostile environment that my research lives and that is part of this research project. As Mies explains, as feminist scholars, "we have to start fighting against women's exploitation and oppression in order to be able to understand the extent, the dimensions, the forms and causes of this patriarchal system," what she also refers to as "if you want to know a thing, you must change it" (1983, p. 125).

As a result, I'll be referring throughout this chapter, and throughout this book, to occasions where I experienced, first-hand, the academic and other hostility aimed at feminist researchers who dare to centre women in their research and action and who dare to question the deeply-embedded academic mantras that 'sex work is work' and 'transwomen are women'. I'm not referring throughout this text to circumstances where I've been challenged or questioned or disagreed with or debated or even offended—those are entirely different, and welcome, interactions. What I am referring to here are the consequences a feminist researcher faces when doing academic research critical of prostitution in Canada. I know that some of the stories I tell will sound ridiculous, because they are. They'll sound unbelievable, like maybe I'm blowing things out of proportion, but the stories I tell are absolutely true and despite the harm they've caused, have given me useful information and insight into the academic workings of patriarchy. This chapter includes a critical discussion of (trigger warning) sex work politics and a (mega trigger warning) analysis of the ways in which transgender politics work to harm and silence feminists in academia.

In Chapter 7, I conclude by contemplating that over the course of my doctoral journey I learned quite a few things, which I guess is the point. In that case, Doctor of Philosophy: mission accomplished. I learned things I didn't expect to learn and I hear that's quite common in these kinds of adventures or at least, it should be. Turns out I needed to define 'colonization' and 'Indigenous feminism' as if women matter as much as men do.[7] This meant not assuming women's interests as a class were considered or included in male-centred Indigenous theorizing. This meant asking uncomfortable questions like what does 'colonization' and 'Indigenous feminism' *actually* mean? Is there one meaning, or many different meanings? Is 'Indigenous feminism' different from 'feminism' and if so, how? Who came up with all these concepts anyways? It became clear that I had no obvious answers to these questions and that I needed

---

7   Women do matter as much as men do.

to clearly define these concepts as part of my research. In other words, I needed to create a female-centred and feminist definition of 'colonization' and subsequently of 'Indigenous feminism' in order to rigorously examine the prostitution of Indigenous women in Canada, and I did.

Notes About Language

There are a few terms used throughout this work that need some clarification. I generally use the term 'Indigenous' when referring to Indigenous peoples—in Canada, this means to First Nations, Inuit, and Métis peoples. Other terms, such as 'Aboriginal', 'native', and 'ndn/NDN' are used as well; 'Indian' is also used to refer to Indigenous peoples although the term is an offensive one; it's only used when referring to the *Indian Act* and when used in direct quotation. In this research, I refer to 'women'. In all other circumstances, I refer to 'women and girls' in recognition of the distinct ways patriarchy impacts adult women and girl children; the distinct ways these groups resist patriarchy; and the particular solutions that are required when working with women versus working with girls. For this research project, I only applied for and received ethics clearance to work with women aged 18 and over and although there's no hard line between 'woman' and 'girl' and there are many connections and intersections and overlapping issues, I use the term 'women' to signal that my research was conducted with adult women. I also use the term 'sex work advocates', meaning individuals and groups, in and outside of academia, who believe and promote the idea that 'sex work' is work, a job like any other. A 'sex work researcher' is a sex work advocate employed by a university in an academic capacity whose scholarship works to normalize prostitution. When I use the term 'feminism', I'm usually referring to radical feminism. Lastly, I refuse to play the out-posture and out-progress all other posturing-progressive-academics game by defining already-defined common-sense terms such as 'woman' and 'man'. When engaged in feminist politics, these terms are self-evident. However, I will define now what I mean when I say 'gender' and 'sex': gender is a bunch of made-up, externally imposed rules and limitations that uphold men's domination and women's subordination in a patriarchy (Jeffreys, 2014); for example, gender tells us that girls are quiet and boys are loud (this is lie). Sex refers to the biological condition of being female or male. Lastly, these terms—the ones I've listed and more —are also political. Language is not neutral and by default, works in the interest of men to disadvantage women (Spender, 1980). Because sex work/prostitution is inherently a political issue (Graham, 2014), so too is the language used to describe, analyze and challenge it or whitewash, abstract, and protect it (Dworkin, 1993). I have no interest in protecting the system of prostitution or of male domination generally, so the terms I use will be considered, by some, to be offensive and unacceptable; in reality, they signify political difference and my unwillingness to use language to kiss the patriarchy's butt so I don't care if I offend all the rapists, pimps, and other men out there.

Notes About Structure: Kind of Like a Collage but Not Really

I wrote a lot, did a lot, and made video diaries throughout the entire research process. I participated in conferences, was kicked out of conferences, engaged in public scholarship and was defamed and attacked on social media (including by distinguished professors and supastar ndns—some at my own university!); I attended rallies, signed petitions, helped women find lawyers, helped women keep their kids safe from their fathers, and helped women make safety plans and leave battering relationships; I made missing persons reports, I spoke to governments, and to the media, and to the public about the issues women, and particularly Indigenous women, confront in a patriarchy. I was, and am, active in the Women's Liberation Movement as part of my work as a researcher and scholar (Mies, 1983). Parallel to Nêhiyaw- and Saulteaux-descended scholar Margaret Kovach's *Indigenous Methodologies* where her "writing often shapeshifts to other forms," I have included some of these reflections, observations, transcriptions, social media posts, doodles, drawings, and web clippings throughout and in the appendices of this text (2010, p. 21). My reflections are marked by italics and a date followed by the phrase 'Dear Diary'. I use the traditional setup of a diary to affirm the scholarly and theoretical importance of women's too-often-internal thoughts and feelings. The tone of my writing is inconsistent, sometimes it's more formal and more often, less so. We often tell stories in a familiar linear narrative, even though they most often didn't happen that way. I made plans, changed plans, had ideas, changed ideas, worked, spoke, broke down, listened, learned, had feelings, squashed feelings, read, cried, dreamed, and thought at different points and at different times about different things; but none of this happened in anything that resembled any kind of straight line, not even a squiggly line—more like a collage of interrelated lines but not even that exactly. There are numerous other transcriptions and video footage that I have from this project that are not directly included in my dissertation or in this book which will see the light of day, just not the light of an academic day. Interviews were conducted in Canada, New Zealand, and Australia over a two-year period, although to constrain the story of this research to those two years would be misrepresenting the journey, so bits and pieces from before, during, and after are also included.

CHAPTER 1

Male Violence Against Indigenous Women in Canada

In this chapter I describe the historical and contemporary landscape as it relates to male violence against Indigenous women in Canada. I discuss responses to the crisis of murdered and disappeared Indigenous women including the theoretical foundations of Indigenous feminism, the road to and what happened during the National Inquiry into Missing and Murdered Indigenous Women and Girls, and the role of mourning and memorialization.

Male Violence

Research has shown that Indigenous women and girls in Canada face disproportionate occurrences of male violence, including being disappeared and murdered at disturbingly high rates for decades and longer. Indigenous women are also funneled disproportionally into poverty, prisons, and prostitution, and continue to be removed from their mothers and placed into the 'care' of the state through the foster care system (Farley et al., 2005). Indigenous women face overwhelmingly disproportionate levels of physical, sexual, and emotional violence, and higher rates of disability, mental health issues, addiction, and suicide (Farley et al., 2005). In these ways, male violence and the threat of male violence severely impacts not only the health of Indigenous women but also impedes our ability to fully participate in social, economic, and political life. In 2015, as a result of mounting public and political pressure from Indigenous women and their allies, the federal liberal government announced a long-awaited National Inquiry into these issues with the following mandate:

> The National Inquiry must look into and report on the systemic causes of all forms of violence against Indigenous women and girls, including sexual violence. We must examine the underlying social, economic, cultural, institutional, and historical causes that contribute to the ongoing violence and particular vulnerabilities of Indigenous women and girls in Canada. The mandate also directs us to look into and report on existing institutional policies and practices to address violence, including those that are effective in reducing violence and increasing safety.
>
> While the formal name of the Inquiry is 'The National Inquiry into Missing and Murdered Indigenous Women and Girls', our mandate covers all forms of violence. This makes our mandate very broad. By not being limited to investigating only cases of Indigenous women who went missing or were murdered, we can include women and girls who died under suspicious circumstances.
>
> It also means we can address issues such as sexual assault, child abuse, domestic violence, bullying and harassment, suicide, and self-harm. This violence is interconnected, and can have equally devastating effects. Expanding the mandate beyond missing and murdered also creates space for more survivors to share their stories. They can help us look to the future from a place of experience, resilience, and hope (National Inquiry into Missing and Murdered Indigenous Women and Girls, 2018a).

Prostitution is one form of male violence that disproportionately targets and harms Indigenous women. Prostitution was brought to Canada by white men with Indigenous women and girls being prostituted around early forts and military bases (Farley et al., 2005) with "Indian teepees pitched on the river flats often [functioning] as the first brothels for the quickly growing prairie cities" (Backhouse, 1985, p. 420). Across Canada today, Indigenous women are overrepresented in prostitution, particularly street prostitution. A 2005 study conducted in Vancouver, B.C. found that 52 per cent of women in street prostitution were Indigenous even though Indigenous peoples generally comprised about 1.7 per cent of the city's population (Farley et al., 2005). Numerous other studies have confirmed the overrepresentation of Indigenous women in street prostitution (Kingsley et al., 2000; Cler-Cunningham and Christenson, 2001; Conseil du Statut de la Femme, 2002; Krüsi et al., 2012). However, a notable gap exists in the quantification of Indigenous women engaging in 'indoor' forms of prostitution such as in brothels or as escorts and those prostituting outside of urban areas in rural areas, small towns, and on reserves (Hunt, 2013). As a result, the overrepresentation of Indigenous women in prostitution in Canada may be more significant than current studies report. Not only are Indigenous women overrepresented in the sex industry, but they also face disproportionate additional male violence in prostitution as the industry categorizes and ranks women according to a racial hierarchy,

> Not unlike other industries, the sex industry is stratified, with white workers (i.e., those defined by others as white or those who can enact whiteness) often occupying the better paying jobs in safer working conditions, and with racialized and Indigenous workers overrepresented as the targets of state, police, neighbourhood, and male violence (van der Muelen, 2013, p. 19).

In Canada, discussion and action on the issues of male violence against Indigenous women and the prostitution of Indigenous women have largely taken place in separate, although at times intersecting and overlapping, spheres.

The Road to the Inquiry

For some people in Canada, the increasing revelations of the consistency and intensity of male violence against Indigenous women was shocking. Indigenous women, however, had been painfully aware of these issues for a very long time, fighting and organizing for Canadian governments and the general public to acknowledge and work to meaningfully address this crisis as far back as 1992 (and earlier). The annual February 14 Women's Memorial March has been held every year in Vancouver since 1992 and continues today not only in Vancouver, but in other cities across Canada as well. While the issue began long before, calls for the federal government to hold a national inquiry into the murders and disappearances of Indigenous women gained steam in the 2000s with the leadership of the Native Women's Association of Canada (NWAC). The fact that women were able to apply enough pressure to governments to force a national inquiry and the increased level of public awareness about this issue in Canada today are victories in and of themselves. It wasn't easy to get to this point and the struggle is far from over but it's important to acknowledge all the work that's been done so far by many different individuals and groups.

In 2002, NWAC, the Canadian Association of Elizabeth Fry Societies, Amnesty International Canada, KAIROS, the United Church and the Anglican Church formed the 'National Coalition for our Stolen Sisters' in response to the disproportionate rates of male violence being committed against Indigenous women (KAIROS Canada, n.d.). In 2004, Amnesty International, with the NWAC, released *Stolen Sisters: A Human Rights Response to Discrimination and Violence against Indigenous Women in Canada*. 2004 also marked the beginning of NWAC's *Sisters in Spirit* campaign to raise awareness about male violence against Indigenous women (Kubik and Bourassa, 2016). In 2005, NWAC and the Government of Canada signed a contribution agreement wherein NWAC would receive five million dollars over a period of five years to research and make recommendations on this issue with goals to

1. Reduce the risks and increase the safety and security of all Aboriginal women and girls in Canada.
2. Address the high incidence of violence against Aboriginal women, particularly racialized, sexualized violence, that is, violence perpetrated against Aboriginal women because of their sex and Aboriginal identity; and

3. To increase gender equality and improve the participation of Aboriginal women in the economic, social, cultural, and political realms of Canadian society (Kubik and Bourassa, 2016, pp. 17–18).

NWAC's *Sisters in Spirit* project reported that 582 Indigenous women had gone missing or been murdered over the last 30 years in Canada and recommended that a national inquiry into missing and disappeared Indigenous women take place. NWAC's *Sisters in Spirit* funding concluded and the project ended in 2010. In 2009, Amnesty International released another report *No More Stolen Sisters: The Need for a Comprehensive Response to Discrimination and Violence Against Indigenous Women in Canada*. In 2011, NWAC launched a new project called *Evidence to Action* in efforts to continue to address the issue of male violence against Indigenous women; however, one condition of this funding was that NWAC couldn't conduct any further research into the crisis of murdered and disappeared Indigenous women (Kubik and Bourassa, 2016).

During that same time period, Robert Pickton was brought to trial and convicted of six counts of second-degree murder and women continued to go missing on Highway 16 known as the 'Highway of Tears'; both of these significant events happened in British Columbia (Kubik and Bourassa, 2016). In 2006, the Highway of Tears Symposium was held in Prince George, British Columbia, producing the *Highway of Tears Symposium Recommendations Report: A collective voice for the victims who have been silenced and launching the Highway of Tears Initiative* (KAIROS Canada, n.d.). In 2010, the government of British Columbia established the Missing Women Commission of Inquiry to investigate any failures that occurred during the investigation and eventual arrest of Pickton (Kubik and Bourassa, 2016). In 2012, the Missing Women Commission of Inquiry released their final report *Forsaken: The Report of the Missing Women Commission of Inquiry*. In March 2011 and December 2011, the Canadian House of Commons and the Standing Committee on the Status of Women released an interim and then final report on male violence against Indigenous women, respectively, with the interim report acknowledging root causes of male violence against Indigenous women as including poverty, racism, Canada's colonial history, and systemic police failures (Kubik and Bourassa, 2016). In 2008, in response to a request by NWAC working in partnership with the Feminist Alliance for International Action (FAFIA), the United Nations Committee on the Elimination of Discrimination against Women announced it would be conducting an inquiry into male violence against Indigenous women in Canada.

In 2013, Human Rights Watch released its report *Those Who Take Us Away: Abusive Policing and Failures in Protection of Indigenous Women and Girls in Northern British Columbia, Canada* and in 2014, the Royal Canadian Mounted Police (RCMP) released its report *Missing and Murdered Aboriginal Women: A National Operational Overview* followed by *Missing and Murdered Aboriginal Women: 2015 Update to the National Operational Overview* (Kubik and Bourassa, 2016). The RCMP's 2014 report disclosed that, according to its own records, nearly 1200 Indigenous women had been murdered or disappeared in Canada over the past 30 years (RCMP, 2014); the 2015 report noted that 11 additional Indigenous women had been disappeared since the conclusion of the 2014 report (RCMP, 2015). In 2015, with a change from a conservative federal government to a liberal one and due to mounting pressure to conduct a national inquiry into male violence against Indigenous women in Canada, the liberal government announced the National Inquiry into Missing and Murdered Indigenous Women and Girls. The Inquiry began in 2016 and concluded in 2019 with the release of the Inquiry's final report *Reclaiming Power and Place: The Final Report of the National Inquiry into Missing and Murdered Indigenous Women and Girls* that included recommendations for action in the form of 231 *Calls for Justice* and supplementary reports on Quebec and Genocide.

Colonization

It has been determined, by Indigenous scholars and other experts, that colonization is a root cause of the disproportionately high rates of male violence against Indigenous women in Canada (Green, 2007; Green, 2017; Bourgeois, 2018; National Inquiry into Missing and Murdered Indigenous Women and Girls, 2019a; National Inquiry into Missing and Murdered Indigenous Women and Girls, 2019b). But what is colonization? We need a noun here, maybe some adjectives, to describe what colonization *is*. Colonization has been described as an annexation (Altamirano-Jiménez, 2012), a structure (Altamirano-Jiménez, 2012; Arvin et al., 2013; Simpson, 2017) and a process (Armstrong, 1996; National Inquiry into Missing and Murdered Indigenous Women and Girls, 2019a; Simpson, 2017). Farley, Lynne (Métis), and Cotton define colonization as a

> ... process that includes geographic incursion, sociocultural dislocation, the establishment of external political control and economic dispossession, the provision of low-level social services, and ultimately, the creation of ideological formulations around race and skin color which position the colonizers at a higher evolutionary level than the colonized (2005, p. 106).

It's important to note that colonization is considered an ongoing series of actions that continue to happen, not a one-time event that occurred in the past (Arvin et al., 2013). The related term 'colonialism' refers to the ideology that informs the process of colonization (National Inquiry into Missing and Murdered Indigenous Women and Girls, 2019a). It's also important to note the differences between colonialism and imperialism as the terms mean different things but are often used interchangeably (Comack, 2018). Imperialism can be defined as

> ... a concept 'which upholds the legitimacy of the economic and military control of one nation by another. Colonialism, however, is one form of practice which results from the ideology of imperialism, and specifically concerns the settlement of one group of people in

a new location. Imperialism is not strictly concerned with the issue of settlement; it does not demand the settlement of different places in order to work'. While settlement is a key element of the colonial process, colonialism has taken different forms within a particular geographical territory, often changing in form over time (quoted in Comack, 2018, p. 456).

English-, Ktunaxa-, and Cree-Scots Métis-descended scholar Joyce Green, in the introduction to the second edition of her ground-breaking edited collection *Making Space for Indigenous Feminism*, states that

> colonialism and its successor settler states are predicated on the theft of and exploitation of Indigenous lands and the oppression of Indigenous peoples, justified by the racist myths that are still encoded in settler cultures (2017, p. 4).

Green describes not only what colonialism is but also what it does—it informs the policies and actions of colonization, a process that works to sever the relationship of Indigenous peoples to land and that exploits and oppresses Indigenous peoples and the land in a variety of ways justified by racism. Other Indigenous feminist scholars (Acoose, 1995; Maracle, 1996; Anderson, 2000; Valaskakis, 2005; Huhndorf and Suzack, 2011; Altamirano-Jiménez, 2012; Nickel, 2017; Simpson, 2017; Bourgeois, 2018) describe a similar analysis that positions land—including the connections to land and the theft of land—as central to the process and to understanding the process of colonization in Canada. As Binizaá scholar Isabel Altamirano-Jiménez states:

> Colonialism can be defined as the territorial annexation of and the structure of domination imposed on non-European peoples by European states. While all colonialisms imply that the colonizers come from away and occupy and conquer sovereign peoples' territories, different colonial formations exist … settler colonialism…focuses on claiming land and on creating permanent settlements that replicate the social, political, economic, legal, and cultural structures of settlers' homeland over the new territories and the colonized (2012, p. 107).

Colonization is about land: the connection of Indigenous peoples to land and the theft and transformation of that land into a thing; a product; a resource by and for settler men. Here, we also see that colonization is about peoples—about severing Indigenous peoples' connections to land and land-based culture and exploiting the land and people for profit. Indigenous women have responded to colonization in different ways: Indigenous feminism and now Indigenous queer theory are two theoretical responses to a gender-based analysis of colonization and ongoing public memorializations continue to dominate action on this issue.

Indigenous Feminism as a Gender-Based Analysis of Colonization

Acknowledging and examining the different impacts colonization has had on women and men is a relatively new perspective. As Green (2007; 2017), and Tk̓emlupsemc scholar Sarah Nickel and Amanda Fehr (2020) note, the importance of including a gendered analysis in the examination of colonization has been increasingly recognized by scholars, organizations, and governments over the past three decades. Many high-profile reports, such as the Inquiry's final report, explicitly recognize the gendered aspect of colonization: "The gendered lens we apply to these contexts is important; while Indigenous men and boys suffered enormously under colonization, with respect to land and governance in particular, Indigenous women, girls, and 2SLGBTQQIA+[8] people were impacted in distinct, though related, ways" (National Inquiry into Missing and Murdered Indigenous Women and Girls, 2019a, p. 230).

---

8   2SLGBTQQIA, more commonly referred to as 2SLGBTQQIA+, refers, in the Inquiry, to "Two Spirit, Lesbian, Gay, Bisexual, Transgender, Queer, Questioning, Intersex, Asexual (National Inquiry into Missing and Murdered Indigenous Women and Girls, 2019). The "+" acknowledges and refers to the identities not captured by this particular acronym (National Inquiry into Missing and Murdered Indigenous Women and Girls, 2019).

Shari M. Huhndorf and Cheryl Suzack, a scholar from the Batchewana First Nations, have identified some of the particular ways that colonization impacts Indigenous women including their removal from previously-held positions of power within their nations, the replacement of Indigenous ideas about gender with patriarchal ones, and the use of Indigenous women's bodies, through sexual violence and other means, to exert control over Indigenous communities (2011). The written and oral historical records have led Indigenous feminist scholars to theorize that most, if not all, Indigenous nations across Canada valued and respected women before white men arrived to settle the country (Huhndorf and Suzack, 2011; Anderson and Lavell-Harvard, 2014; Lavell-Harvard and Brant, 2016; Anderson et al., 2018). This meant that Indigenous women had more ability to make decisions for themselves and for their nations in leadership positions (Huhndorf and Suzack, 2011). Pre-colonization, the systemic mass violations of the safety and dignity of Indigenous women didn't exist. However, Indigenous feminist scholars assert this is certainly not the case in Canada today, where the foreign institutions of patriarchy, capitalism, and racism, brought over by white male settlers, have become embedded in Indigenous communities, threatening and taking the lives of Indigenous women now for hundreds of years (Anderson and Lavell-Harvard, 2014; Lavell-Harvard and Brant, 2016; Anderson et al., 2018). The devaluation of Indigenous women was and is essential to the ongoing processes of colonization, as women were traditionally considered life-givers, a position that Cree/Métis scholar Kim Anderson calls "empowered motherhood":

> Women were considered the head of the household because they were primarily responsible for the work involved in child rearing and in managing the home and home community. Empowered motherhood was not only a practice but also an ideology that allowed women to assert their authority (2011, p. 83).

By targeting the social and political status of Indigenous women, white male colonizers were able to interfere with matriarchal cultural transmission from grandmother to mother to daughter (McIvor, 2004; Brodsky, 2016).

From first contact between Indigenous women and white men, men set about physically removing Indigenous peoples from their traditional territories, legislating them onto white-man-created small pockets of land called 'reserves' and removing Indigenous children from their mothers and communities through forcible placement into the Indian Residential School system (Farley et al., 2005). The creation of nation-wide racist lies about Indigenous peoples continues to sustain the underlying colonial ideologies that guide these horrific practices. One of the ways that colonization impacted Indigenous women in particular was through the construction of Indigenous women as either 'savage squaws' or 'Indian princesses'.[9] Since the invasion of Canada by white men, Indigenous women have been constructed as hyper-sexualized, savage squaws or as passive—yet still sexually-available—Indian princesses who display stereotypical markers of Indigeneity and femininity (Green, 1975; Acoose, 1995; Anderson, 2000; Valaskakis, 2005; Lajimodiere, 2013). 'Squaw-ness', the idea that Indigenous women are hyper-sexual, deviant, and dirty, was imposed historically on Indigenous women and has resulted in particularly devastating consequences then and today including the normalization and justification of male violence. While many theorists (Acoose, 1995; Anderson, 2000; Bourgoise, 2018) have proposed that constructing Indigenous women and girls as squaws and/or princesses objectified women and that it's this objectification that allows for men to more easily commit acts of violence against these non-women 'objects' (Lederer, 1982) what this dominant ideology actually did at the time (and today), is construct all Indigenous women and girls not as objects, and especially not as just any old object, but instead as women and girls sexually available to all men. In patriarchy, it's important that women are sexually

---

9   In a forthcoming text (Smiley 2023), I critique the concept of the 'squaw' vs the 'Indian princess' and instead propose the concept of 'squaw' vs 'squaw'.

assaulted by men as women—not as objects; otherwise, men could simply batter, assault, and sexually penetrate blow-up dolls that represent women or detached sex toy 'vaginas'—which men do, but this alone is insufficient for male domination. As Robin Morgan has theorized, women are the evidence of male domination (1977). This means in her assault, rape, and murder by men, she must be a she—a female human—not an 'it' object without any humanity at all. In this way, women aren't objectified so much as male violence against women—not male violence against objects— is normalized. As Black feminist scholar Patricia Hill Collins states regarding sexist and racist representations of Black women: "these controlling images are designed to make racism, sexism, poverty, and other forms of social injustice appear to be natural, normal, and inevitable parts of everyday life" (1990, p. 69). In 1883, Member of Parliament Edward Blake stated in regard to the Indian Residential School (IRS) system:

> If [we] leave the young indian girl who is to mature into a squaw to have the uncivilized habits of the tribe, the Indian, when he married such a squaw, would likely be pulled into Indian savagery by her. If this scheme is going to succeed at all, you will … have to civilize the intended wives … I have known … how difficult it is to eradicate that hereditary taint (Stote, 2015, p. 34).

MP Blake's expression of the patriarchal ideology that all Indigenous girls will become squaws; that being a squaw is genetic and hereditary; and that Indigenous women are to be blamed for the 'savageness' of men was also expressed and acted upon by Indian agents and other men who perpetrated violence against Indigenous women at the time.

This classification of Indigenous women as either squaws or princesses (akin to the more generalized classification of women as 'virgins' or 'whores') (Anderson, 2000) is an inaccurate construction and description of ourselves. In reality, we are women—complex, and from many different nations with many different personalities and desires—not 'squaws' or even 'princesses', at that. A 'squaw', like a 'whore' or a 'slut', and a 'princess, like a 'virgin' or 'prude', doesn't exist: these are lies—false constructions and false representations—created and told about Indigenous women by men to categorize, rank, degrade, and separate women from each other. The creation of these harmful myths about Indigenous women in particular, continued to legitimate and encourage colonial policies to be carried out with no remorse, even reframed as being 'for their [Indigenous women's] own good'.

Indigenous feminist scholars have theorized that the attack on Indigenous women by white men functions primarily to secure access to Indigenous lands and resources:

> Canada is just quite simply a settler society. A settler society whose multicultural, liberal, and democratic structure and performance of governance seeks an ongoing settling of land. This settling is not, of course, innocent either. It is dispossession: the taking of our land from us. And it is ongoing. It is killing our women in order to do so; and has historically done this to do so. So that allows me to qualify the governance project here as also fundamentally gendered (Simpson, 2016).

Destruction of Indigenous women thus became paramount in the attempt to destroy Indigenous communities to gain access to lands and 'resources', redefining what was once a spiritual and loving relationship with the earth to an inherently destructive one motivated by profit. Colonization is about lands and peoples, according to Indigenous feminist theorists, but it's also a gendered process because it

> ... intentionally targets Indigenous women in order to destroy families, to sever the connection to land-based practices and economies, and to devastate the relational governance of Indigenous nations. Indigenous women's role as decision makers, keepers of tradition, holders of oral knowledge, and matriarchal governors in many nations through house groups and clan systems was disrupted through colonization (Martin and Walia, 2019, p. 39).

Culture, intimately intertwined with land, is seen as a primary foundation of Indigenous feminism and its priority. As Anderson (2011) states:

> For me, Indigenous feminism is about creating a new world out of the best of the old. Indigenous feminism is about honouring creation in all its forms, while also fostering the kind of critical thinking that will allow us to stay true to our traditional reverence for life (p. 89).

Decolonization then, a central goal of Indigenous feminism, is defined as a return to traditional values and principles that ensure respect for Indigenous women (Green, 2007; Altamirano-Jiménez, 2011; Anderson, 2011; Green, 2017; Nickel, 2017). In turn, because Indigenous feminism is not primarily concerned with women, men have an active role to play in this gender-inclusive movement:

> With an acknowledged goal of renewing tradition (in which gender roles were interdependent), it follows that Native women require the participation of men in the social, political and spiritual life of the community. The survival of culture and perpetuation of tradition necessitate the fostering of collective experience; exclusion of any segment of the population is not a viable option. Many Native women see themselves as having a key function in the restoration of traditional male roles; historically, in many Aboriginal societies, women were the selectors and trainers of appropriate male leaders (Grey, 2004, p. 14).

Indigenous Feminism Is Not Feminist

In my review of Indigenous feminist literature, the most striking and common message that came across was that Indigenous feminism is not 'white feminism' (sometimes called 'Western feminism' or 'mainstream feminism'). What is meant by 'white feminism' however, we don't know, because 'white feminism', such as who and what theories and practices would fall under this heading, aren't specified. Whether Indigenous feminists are more or less critical of 'white feminism', there is a noticeable lack of clarity around the concept. For example, 'white feminism' is often criticized for focusing on rights as opposed to responsibilities; individualism as opposed to collectivism (Anderson, 2011). When looking at liberal feminist politics that, for example, promote the idea that 'sex work is work' I agree that this liberal gender-based individualism (I wouldn't call it feminism) harms women. On the other hand, 'white feminism' is also often criticized for defining collectivity as sameness and overemphasizing sameness while ignoring difference amongst women in calls for a 'global sisterhood' (Maracle, 1996; Oulette, 2002; Grey, 2004). This criticism is directed more toward radical feminist politics and homogenizes and misrepresents or outright ignores the meaning of 'sisterhood' and the discussions, debates, and disagreements that have happened (and continue to happen) about this concept within the radical feminist movement. In this way, criticisms of generic 'white feminism' confuse liberal and radical politics by lumping these two very different traditions under one 'white feminist' umbrella.

Criticisms of 'white feminism' also unfortunately rely on anti-feminist and often homophobic stereotypes that construct feminist activists as 'man-haters', 'homewreckers', and all manner of 'hostile', 'angry', or 'negative' women: "the majority of Canadians do not understand feminism well, and disparaging feminism has been in vogue in the dominant as well as Indigenous cultures" (LaRocque, 2017, p. 123). Feminism is also dismissed as not only being 'white', but also 'middle-class' by Indigenous and other women of colour. As Morgan argues, however, feminists of the past (and present) inherit their class status through their fathers and then their husbands (Morgan, 1970)—the reality of the second wave Women's Liberation Movement was that many women active in the movement came from poor or working-class backgrounds (Hawthorne, 1994) and if they were considered middle-class, it was only because they had 'married well' to a middle-class man who then imparted his class status onto *his* wife—an issue the Women's Liberation Movement rallied against (Morgan, 1970). LaRocque suggests that these misunderstandings are a result, in part, of Indigenous women's disadvantaged socio-economic position and lack of access to education, among other factors while also recognizing that some Indigenous scholars "… charge white feminism with having little or no understanding of colonial history, Aboriginal peoples, or race oppression" (2017, p. 123). Feminism has long been misrepresented, mischaracterized, lied about, and purposefully disparaged by the dominant patriarchal culture because feminism actually challenges the status quo (i.e. patriarchy). Feminism is a threat to patriarchy and as a result, to power; it makes women and men uncomfortable. For these reasons, an anti-feminist campaign that lies about what feminism actually wants, does, and can, offer to women has been essential in maintaining patriarchy.

Indigenous Feminism Is Feminist

Some Indigenous feminist scholars have theorized Indigenous feminism as a response to colonization rooted in the material realities of women's lives. Sámi scholar Rauna Kuokkanen has theorized that our current understanding of colonization positions Indigenous women as mere conduits through which colonization and resistance happens; what Crenshaw and Kuokkanen call 'instruments' of colonization as opposed to 'beneficiaries' or victims in their own right (Bell and Nelson, 1989; Crenshaw, 1991; Kuokkanen, 2015). Indigenous sovereignty and the 'Nation' that men fight for is composed of men (Simpson, 2016); it excludes Indigenous women in many ways, with "Aboriginal women's contestation of their subjugation … commonly perceived by male leadership as a threat to the security and unity of their nations" (Kuokkanen, 2015, p. 276).

Using Black scholar Kimberlé Crenshaw's (1991) concept of intersectionality, Kuokkanen examines the ways in which patri-archal violence within Indigenous communities in Canada and Scandinavia is depoliticized and silenced in order to protect Indigenous men and their agendas (2015). She examines the danger in analyzing male violence within Indigenous communities only through a lens of colonization; this, she argues:

... risks considering internal oppression based on gender as merely a consequence against the entire indigenous community. Rather than victims of gendered violence in their own right, indigenous women become simply the means by which discrimination against indigenous communities at large can be recognized (Kuokkanen, 2015, p. 272).

Kuokkanen calls for an analysis of the adoption of patriarchy by Indigenous men in addition to an examination of colonization in order to fully understand the issue. She cautions:

... the failure to deal with gendered, in-community violence creates a cycle allowing indigenous leaders and laypersons alike to consider violence a non-issue, which in turn leads to condoning violence through silence, and to the complicity of politicians, academics and authorities spurning calls to action or discussion (Kuokkanen, 2015, p. 282).

Other Indigenous feminist theorists have voiced concern about degendered Indigenous movements, comprised primarily of men, that focus solely on land and sovereignty:

... centering the experiences of women and children—their homes and bodies, their feelings and emotions—is a crucial corrective to theoretical accounts of colonialism that focus solely on the level of lands and resources (De Lueew, 2016, p. 15).

Nlaka'pamux lawyer and educator Sharon McIvor examines the ways that both the male-dominated Canadian State and Indigenous men have benefitted from patriarchy and how both contribute to the oppression of Indigenous women:

... [Indigenous women] are not equal in their enjoyment of Indian status and band membership, and they are denied matrimonial property rights enjoyed by all other Canadians. Further, because government legislation, policies, programs, and services constantly reinforce this systemic patriarchy, many in the Aboriginal communities now believe that their traditions were originally patriarchal, and men are accepted as the 'boss', politically, economically, spiritually, psychologically, and physically. In turn, Aboriginal women have been denied opportunities to hold leadership positions within their communities and organizations and have been excluded from high-level negotiations among Aboriginal and Canadian political leaders. Male Aboriginal leaders and male Canadian politicians have colluded in excluding Aboriginal women from participation in governance (2004, p. 108).

It comes as no surprise then, that Indigenous men would privilege the struggle for lands and sovereignty over issues that profoundly impact women, such as male violence, reproductive rights, women's health, and other issues. "It's all about the land" is a common response accompanied by demands to focus on land claim and sovereignty issues first with a promise that women's issues will be dealt with after, but as McIvor states, "[a]fter 135 years of sex discrimination by Canada, we were afraid of self-government. Why would neo-colonial Aboriginal governments, born and bred in patriarchy, be different from Canadian governments?" (McIvor, 2004, p. 128). As Nickel explains:

> Citizenship and sovereignty, then, took on a "hypermasculinist" character where men enjoyed stable citizenship and political authority while women's political presence (both physical in terms of membership status and conceptual in terms of political concerns) was seen as irrelevant (2017, pp. 319–320).

These theorists, among others (Simpson, 2016), argue that the political, social, and economic status of Indigenous women must be addressed at the same time and in conjunction with issues of land rights and sovereignty.

Some Indigenous feminists are critical of aspects of Indigenous cultures that limit or discriminate against the full participation of Indigenous women in social, political and spiritual life (LaRocque, 1994; Maracle, 1996; Bear, 2007; Anderson, 2011). A controversial and unpopular line of inquiry and questioning, Indigenous feminism provides a framework for Indigenous women to examine, evaluate, and explain patriarchal ideologies and behaviours within their own cultures:

> Incorporating traditional elements into our modern lives is more complicated, and it is at this stage that I find feminist thought to be critical. Feminism of all stripes can help us to tease out patriarchy from what is purportedly traditional and to avoid essentialist identities and systems that are not to our advantage as women. Studying feminist theory and history has been helpful to me, for I can draw parallels between some of what we call traditional and that which has been undoubtedly patriarchal in other contexts worldwide (Anderson, 2011, p. 86).

Due to racism within the Women's Liberation Movement and elsewhere, critically examining one's own culture is something usually only reserved for white women. Indigenous feminism, thus, provides much-needed tools that Indigenous women can use to build theory and practice from their own experiences of sexism in and outside of Indigenous communities and come to terms with the idea that some Indigenous traditions are born and bred of patriarchy.

Indigenous Queer Theory

In contrast, other theorists (Driskill, 2011; Hunt and Holmes, 2015; Belcourt and Nixon, 2018) take a less material and more theoretical, conceptual, academic, and I would argue confusing and nonsensical, approach to Indigenous women's issues that mirrors the shift in feminist politics from that of the 'second-wave'[10] to what is commonly called 'third-wave feminism',[11] although some radical women have characterized 'third-wave feminism' as rooted primarily in 'queer theory' (Butler, 2006; Rubin, 2012) and understood as an anti-feminist backlash rather than a continuation of the feminist movement (Waters, 1996; Jeffreys, 2003). Queer theory doesn't have an agreed-upon definition (Nash, 2011).

---

10 Second-wave feminism generally refers to feminist thought and action that occurred between the 1960s and 1990s; First-wave feminism generally refers to women's fight for the right to vote and third-wave feminism is considered to be the 'wave' we're currently in, from the 1990s until present.

11 Ibid.

Indeed, this fluidness seems to be a hallmark of queer theory itself. Hunt and Holmes define queer politics as such:

> While queer is often used as an identity category or umbrella term for non-normative sexual and gender identities, it emerged as a critique of essentialist constructs and identity politics. As a verb, queer is a deconstructive practice focused on challenging normative knowledges, identities, behaviors, and spaces thereby unsettling power relations and taken-for-granted assumptions. Queerness is then less about a way of 'being' and more about 'doing' and offers the potential for radical social critique (2015, p. 156).

Further, they go on to explain queer decolonial politics:

> A decolonial queer politic is not only anti-normative, but actively engages with anti-colonial, critical race and Indigenous theories and geopolitical issues such as imperialism, colonialism, globalization, migration, neoliberalism, and nationalism (Hunt and Holmes, 2015, p. 156).

Indigenous queer theory (Driskill, 2011) and Indigenous feminism are often collapsed together in methodology, theory, practice, and politics, even though the two ways of thinking are incongruent. What happens is that, intertwined with queer theory, Indigenous feminism loses any definition based in the materiality of women's lives: that is, Indigenous feminism becomes Indigenous *feminisms* having multiple and individualized definitions unique to each person (Anderson, 2011; Yee, 2011; Arvin et al., 2013), or is defined as being simply undefinable (Green, 2007; Green 2017)—at any rate, a perspective that, like queer theory, is not about women. An example of the colonization of Indigenous feminism by queer theory is visible in the focus on the examination of violence against Indigenous 2SLGBTQQIA+ peoples. Many Indigenous feminists (and others) claim that Indigenous 2SLGBTQQIA+ peoples face the worst forms and highest amounts of violence compared to any other marginalized group (Vowel, 2016; Simpson, 2017; Bourgeois, 2018) even though a body of research hasn't established this in Canada (National Inquiry into Missing and Murdered Indigenous

Women and Girls, 2017). While we do know that lesbian, gay, and bisexual Indigenous people face discrimination and male violence due to their sexuality (Statistics Canada, 2021), we don't know this in the same way in regard to discrimination and violence based on one's internal, unseen, undefinable and indescribable "gender identity."[12] Additionally, other factors such as sex, age, and economic status, for example, also play a role in the construction and expression of homophobic ideologies. To remove sex as a factor when examining violence against 2SLGBTQQIA+ people makes it impossible to get to the root of the issue—for example, most of this violence is committed by men and this is an important piece of information we need to know when examining these particular forms of violence.

Identity, including the deconstruction of identity, is a central area of inquiry in Indigenous queer theory. A shift from a focus on women to a focus on identity confuses and obscures the realities of patriarchy and makes political action difficult:

> The deconstruction of identity in queer theory has been criticized for making political action difficult, since people determinedly unsure of who and what they are do not make a powerful revolutionary force (Jeffreys, 2003, p. 39).

Fighting to end male violence against Indigenous women in Canada has become discourse—and not just discourse about *male violence against Indigenous women* in Canada but discourse about *violence against Indigenous peoples* in Canada. In addition to ignoring or outright disputing male violence against Indigenous women, in many ways, postmodern, queer, and other anti-feminist academic theories have complicated and nuanced the issue to the point where we have less understanding instead of more: we are less sure of our realities as women and as Indigenous women and we

---

12   Justice Canada (2016) defines gender identity as "… each person's internal and individual experience of gender. It is their sense of being a woman, a man, both, neither, or anywhere along the gender spectrum." This definition is a terrible definition. It doesn't tell us anything.

are less confident and able to communicate those realities in fewer and fewer spaces.

Memorialization and Trauma

The current landscape in regard to male violence against Indigenous women, particularly murders and disappearances, is dominated by discourses of trauma, grief, and memorialization. For example, 2022 Memorial March guidelines from the Vancouver march state:

> … The Memorial March is an opportunity to come together to grieve the loss of our beloved sisters in the Downtown Eastside and to dedicate ourselves to justice. This event is organized and led by women and non-binary people because Indigenous women, girls, two spirit trans people face physical, mental, emotional, and spiritual violence on a daily basis … We respectfully ask that you please do not bring your agency or group banners, flags, or leaflets as the march only carries signage remembering our sisters. Signs to honour womens' lives are welcome (ajik, 2022).

While the Memorial March wasn't always 'political banner-free', this has been the case for many years while the March remains, as it always has been and despite claims otherwise, political. The Toronto 10th Annual Strawberry Ceremony for Missing and Murdered Indigenous Women and Girls Facebook page states: "Please leave your agency and organization banners at home and instead make signs in honour of women, girls, Trans, and Two Spirit people who have died violent and premature deaths" (Huntley, 2015); the Montréal Memorial March, organized by the Centre for Gender Advocacy's Indigenous solidarity group, Missing Justice, stated on their 2016 Memorial March Facebook page,

> the march commemorates women of all backgrounds, with emphasis given to Indigenous women, who are the disproportionate victims of such violent crimes. On Feb. 14, we honour Indigenous womxn, two-spirits and transwomen, including transwomen of colour, immigrant, refugee, and nonstatus womxn, sex workers and all womxn who've

gone missing or been murdered. We remember and we continue to demand justice (Missing Justice, 2016).

And the art installation *Walking With Our Sisters* states:

> *Walking With Our Sisters* is a commemorative art installation to honour the lives of missing and murdered Indigenous Women of Canada and the United States; to acknowledge the grief and torment families of these women continue to suffer; and to raise awareness of this issue and create opportunity for broad community-based dialogue on the issue (Walking With Our Sisters Collective, 2017).

Previous personal (and public) experiences of non-Indigenous march organizers, Missing Justice, attempting to physically silence me at the 2010 Annual Montréal Memorial March for speaking critically about prostitution, as well as having a 2015 Facebook post that shared my work on prostitution removed and my presence as well as any statements critical of the sex industry banned from the *Walking with our Sisters* Facebook page, in addition to informal conversations with Indigenous women friends and allies, has brought to light a previously hidden connection that warrants further investigation: connection between sex worker advocates and the ways in which discourses of Indigenous women's trauma, grief, and memorialization are used to highlight particular (patriarchal) agendas and silence others (feminist).

While acknowledgment of trauma and grief and the memorialization of our dead and disappeared is certainly necessary and important, a focus *only* on these processes with little to no space for political action that includes a naming and critique of structures, systems, and perpetrators can continue a discourse of abstracted victimization that requires, "... a recovery process which typically emphasizes personal, often professionally mediated, transformation, rather than broader changes in the social and political order" (Maxwell, 2014, p. 409). While Indigenous scholars such as Maria Yellow Horse Brave Heart have adapted the concept of historical trauma to better suit the context and needs of Indigenous peoples, a focus solely on trauma can medicalize the issue,

... refram[ing] contemporary social suffering and interlinked political struggles of indigenous and other marginalized populations as, on the one hand, problems of behaviour to be remedied by professional interventions, and on the other, problems of individual victimhood to be remedied by financial compensation (Maxwell, 2014, p. 413).

Thus, trauma and victimization are intimately linked, both directing the focus to the behaviours and responses of individual Indigenous women victims and invisibilizing "who is doing what to whom"; this abstracts and normalizes the male violence we experience. As Sherene Razack states, "... utilizing an optic of vulnerability it is difficult to consider the perpetrators of the violence and to consider what sexualized violence has to do with colonialism" (2016, p. 292). Male violence against Indigenous women is increasingly normalized as discourses of trauma, grief, and memorialization continue to dominate discussion and action. While the issue of male violence against Indigenous women has become increasingly visible in the past decade due to the hard work of Indigenous women and their allies, the issue has simultaneously become de-gendered in that the perpetrators of the violence are rarely named—for example, the issue is referred to as violence against Indigenous women, not *male* violence against women; or women are referred to as *missing* and murdered, as opposed to *disappeared* and murdered. Not unique to this issue, we see a similar process occurring in other areas of male violence against women as well:

Examples of the process by which social movement frames achieve wide acceptance and become institutionalized in various social practices but lose the critical feminist or progressive intent can be found throughout feminist praxis, from the transformation of 'battered women' into the 'battered woman syndrome' to the depoliticization of 'sexual harassment' (Naples, 2003, p. 89).

The Importance of a Sex-Based Feminist Analysis

You'd think that working to end male violence against Indigenous women in Canada would be a straight-forward goal. Male violence against women is harmful and wrong, right? Men raping women is harmful and wrong, right? Right, but wrong in that this issue is presented as way more complicated than it actually is. What counts as 'violence'? Who is a 'woman'? Among feminists and academics in Canada, two of the most controversial topics today include gender and prostitution. So controversial, in fact, that many organizations and individuals distance themselves from discussing these important issues out of fear, or adopt dominant positions due to pressure or without exposure to, and respectful engagement with, feminist perspectives. As an example, the Inquiry adopted dominant perspectives very early in their process in regard to gender and prostitution meaning feminist analysis was booted right out of the Inquiry from the get-go, meaning that Indigenous women lost out, again, in our own inquiry.

National and international homicide statistics and research demonstrate that women and men are generally killed for different reasons by those with differing relationships to the victim, although in both cases the perpetrators are overwhelmingly male (Canadian Femicide Observatory for Justice and Accountability, 2018). The 2017 Midterm Report of the National Inquiry into Missing and Murdered Indigenous Women and Girls stated that the inclusion of LGBTQ2S was due to pressure by LGBTQ2S, Transgender, non-binary, and/or Two-Spirit people to include examination of the male violence they endure. The Inquiry states that by inclusion of these issues into the scope of the Inquiry a "… critical knowledge gap [is addressed], as very few previous reports have looked at how violence is different for Indigenous LGBTQ2S people" (National Inquiry into Missing and Murdered Indigenous Women and Girls, 2017, p. 20). Here, the Inquiry has acknowledged that male violence impacts different groups in different ways, consistent with research into male violence. Yet, the inquiry made the decision to include the particular male violence that LGBTQ2S *people* face into an under-funded inquiry with a very limited timeframe. This position, that males who identify as lesbians, gay, bisexual, transgender and/or women, queer, and/or Two-Spirit should be centred in feminist work, is one that critically impacts Indigenous women and women generally, in regard to the historical ways male violence has impacted us, what potential solutions can work for us, and compromises our ability to organize politically with those we choose to.

The Inquiry also decided very early on that prostitution is, in fact, a form of work, stating in their lexicon of recommended usage terms, "Most self-identified sex workers define sex work as work" (National Inquiry into Missing and Murdered Indigenous Women and Girls, 2018b; National Inquiry into Missing and Murdered Indigenous Women and Girls, 2019). What does this even mean? This kind of statement is deliberately misleading and confusing, or demonstrates fundamental lack of knowledge about the issues, debates, and controversies in regard to prostitution/ sex work. A position such as 'sex work is work' is about further normalizing and entrenching the ability of men to purchase sex acts from women who almost always do not want to have sex with them and to their ability to sell women to other men for a profit. A sex work perspective agrees that men are entitled to sex on demand. A more critical investigation into the issues and the controversies surrounding prostitution would only have benefitted the processes and outcomes of the inquiry. Both of these issues—gender and prostitution—are controversial and often difficult to speak about. But issues being controversial and difficult to speak about is not a reason to stay silent or to quickly adopt a more popular, non-critical, position in order to protect one's self or ease the process, but this is what's happening.

Conclusion: Male Violence Against Indigenous Women in Canada

While there may not be agreement on a definition or definitions of Indigenous feminism(s), there is a general consensus that colonization is primarily about settler theft of Indigenous lands and 'resources' and dispossession (Simpson, 2017) of Indigenous peoples from their connections to land, cultures, and each other. There is also a general consensus that Indigenous feminism is not 'white feminism' although there are no descriptions of what this 'white feminism' is, who the theorists and activists are, and what parts of 'white feminist' theory and/or action are being challenged. This overwhelming hostility toward an undefined 'white feminism' demonstrates how deeply rooted patriarchy and the ideology of 'woman-hating' is, even among women. This, in itself, is more a symptom of oppression than a cause, but it does expose a fundamental weakness of current Indigenous feminist theorizing: that is, either the intentional devaluation and disregard of hundreds of years of feminist theorizing (for example, scholars did not adequately—or in some cases, at all—learn about and consider feminist theory) or intentionally generalizing, stereotyping, and dismissing feminist theory and action (for example, scholars did learn about and consider feminist theory but didn't describe these theories or provide citations to these theories in their writing). In either case, Indigenous feminist theory as a theory itself suffers because previous feminist theories—whether someone agrees with these theories or not—are pulled out and away from under Indigenous feminist theory. We build theory and practice and take action in part by learning from those who came before us—we learn and grow by agreeing, disagreeing, criticizing, debating, and building on the work that women have done in the past. It becomes much more difficult to build a theory, and we lose out on the potential for radical ideas and new directions, when its foundations are ignored.

A second weakness of current Indigenous feminist theory is that both understandings of Indigenous feminism—one that is more based in the material realities of Indigenous women's lives and calls for the inclusion of a gendered analysis of colonization at the same time as issues of land and sovereignty, and one that adopts a highly individualized non-definition of Indigenous feminisms that's not actually about women at all—both respond to an understanding of colonization that is about land and that prioritizes issues of race, racism, and white supremacy over issues of sex and gender. In this way then, the theories I've discussed earlier, and really all current theories of Indigenous feminism, fail Indigenous women because they don't explicitly and consistently centre women in their understandings of colonization and women's resistance to colonization. What if we were to centre women in our definitions of colonization and decolonizing feminism? What if we examined colonization as a process of male entitlement and female obligation? What if we built on—instead of dismissed—the work of feminists, such as Ann Stoler, Maria Mies, Robin Morgan, and Kathleen Barry who courageously theorized colonization as a sex-based practice?

From 1992 (and earlier) until present (and ongoing), many other local, regional, national, and international events, reports, and actions have been organized to address the murders and dis-appearances of Indigenous women in Canada. While many of these activities have helped the healing process of Indigenous women who have survived male violence and the family and community members of those women who were taken or murdered, influenced government actions and policy, forced positive social change, and greatly increased public awareness of the issue, among other important victories, for all the increased *awareness* of the issue of murdered and disappeared Indigenous women, governments, academia, non-governmental organizations (NGOs), the Canadian public, and even Indigenous women themselves have yet to increase *understanding* of the issues. As feminist Louise Armstrong writes after ten years of feminist struggle to identify and end incest:

> When we first spoke out, ten years ago, on the subject of incest, of our abuse, as children, by fathers and stepfathers, of our childhood rape by older brothers, stepbrothers, funny uncles, grandfathers—there was, for all the pain, sometimes humour.
>
> And there was, even through the anguish, a terrific mood of ebullience, of fantastic hope. Not only was it thrilling to pull insight and clarity from turmoil. By then—in the late 1970s—there was that sense of empowerment, of possibility for real change.

In these ten years things have become unimaginably worse—for child victims, now, and for the women, their mothers, who try to protect those children. And for survivors, who now find the very stuff of their trauma, their degradation, their violation as children, the common currency of talk show guest 'experts' and 'professionals'; find their courageous speaking-out transformed into no more than a new plot option for ongoing dramatic series.

People say to me, "Well, but at least we're talking about it now."

Yes. But it was not our intention merely to start a long conversation.

In breaking the silence, we hoped to raise hell. Instead, we have raised for the issue a certain normalcy. We hoped to raise a passion for change. Instead, what we raised was discourse—and a sizable problem-management industry ... (1990, p. 43).

Redefining Colonization and Indigenous Feminism

In this chapter, I redefine 'colonization' and 'Indigenous feminism', proposing feminist understandings of both.

Colonization

Cherry Smiley @_cherrysmiley_ · Jun 3, 2019 ···
#MMIWG I saw a paper bag to collect tears earlier. That's fine, but where is the paper bag that I put my anger in? #wheresthefeministragebag

Figure 2: A marvellous screenshot of a statement I made on Twitter during the closing ceremonies of the National Inquiry into Missing and Murdered Indigenous Women and Girls.

As discussed elsewhere in this book, patriarchy is our world's default ideology. Men and their interests are centred in everything we do, consciously or unconsciously, unless we intentionally apply feminist thinking (Spender, 1980; Jeffreys, 2003; de Beauvoir, 2011). And even when that's the case, that we're consciously applying feminist theory to a particular situation, it's so easy to slip back into the lifetime of patriarchal brainwashing we've received and centre men, again; and this happens, all the time. Feminism is, and must be, intentional: you can't accidentally be a feminist or be a feminist when you say you aren't a feminist. Feminism is an ongoing political choice and an ongoing political struggle within and outside of ourselves. Given that we live most of our lives submerged in the woman-hating ideology of patriarchy which constructs men as the most important everything and anything, people—even Indigenous and even with an 's'—means men: the default, the man-everything to the woman-nothing, the man-centre to the woman-margin (Spender, 1980). Unless women are intentionally and explicitly specified, we're absent (Spender, 1980). For example, 'mankind' means everyone; 'womankind'[13] only means women. Inspired by feminist thinkers and activists, I intentionally write and say 'women and men' instead of 'men and women'. This felt and sounded strange to me at first but now, after many years of practice, it sounds normal. Give it a try. Sure, it's symbolic that men come first, but guess what: men do come first, unless we make an intentionally feminist decision otherwise.

Toward a Feminist Definition of Colonization in Canada

What if we started with women first? What if we put women, who are humans like men, at the centre of our thinking about the world? What would a female-centred, feminist understanding of colonization look like, and how would this alter Indigenous and feminist theorizing, action, and politics? Building on the work of feminist scholars such as Gerda Lerner, Anne Stoler, Maria Mies, Kathleen Barry, Robin Morgan, Diane Bell, Napurrula Nelson, Kimberlé Crenshaw, and others, I propose a feminist definition of colonization where a) colonization is primarily a hierarchal sex-based process where men dominate women; and b) colonization is a process of male entitlement and female obligation.

---

13 The term 'womankind' is not widely used, if at all.

Colonization is a Hierarchical Sex-Based Process Where Men Dominate Women

> I was able to link the deplorable conditions of many contemporary Native women and children to colonization and its handmaiden, patriarchy (Anderson, 2011, p. 83).

Similarly, this PhD journey has provided me with energy and time to link our current situation as Indigenous women to patriarchy and its handmaiden, colonization. As Māori author Annie Mikaere writes:

> The position of women in English law was derived directly from their status in Roman law: The term [family] was invented by the Romans to denote a new social organism, whose head ruled over wife and children and a number of slaves, and was invested under Roman paternal power with rights of life and death over them ... according to the English common law, the head of the family (the husband/father) was in control of the household, 'women and children were chattels to be used and abused by the paterfamilias as he chose' (1994, section III, para. 2).

Women were the first people to be colonized and they were colonized by men. As part of that process of colonization, women become dependent on men for their survival and were forced to acquiesce to the lie that men, because they are male, are superior in every way to women, because they are female, and that this is the natural, inevitable, and unchangeable order of things (Lerner, 1986; Daly, 1985). Men's domination, including sexual domination, over women was enforced through a variety of different methods: women 'cooperated' with patriarchy due to the gendered patriarchal socialization all women and men receive, but men's domination over women was also enforced with male violence and the threat of male violence and women's economic dependency on male relatives then husbands (Lerner, 1986). Women were further coerced into 'cooperating' in their own oppression through the awarding of (relative) privileges to conforming women of the upper classes and through the division and ranking of women into 'good respectable women' and 'bad worthless women' (Lerner, 1986). Women were rewarded (relatively speaking, of course) for conforming to the expectations of their sex-class and women were punished for questioning or challenging these expectations, although it's important to note that any (relative) privilege a woman was granted didn't undo the realities of the woman-hating world she lived in—it wasn't a 'one-or-the-other' kind of deal where women were respected or not; more of a 'better-chance-of-having-insecure-access-to-some-material-comforts-than-other-women-did' kind of deal but even then, there were no guarantees and this didn't alter the relationship of any individual woman or woman as a class to patriarchy; for example, any relative privilege a woman may have didn't protect her from male violence or the threat of male violence and this remains true today.

Evidence for colonization as being primarily a sex-based hierarchal process can be seen in the epic journeys of 'explorers' such as Christopher Columbus, Juan Ponce de Leon, James Cook, Jacques Cartier, and Giovanni da Verrazano, among others, who, already practiced in the colonization of women (Lerner, 1986) explored 'new lands' and 'new worlds', invaded these territories and claimed them on behalf of England or France or Spain or wherever; occupied, settled, and colonized them. What do these invaders—all of them, including those not mentioned here—have in common? They were all men. Women did not "... [sail] the ocean blue ... in fourteen hundred ninety-two"[14] or in any other year for that matter during the 'Age of Discovery'. White women, instead, were eventually brought to the colonies as chattel, as property of their male relatives or husbands (Carter, 1997) where they were still considered subordinate to men and treated accordingly (Lerner, 1986). As Ann Stoler, Gerda Lerner, Sarah Carter and other feminist historians have argued, the category of 'colonizer' is more complicated than presented:

---

14 The author of this poem is unknown.

Colonial authority was constructed on two powerful, but false, premises. The first was the notion that Europeans in the colonies made up an easily identifiable and discrete biological and social entity; a 'natural' community of common class interests, racial attributes, political affinities and superior culture. The second was the related notion that the boundaries separating colonizer from colonized were thus self-evident and easily drawn. Neither premise reflected colonial realities … (Stoler, 1989, p. 635).

The men who invaded and colonized territories across the globe, including what we now know as Canada, and the patriarchal nations they represented, weren't out there 'exploring' and 'discovering' because they didn't have enough: they already had land and they had already turned this land into a resource exploited for profit and these male invaders had already colonized the women around them into 'accepting' their role as subordinates. These male invaders had already exploited women's labour, reproductive capacities, and sexuality for fun and profit. Capitalism, tied to immediate material comforts, encouraged more, more, more: it provided a way for men, who already had so much, to act on and materially benefit from the belief that they were entitled to so much more.

In *Capturing Women: The Manipulation of Cultural Imagery in Canada's Prairie West*, Sarah Carter examines historical representations of Indigenous and non-Indigenous women in the Canadian prairies from 1885–1900. She notes that historically, "it is difficult to uncover the 'real', since we have access to the 'real' only through representation" (Carter, 1997, p. 9). In this time period (and today) women were constrained by expectations of femininity and the conditions of their material realities and were not free to tell and record their own stories, in their own words (Carter, 1997, p. xv). Women were not (and are not) able to construct and freely project our own images, identities, and representations out into the world (Carter, 1997, p. xv). The systems of power that determine who gets to construct identities, who gets to project these identities, and whose representations are seen as legitimate have real consequences in our real world, regardless of the accuracy of the representation, as Carter states, "just as few white women actually lived up to the virtues they were said to exemplify, few Aboriginal women actually behaved in the way fixed in the colonial imagination" (1997, p. 185). The representations constructed by white men of both Indigenous and non-Indigenous women were used in the creation of a Canadian narrative that supported colonial actions, attitudes, and policies in the settlement of Canada by white men (Carter, 1997).

In contrast to Indigenous women, white women were viewed as civilized, virtuous, vulnerable property who were always in need of male protection (Carter, 1997). As Carter states, "... white women became essential symbols, or key icons, around which the new society was to be built. White women were the true 'empire builder', their children the cornerstone of a strong nation" (Carter, 1997, p. xiv). In these ways, the supposed vulnerabilities of white women were used to justify the horrific treatment of the savage, dangerous, and uncivilized Indigenous women in a legitimation of the male colonial agenda (Carter, 1997). The constructions of women, Indigenous and non-Indigenous, by men in this time period also served to control women, as "[t]he powerful ideologies of white and Aboriginal femininity functioned to inform both groups of their appropriate space and place" (Carter, 1997, p. 205). Since the invasion of Canada by white men, Indigenous women's 'appropriate place' has long been constructed as that of a 'princess' or a 'squaw' (Green, 1975; Acoose, 1995; Anderson, 2000; Valaskakis, 2005; Lajimodiere, 2013). While an 'Indian princess' is a 'beautiful', youthful Indigenous woman or girl who displays stereotypical markers of Indigeneity and femininity, it is important to note that both the princess and the squaw exist only in relation to non-Indigenous men:

> From the 'ministering maiden' image of the princess Pocahontas to her darker twin, the squaw, both the nobility and the savagery of Indian women have been defined in relation to white males—as women who rescued them, served them, married them, and who even gave up their Indian nation for them (Valaskakis, 2005, p. 134).

The squaw, the 'darker twin', is an Indigenous woman or girl with a savage sexuality (Valaskakis, 2005). She is always sexually available and exchanges sex for material benefit; importantly, she desires and enjoys these sex acts with multitudes of unknown men. In the construction of Indigenous and white women, men were able to turn Indigenous and white women against each other (Carter, 1997).

Colonization is a Process of Male Entitlement and Female Obligation

> I suggest that the very categories of 'colonizer' and 'colonized' were secured through forms of sexual control which defined the domestic arrangements of Europeans and the cultural investments by which they identified themselves. Gender specific sexual sanctions demarcated positions of power by refashioning middle-class conventions of respectability, which, in turn, prescribed the personal and public boundaries of race (Stoler, 1989, p. 635).

If we think about colonization as first a process of male domination and female subordination, this helps us to understand how women came to be viewed as the property of men—men owned (and still do own) women. In order to practice ownership over women though, men first had to feel entitled to that ownership and they did, and they do, because they're men and in patriarchy, men are superior to women. Men get a pretty sweet deal and women get fuck all in patriarchy. This is also why our only road to Women's Liberation is to overthrow and burn the patriarchy to the ground; not reform or rearrange it by making it more inclusive.

Old Skool Patriarchy?

Most feminists and Indigenous women in Canada believe that most or all pre-colonial Indigenous societies were matriarchal. For example, Dawn Lavell-Harvard, from the Wikwemikong First Nations, and Kim Anderson argue that prior to the invasion of

Canada by white men, many Indigenous cultures had egalitarian social structures that reflected and promoted respect for women and girls (Lavell-Harvard and Anderson, 2014). Indigenous women were believed to be fully human, as opposed to second-class, disposable subhumans (Razack, 2015); and women were autonomous and important in their own right with very deep ties to their families and communities:

> In land-based communities, given that the men were often away from the community for long periods, women were not only encouraged, but expected to be independent and self-reliant ... relationships [were] characterized by interdependence and equality (Lavell-Harvard and Anderson, 2014, p. 6).

The majority of Indigenous research, including oral histories, has consistently shown that systemic patriarchy, capitalism, and racism were not widely present among pre-colonial Indigenous communities in Canada. While by no means a utopia, the systemic issues that confront Indigenous women today, such as male violence against women, poverty, homelessness, and land destruction, and the underlying dominant ideologies that drive those issues, were not present to the same extent—if at all—they are now in contemporary Canada.

However, even though patriarchy may not have been present as it is today, male violence against women did exist in pre-colonial Indigenous communities:

> ... there are indications of violence against women in Aboriginal societies prior to European contact. Many early European observations as well as original Indian legends (e.g., Wehsehkehcha stories) point to the pre-existence of male violence against women. It should not be assumed that matriarchies necessarily prevented men from exhibiting oppressive behaviour toward women (LaRocque, 1994, p. 75).

Other evidence of the existence of male violence against women in pre-colonial times can be seen in the different strategies Indigenous women used to prevent and contend with male violence when it did happen, such as retaining their own identities and living with their relatives and other women in community during marriage (Mikaere, 1994; Bourgeois, 2018) or divorcing men in a simple process that carried no shame or stigma (Mikaere, 1994; Bourgeois, 2018). Men who committed acts of violence against women or children received consequences that clearly demonstrated the severity of the crime:

> ... assault on a woman, be it sexual or otherwise, was regarded as extremely serious and could result in death or, almost as bad, in being declared 'dead' by the community and ignored from then on (Mikaere, 1994, Section II, para. 5).

It seems likely that the underlying dominant ideologies in pre-colonial Indigenous communities didn't stem from woman-hating, male entitlement, and ownership and as a result, it was socially unacceptable behaviour for men to assault, rape, and murder the women around them.

While it seems that it was socially unacceptable to commit acts of violence against women, some men in pre-colonial Indigenous communities did just that, acceptable or not. In response, Indigenous women employed a number of preventative strategies and appropriate punishment to discourage this type of behaviour:

> ... importantly, Indigenous women are in no way suggesting that violence originated with colonialism: they acknowledge its existence in pre-colonial Indigenous societies, but also point out that the matriarchal organization and/or strict anti-violence policies of many Indigenous societies provided Indigenous females with security against violence (Bourgeois, 2018a, pp. 68–69).

Patriarchal thinking and behaviour didn't flourish into a systemic cultural foundation because most cultures weren't built on a foundation of entitlement and ownership that produced a situation where only some (men) were owners while others (women) were owned. Instead, Indigenous women were largely self-sufficient. That is, they had the knowledge of, practice, and access to what they needed to survive. My grandma would say, "if you were thirsty, you went to the river and drank; if you were hungry, you found something to eat; if you needed somewhere to live, you built a house." Women were not economically or otherwise dependent on men for what they needed to survive and this gave women more autonomy and control over their own lives (Anderson, 2016).

Another strategy that kept patriarchal thinking and behaviours in check was a more collective structure of social organization. In a more open and communal culture, women are less isolated. This is particularly true for women who have children as the structure of the nuclear family is set up to isolate women from each other and facilitates economic and other dependence on men (Mikaere, 1994; Carter, 1997; Green, 2017). In contrast, Indigenous forms of collective social organization

> … ensured a degree of flexibility for women not possible within the confines of the nuclear family. The presence of so many caregivers, and the expectation that they would assume much of the responsibility of child rearing, enabled women to perform a wide range of roles, including leadership roles (Mikaere, 1994, section II, para. 8).

Really Though, It Wasn't a Feminist Utopia

While it seems that systemic male violence against women in pre-colonial Indigenous cultures didn't happen to the same all-encompassing life-shattering consistency that it does today, this doesn't mean that the world was a perfect place for women. On the contrary, "one must also note that in all hunting/gathering societies, no matter what women's economic and social status is, women are always subordinate to men in some respects" (Lerner, 1986, p. 30). For example, Sto:lo women were rarely 'chiefs' as in leaders while men were (Knickerbocker, 2020) and Māori women traditionally didn't speak on the marae while men did (Du Plessis et al., 1993). Indigenous women scholars, however, have argued that when Sto:lo and Māori cultures are evaluated on their own terms and not that of 'white feminism', that these sex-based roles are not based in inequality between women and men: Sto:lo women, while not chiefs, did guide their communities through their roles as matriarchs (Knickerbocker, 2020) and Māori women did speak on the marae when speaking is defined from a Māori perspective (Du Plessis et al., 1993). Yet, there is a very serious danger to women when cultural relativism is used to explain and justify any exclusion or limitation of women from social, political, spiritual, or economic life. While there are cultural practices that are segregated by sex, men, unlike women, are never excluded or limited from participating as full and equal members of their communities due to their sex.

Indigenous women and feminists have long argued that women are—are seen to be, or should be seen to be—closer to 'nature than 'culture' (Ortner, 1972). For example, Robin Morgan theorized that women were a colonized people because men had seized control over women's 'land'—'land' meaning women's bodies (Morgan, 1977; Morgan, 2000). Today, this point is often made from a cultural perspective by Indigenous women across Canada who use this perspective to draw political connections between the destruction of Indigenous women and the destruction of the land with the two bodies (women and land) equaling one to the other:

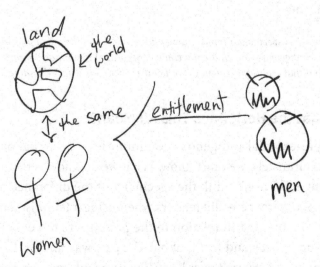

Figure 3: A dazzling hand-drawn image that shows the dominant idea that Indigenous women are equivalent to/the same as the earth.

I disagree with this analysis: women and the land are not the same. There are deep relationships and cultural connections between women and the land to be sure but folding the two into one concept makes it hard to see how men's colonization of women operates. What is the same, or similar, is the relationship men have to women and the relationship men have to the land—a relationship of entitlement and ownership:

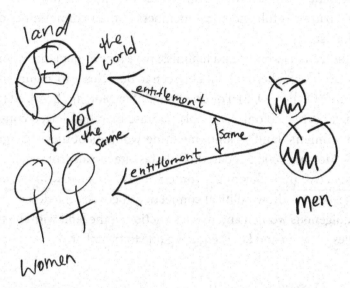

Figure 4: A spectacular hand-drawn image that shows the unpopular idea that Indigenous women are not equivalent to/not the same as the earth, but that male entitlement to both of these bodies is what's the same.

So, What the Heck Does This All Mean?

Were pre-colonial Indigenous communities patriarchal or not? I think, ultimately, we don't know. What we do know is that it was different and I don't think the specificity of the difference or the degree of difference really matters when using a feminist analysis to examine the past in relation to the present. It's too easy to get caught up in back and forths about 'the past was this' or 'the past was that' when we can't ever know for sure and we don't need to. Culture, and the ideologies that governed pre-colonial Indigenous cultures, were different—not perfect—but different and that's all we need to know. Indigenous cultures weren't based on these same fundamental concepts of entitlement and ownership, whether that be male entitlement or even female entitlement. What this says is that systemic patriarchy, capitalism, and racism are not the natural, inevitable, and unchangeable order of things; they are not ideologies that sprout from our biological destinies as female and male human beings; they are *ideas and behaviours* and ideas and behaviour are chosen and can change (Mies et al., 1988). These changes can be positive or negative. Indigenous men recognized the benefits patriarchy offered to them and decided that these benefits outweighed the disadvantages created by the hierarchies of class and race that accompanied patriarchal culture. Patriarchy wasn't imposed on Indigenous communities, *Indigenous men chose to adopt patriarchy as a fundamental ideology.* Patriarchy is a choice and all men benefit from this system to a greater or lesser extent depending on where they're placed in the hierarchies of class, race, and sexuality (McIntyre et al., 2000).

Importantly, aspects of patriarchy weren't unfamiliar to Indigenous men as male violence against women, cultural limitations placed on women, and discriminatory practices against women pre-existed the invasion of white men; it was the adoption of patriarchy and capitalism that turned individual acts of male violence and discriminatory practices against women into a systemic patriarchal and profit-oriented culture where men were not only able to benefit from patriarchy but now also able to immediately and materially profit from the subordination of women. Male entitlement and ownership, the accumulation of always-more, and class-, race-, and sexuality-based hierarchies allowed men to exploit women as they kept taking what they felt they were entitled to, which was basically everything. Indigenous men chose to adopt patriarchy as a system and keep choosing to do so because it benefits them. If we look, for example, at the system of capitalism, we don't say that capitalism was imposed on the wealthy businessmen who benefit from capitalism—these businessmen adopted the values of capitalism and continue to do so because it benefits them (some more than others). Capitalism benefits the wealthy as patriarchy benefits men.

Making Deals

While there's a lot we don't and can't know, what we do know is that once white men invaded Canada, Indigenous men colluded with white men to institutionalize male domination to their benefit. White and Indigenous men worked together, and continue to work together, to maintain the subordination of women and to legally, socially, and politically exclude Indigenous women from everyday life. Two of the ways in which men institutionalized patriarchy are through the legal and political ejection and exclusion of Indigenous women from their communities and through the use of male violence to protect male entitlement, ownership, and their patriarchal benefits. As Dworkin stated about the false divide between conservative and liberal men, "pretending to argue, they collude. And if one don't get you, the other will" (1997, p. 199).

Treaties as the First Formal Collusion Between Indigenous and White Men

I was in New Zealand in 2019 on the Treaty of Waitangi Day.[15] We had planned to attend the events being held in Waitangi on that day but unfortunately had to change our plans at the last minute. Speaking with a Māori friend, I remember asking how many women were present during the initial signing of the treaties and how many women ultimately signed. Her responses sparked questions that led to the adjustment of my dissertation: maybe one or two women were present at the initial signing at Waitangi on February 6, 1840 but this isn't confirmed and it's possible no women were present at the initial signing at all. At first, it was believed three or four

---

15   Every February 6, Aotearoa/New Zealand marks the signing of the Treaty of Waitangi between Māori and white male colonizers in 1840.

women had signed the treaty as it circulated Aotearoa, but it has been determined that at least thirteen Māori women had signed the Treaty of Waitangi (Mikaere, 1994). Out of approximately 540 signatures, 527 of the signatures are from men—99% of the Treaty of Waitangi signatories were men.

A similar pattern emerges when looking at the numbered treaties across Canada signed between 1871 and 1921—women were not signatories to treaties. Many Indigenous feminists understand this exclusion of women as due to the *imposition* of patriarchy onto and into Indigenous communities: "Native men are domesticated into the wage economy and taught their only power is to ally with white men in the oppression of Indigenous women through church, school, law, and policy" (Simpson, 2017, p. 89). With so much discussion of 'Indigenous women's agency' and how feminism supposedly denies the agency of Indigenous women to suck the dicks of men whose dicks they don't want to suck, you'd think there'd be similar discussions around the removal of Indigenous men's agency to cut a deal with white men when it works for them. Surprisingly,[16] there's no discussion around this double standard (that's false in the first place): Indigenous women *are not* passive victims of colonization but active agents who make their own completely valid choices to perform sex acts with multitudes of unknown men for some type of benefit but Indigenous men *are* passive victims of colonization who have no other choice but to forcibly accept a patriarchal system that benefits them at someone else's (women's) expense. This idea that a system that benefits men was forced onto men, or that these poor Indigenous men were so completely bamboozled and somehow didn't realize that they were "… targeted by white men working strategically and persistently to make allies out of [them]," using neoliberal academic concepts and language, "erases Indigenous men's agency." The reality is that it took both parties, together—white men and Indigenous men—to exclude Indigenous women and white women from participating

---

16   It's not surprising, I'm being sarcastic.

as equals—if at all—in decisions that directly and profoundly impacted their lives (McIvor, 2004).

None of this, of course, meant that the treaties were fair, for Indigenous women or men. They were not at all fair to Indigenous peoples and white male settlers used their power to get themselves the best deal possible by embedding concepts such as "... cede, surrender, extinguish, yield, and forever give up all rights and titles ..." (qtd. in Comack, 2018, p. 461) into the treaties when these foreign concepts had no translation in Indigenous worldviews: "ownership of the land is inimical to Indigenous ways of knowing, and Indigenous languages have no translation for words like 'cede' or 'surrender'" (Comack, 2018, p. 461):

> The situation varied from one treaty to another, but in general the Indian nations, based on their cultural and oral traditions, understood they were sharing the land, not 'surrendering' it. While the surrender clauses of the early land sales in Ontario were included in the later written numbered treaties, it is questionable whether their implications were known to the Indian parties, since these legal and real estate concepts would have been incomprehensible to many Aboriginal people. Further, it would have been difficult, if not impossible, to translate the legal language expressing these concepts into the Indian languages. Aboriginal people often understood that they were being compensated for the use of their lands and that they were not being asked to give up or surrender them, but to allow settlers to move onto their lands peaceably (RCAP, 1996, p. 148).

Had these concepts been translated and their consequences understood by the Indigenous men signing the treaty, it's doubtful they would've agreed to such an unfair and exploitative deal for themselves and their nations (Comack, 2018). It's here that we can begin to see the patriarchal foundations of the treaties. According to the Royal Commission on Aboriginal Peoples (RCAP):

> In these negotiations the Indian parties were concerned primarily with retaining and protecting their lands, their ways of life, and the continuation of their traditional economies based on hunting, fishing, trapping and gathering. In these areas they were firm and

immovable in treaty negotiations. Though they were agreeable to sharing, they were not agreeable to major changes in their ways of life. Further, they were not asked to agree to this; it was common for Crown representatives to assure treaty nations that their traditional way of life would not be affected by the signing of the treaty. Indeed, an examination of the reports of the treaty commissioners reveals that these matters, not the sale of land, occupied most of the discussion during treaty negotiations (RCAP, 1996, pp. 148–149).

What this suggests is that Indigenous men would have been completely unwilling to surrender their territories to Canada had this foreign concept and its consequences been explained and understood by both treaty parties. This makes complete sense. However, the RCAP and other sources also reveal that, for some of the treaty negotiation processes at least, the discussions focused on assurances that Indigenous peoples would be able to continue their ways of life, culture, and traditions in Canada. Today, we know this isn't what happened. At the time though, Indigenous ways of life had already changed, only these changes most profoundly and negatively impacted Indigenous women. At the time the numbered treaties were signed, for example, Indigenous women were already being prostituted. There's no evidence that this practice existed prior to white men's invasion and I'd argue that this is a very profound change to Indigenous women's ways of life. Capitalism allowed entitlement and ownership (communal or individual) to turn a profit and helped to institutionalize patriarchy—now, there was an immediate economic benefit to patriarchy in that, for example, men could acquire extra food rations by pimping their Indigenous female relatives out to white men (Backhouse 1985; Mawani, 2002). Capitalism monetized patriarchy and racism as well to benefit some (men) at the expense of others (women). Additionally, that Indigenous women were excluded from the treaty-making process was another profound change in Indigenous women's ways of life as Indigenous women generally had more decision-making ability prior to the arrival of white settler men (although how much more is up for debate). By the time the treaties were signed, life had already changed in profound and negative ways for Indigenous women. What Indigenous men were attempting to negotiate in the treaty process was assurance that *Indigenous men's lives* wouldn't change in profound and negative ways. Surrendering land, it seems, had there been mutual understanding between the treaty parties, would have been completely unacceptable and negotiations could have possibly broken down. Assurances that Indigenous men's ways of life and relative privilege in patriarchy would be respected was also a key issue in negotiations. Indigenous women, however, already reeling from the impacts of patriarchy and its terrible cousins capitalism and racism, were of no real concern to the Indigenous and non-Indigenous men that colluded then and who continue to collude today.

The Indian Act

As many Indigenous feminists (McIvor, 2004; Vowel, 2016; Eberts, 2017) have analyzed, the implementation of the Canadian government's 1876 *Indian Act* has had, and continues to have, significantly negative impacts on Indigenous peoples and particular consequences for Indigenous women. Up until 1985, Indigenous women with Indian status who married non-status men forfeited their Indian status while Indigenous men who married non-status women conferred Indian status to their wives and children. After numerous legal challenges and advocacy campaigns by Indigenous women such as Mary Two-Axe Early, Sandra Lovelace, the women of Tobique,[17] and Jeanette Corbiere-Laval,

> in 1985, the federal government enacted Bill C-31, both in response to Lovelace and because of section 15 of the *Canadian Charter of Rights and Freedoms*. The promise was to eliminate all of the sex-based discrimination against women in the *Indian Act*. Instead, Bill

---

17 See *Enough is Enough: Aboriginal Women Speak Out* (Silman, 1987) for an excellent account by the women of Tobique about their struggle against sex discrimination in the *Indian Act* and elsewhere.

C-31 removed some of the sex discrimination and carried forward the rest (Brodsky, 2016, p. 316).

In 1985 until 2009, Sharon McIvor and Lynne Gehl continued to legally challenge the ongoing sex-based discrimination in the *Indian Act*, eventually winning another partial victory (Brodsky, 2016). In 2017, with the assistance of many feminist allies, the Government of Canada finally agreed to remove all sex-based discrimination from the *Indian Act* and the process was completed in 2019, restoring Indian status to hundreds of thousands of Indigenous peoples who were wrongly denied or who had lost their Indian status because they were female or because an ancestor was female.

While Indigenous feminists and many others across the country celebrated this important victory, the journey to this point had been incredibly difficult. The use of the justice system by Indigenous women was (and still is) seen as using the 'Master's Tools';[18] In this case, each of the women who attempted to claim their rights and remedy sex-based discrimination in the *Indian Act* using the Canadian legal system were harshly criticized not only for their strategic decisions, but because they were women challenging patriarchy. As McIvor states:

> [f]or the women, to stand up in court is to be subject to the harshest treatment from their own communities locally, regionally, and nationally – be they Indian, Inuit, or Métis. It is a hard and lonely road, but sometimes a necessary one (McIvor, 2004, p. 111).

Until the most recent court battles, Indigenous men's groups and male-dominated First Nations overwhelmingly sided with the Canadian government against Indigenous women in favour of continuing the legal practice of sex-based discrimination in the *Indian Act* (Silman, 1987). McIvor (2004) and other Indigenous women, have also written of the sexist opposition by the Canadian government and Indigenous men's organizations to allow Indigenous women, represented by the Native Women's Association

---

18   See *The Master's Tools Will Never Dismantle the Master's House* by Audre Lorde (1984).

of Canada, to have dedicated funding and 'a seat at the table' during the Charlottetown Accord negotiations.[19] We continue to see the patriarchal attitudes present in Indigenous men's organizations: In 2020, the Assembly of First Nations (AFN, founded as the National Indian Brotherhood) engaged in internal heated debate after a resolution was brought forward by a woman to conduct an independent investigation into the AFN's treatment of women and of homosexual people with some AFN members refusing outright to support the resolution and others attempting to modify it so as not to disrupt the status quo (i.e. patriarchal) operations of the AFN (Bellrichard, 2020). That this resolution would even cause a debate as to whether or not it should move forward shows the patriarchal foundations of the AFN. Another example of the patriarchal attitudes present in Indigenous men's organizations is that out of five national native organizations, only one (the NWAC) is a women's organization.[20] This alone is concerning or should be, at least, that Indigenous women's needs and interests are folded into Indigenous men's needs and interests. What happens when these needs and interests conflict with each other, such as when the need for Indigenous women to be safe in their homes conflicts with Indigenous men's interests in raping and battering their girlfriends, wives, sisters, and daughters? Our poor men, we say, they've been hurt and that's why they're hurting us or those poor men, they say, they've been hurt and that's why they're hurting their women. Bullshit. If "hurt people hurt people" as former DIA[21]

---

19 See McIvor's article, *Aboriginal Women Unmasked: Using Equality Litigation to Advance Women's Rights* (2004) for an excellent account of the ways in which Indigenous women were discriminated against by Canadian Governments and Indigenous men's groups during the Charlottetown Accord negotiations.

20 Some Indigenous women, myself included, argue that NWAC is no longer a women's organization as their mandate has expanded to include not only politically representing the voices of Indigenous women and girls, but also representing the political voices of men who identify as anything other than 'men' including 'gender diverse', 'trans', 'Two-Spirit', 'non-binary' and so on.

21 The Canadian Federal Government has changed the name of what was originally called "the Indian Department" so many times, it's hard to keep track. Currently, there are two departments known as Indigenous Relations and Northern Affairs

agent Carolyn Bennett said to me in a short conversation, women would overwhelmingly be violent predators; but this isn't the case.

Colonization as an Excuse for Male Violence Against Women

The idea that Indigenous men are benefactors of an adopted patriarchy and that Indigenous men also commit violence against Indigenous women continues to be controversial despite the fact that Indigenous men are committing acts of violence against Indigenous women. Saying this out loud or writing this down doesn't mean that only Indigenous men are committing acts of violence against Indigenous women; it means that in patriarchy, men target women—and Indigenous women in particular—for acts of violence and that Indigenous men are included in the category of men because they are male. The pressure that Indigenous women are under to ignore, excuse, or even justify violence against Indigenous women by Indigenous men in particular, is immense. As Farley et al. stated:

> Sexual violence and other family violence are major social problems in First Nations communities. [citing Lynne] A Dene woman described communities in which the entire female population had been sexually assaulted by men. She had been threatened with further violence if she spoke out against this ... (Farley et al., 2005, p. 258)

Other researchers have found similar rates of male violence against Indigenous women and particularly, of Indigenous girls, within Indigenous communities. One study found that up to 75 per cent of sex crime victims in some Indigenous communities are girls under the age of 18, 50 per cent of those are under the age of 14, and almost 25 per cent of those are under the age of seven (cited in McIvor and Nahanee, 1998). High rates of sexualized male violence

---

Canada and Indigenous Services Canada. Some Indigenous peoples, like my mom, just refer to this department as the Department of Indian Affairs (DIA) because while its name may have changed many times over the years, its purpose and consequences are still the same.

against Indigenous girls have also been found outside of Indigenous communities. For example, a 2016 study found that over 61 per cent of children sexually abused in British Columbia's foster care system are Indigenous girls although Indigenous girls comprise approximately 25 per cent of the total children in the system—an overrepresentation in itself (B.C. Representative for Children and Youth, 2016).

The disproportionate rates of male violence against Indigenous girls allows us to better see the connection between the sexual assault of girls, particularly incestuous male violence, and the disproportionate prostitution of Indigenous women:

> Incest is boot camp. Incest is where you send the girl to learn how to do it. So you don't, obviously, have to send her anywhere, she's already there and she's got nowhere else to go. She's trained. And the training is specific and it is important: not to have any real boundaries to her own body; to know that she's valued only for sex; to learn about men what the offender, the sex offender, is teaching her (Dworkin, 1993, pp. 4–5).

Research on adult women in prostitution has confirmed this link between sexual assault in girlhood and prostitution with a nine-country study on prostitution finding that across the countries, 65 per cent to 95 per cent of prostituted women were sexually assaulted as children (Farley et al., 2004, p. 56). Another study found:

> Eighty-two percent of our respondents [women in prostitution] reported a history of childhood sexual abuse, by an average of four perpetrators. This statistic (those assaulted by an average of four perpetrators) did not include those who responded to the question 'If there was unwanted sexual touching or sexual contact between you and an adult, how many people in all?' with 'tons' or 'I can't count that high' or 'I was too young to remember' (Farley et al., 2005, p. 249).

While not all of these assaults may have been committed by family members, at least some, likely many, were. As Farley et al. state:

> Like adult prostitutes, incested children are bribed into sex acts by adults and offered food, money, or protection for their silence. Use

of a child for sex by adults may thus be understood as prostitution of a child ... when a child is incestuously assaulted, the perpetrator's objectification of the child victim and his rationalization and denial are similar to the john's in prostitution. The psychological symptoms resulting from incest and prostitution are similar (Farley et al. 2003, p. 57).

In addition to committing acts of male violence against women themselves, Indigenous men have also facilitated and benefitted from male violence against Indigenous women. When we understand that Indigenous women are not simply conduits for the violence of colonization, we can more accurately name the violence perpetrated against Indigenous women as femicide,[22] as opposed to genocide. While there are numerous accounts of white men in positions of power demanding or offering the exchange of sex acts from Indigenous women for food rations and other necessities needed in order to survive in the past (Carter, 1997), there are also accounts of Indigenous men acting as pimps or facilitators of Indigenous women's prostitution (Backhouse, 1985; Mawani, 2002). While at least some or perhaps many of these allegations are suspect, coming from missionaries, government officials, and racist and sexist sensationalized media reports such as 'Indian Girl Sold for 1000 Blankets and Five Little Girls Sold at Alert Bay Potlatch' as justification for the colonial project that was Canadian-nation building (Backhouse, 1985; Mawani, 2002, p. 43), Indigenous men participated in some way in the prostitution of Indigenous women. The 2011 murder of Cree woman Cindy Gladue, who bled to death in a motel bathtub from an 11cm tear in her vaginal wall admittedly caused by Bradley Barton, a white truck driver, demonstrates this very scenario. Barton, who had purchased sex from Gladue on two occasions including the night she bled to death, claimed that Gladue's fatal injury was caused by consensual 'rough sex' (Razack, 2016). As Razack states, "in the initial reporting of the

---

22 In 2012, Diana Russell defined femicide as "... the killing of one or more females by one or more males *because* they are female" (p. 2); Russell defines and examines femicide in many of her works (1976; 1992; 2001; 2012).

murder, Gladue's Indigenous origin did not merit a mention, and media coverage was sparse. Few seemed to notice the death of an Indigenous woman in the context of prostitution" (2016, p. 286). In 2015, the trial of Barton and the death of Gladue became national headlines when Gladue's vaginal tissue was brought into the courtroom as evidence and when Barton was initially acquitted on all charges (Razack, 2016); Barton has now been found guilty of manslaughter in the death of Gladue (Russell and Snowden, 2021). While a dehumanizing act, the initial violence that Barton committed against Gladue in her life and death and certainly the role of Gladue's boyfriend at the time of her death, Steven Reid, who stated that "… he was the one who connected Ms. Gladue with Mr. Barton after the trucker said he wanted to 'be with a woman'" (Carlson, 2015) was de-emphasized or completely ignored.

As much as we don't want this to be the case, this is the case. I, and other women who have worked in paid or unpaid, formal or informal positions as feminist anti-violence workers, have heard similar stories and we believe these women. It's no small task to bring up Indigenous men's violence against women as a constant threat and an urgent issue—this is when your commitment to feminist analysis is challenged because believe me, it's much easier in most situations to just blame those white guys over there. Yes, white guys choose to beat, rape, and murder Indigenous women and they should be blamed and held to account for these actions, as should all men—white, Indigenous, black, Asian, able-bodied, physically disabled, tall, short, long hair, short hair—all men who choose to commit acts of violence against women should be blamed and held to account for their actions. Academic nonsense, in all its racist woman-hating glory, encourages complexity and nuance here when it's actually not complex at all. We either stand with women who have been raped or we stand with the men who rape them. Of course, when 'professional considerations' come into play, this can make the decision a difficult one: Do I potentially limit my career opportunities by using my academic platform to support a woman who has been sexually harassed by a very powerful, well-connected Indigenous man or do I stay quiet, knowing it's not right, but better her than me and dang academia is so competitive and I really want tenure? For some women, there's no hesitation and the decision to stand with and for women is an easy one, whatever the potential personal or professional costs may be. For others, this is a very difficult decision but it's just that—difficult, not complicated: do you do what's right and fight with and for women against the patriarchy, or do you do what's right for you as an individual woman with some class privilege and lofty 'feminist' career aspirations? As Ware stated:

> The black middle class has not joined the militant movement. As a class, it has closely identified with white America. Up until now it has been a conservative force in the black community. This middle class, largely descended from lighter-skinned slaves, has been the segment of black society that has benefitted most from things as they are. They have preferred the advantages they know to the mere possibilities of a black revolution (2000, p. 99).

Police: Defenders and Protectors of the Patriarchy

Many Indigenous feminist scholars have presented courageous and blistering critiques of the police as an anti-Indigenous institution in Canada (Palmater, 2016; Eberts, 2017). If we examine colonization as a sex-based oppression of women by men though, we can analyze the police as a mechanism to protect patriarchy and particularly the male sex-right. Police officers in Canada are overwhelmingly male and this has been the case since this manstitution began. For at least the past 30 years, there have been repeated calls to investigate the sexual harassment of female police officers by male police officers that occurs within the Royal Canadian Mounted Police (RCMP) (Bastarache, 2020). In the final report on the implementation of the Merlo-Davidson settlement agreement,[23] *Broken Dreams, Broken*

---

23 The Merlo-Davidson Settlement Agreement assessed "… claims for compensation made by women who had experienced sexual harassment and gender or sexual orientation based discrimination while working for the RCMP as a regular

Lives: The Devastating Effects of Sexual Harassment on Women in the RCMP, Bastarache states:

> One of the key findings of this Report is that the culture of the RCMP is toxic and tolerates misogynistic and homophobic attitudes amongst its leaders and members. This culture has resulted in incalculable damage to female members of the RCMP as well as those working for the public service. A change in the culture of the RCMP is essential. This Report concludes that change cannot come from within the RCMP but must be initiated from external sources (2020, p. i).

The report details some of the incidences of sexualized violence and sexual harassment that male officers and employees of the RCMP perpetrated against their female colleagues, including over 130 claims of sexual assault (Bastarache, 2020):

> Claimants told the Assessors that male RCMP members would call women sickening and humiliating names like 'split-tail', 'cunt', 'canoe-licker', 'bitch', 'ball-breaker', 'fresh meat', 'beaver tails', 'WREN (wasted regimental number)'. If a woman happened to also be Indigenous she was called a 'squaw', 'smoked meat' … Dildoes placed in women's desks were not uncommon. At least one woman found used condoms in her desk drawer. Other women were handcuffed to the toilet in the men's washroom or to chairs, or in a cell. Other examples included leaving tampons covered in ketchup in a woman's desk drawer, forming a wool hat into the shape of a 'beaver', putting dog turds in boots, putting ink on a toilet seat, invading a woman's personal space in a locker, putting up doctored photos of women on detachment bulletin boards suggesting that they are selling sex and the list goes on … Women also recounted being given menial tasks, i.e. being told to empty garbage cans, clean kitchens, wash cars or make coffee with the goal of making them feel "less than", of humiliating them. They were told that they had to do these tasks because it was women's work … Sexual misconduct in the RCMP appears to occur with a surprising frequency. The Assessors were told of drunk male members at Regimental dinners, standing on the table and waving their penises

---

member, a civilian member or a public service employee …" (Bastarache, 2020, p.1). Over 3000 claims were made (Bastarache, 2020).

at the women; sexual assaults when members are out of town on courses and staying at hotels were frequent … Indigenous women, particularly those who had been abused as children, were preyed upon by their male colleagues for sexual favours … Pornography on RCMP computers and phones was raised in many claims. Some of this material was violent and obscene. The Assessors were told of seized pornography being passed around as amusement. Sometimes male RCMP members would spend time at the scene of the search, viewing it with relish and requiring female members to come and watch with them. In earlier times, pornography was sometimes displayed at the detachment; it can now be emailed or texted to women members … (Bastarache, 2020, pp. 46–47).

Given the internal woman-hating culture of the RCMP and horrific misogynist treatment of female RCMP officers and other female employees by male RCMP officers, it's not surprising to learn that sexual assaults, a crime overwhelmingly perpetrated against women by men, is the most underreported crime to police in Canada and when reported, is the least likely to result in a criminal conviction (Benedet, 2013). Johnson estimates that 0.3 per cent of sexual assault cases in Canada result in a criminal conviction (Benedet, 2013). When we see the woman-hating workplace culture of the RCMP combined with the fact that sexual assault is the least reported, least investigated and least prosecuted crime, it becomes clear that one of the primary functions of the RCMP is to protect men's entitlement to sexually access women's bodies.

CHAPTER 3

Toward a Decolonizing Feminist Methodology

In this chapter I describe the methodological foundations of my research including what the heck happened and what I learned during the research process. I suggest a framework for a decolonizing feminist methodology and present research-creation as a methodology.

Methodology?

> Methods and methodology are not simply techniques and rationales for the conduct of research. Rather they must be understood in relation to specific historical, cultural, ideological and other contexts (Reinharz, 1983, p. 162).

I begin by describing what I mean by methodology. In this research, I borrow from Renate Klein's concept of methodology that refers to the overall research project, the choices made about and within that project, the doing of the research itself, and the presentation of the research results (1983). The purpose of my research is political and aims to contribute to furthering the theory and goals of the Women's Liberation Movement. I make no claims to neutrality or objectivity; rather, I position myself with honesty and transparency in relation to the issue and to those I engage in research with while remaining open-minded. As Erin Graham has noted, however, while it's important to keep an open mind, it's also important that your mind is not so open that your brains fall out.[24]

Feminist Methodological Foundations

This research is firmly grounded in feminist methodological guidelines developed by Maria Mies and described in 'Towards a Methodology for Feminist Research'. Mies' guidelines draw on her experiences as both a social scientist and as an active participant in the Women's Liberation Movement, a position she recognizes as contradictory but that also informs her work (Mies, 1983). Mies goes on to briefly describe seven methodological guidelines for feminist research: (1) the idea of value-free, neutral, objective research must be replaced with conscious partiality, "which is achieved through particle identification with the research objects" (122); (2) the relationship between researcher and researched should be one of 'a view from below' as opposed to 'a view from above'; (3) neutral, uninvolved 'spectator knowledge' must be replaced with active participation in the Women's Liberation Movement; (4) changing the status quo must become the starting point for research; (5) the research process, for both the researcher and those being researched, must become a process of problem-formulating consciousness-raising, what Paulo Freire calls 'conscientization'; (6) the study of women's individual and social history must accompany the problem-formulating conscientization of women; and (7) in order to appropriate their own history, women must collectivize their own experiences (Mies, 1983). Mies describes how she applied these principles in a research action project in Cologne, Germany, at a battered women's shelter called Women's House (1983). This process began with the organization of a street action about the need for a shelter for battered women in order to

---

24 Personal communication.

learn about the issue and to pressure the government to take action against men's abuse of women in the home. The research process also included interviewing individual women and transcribing their life histories up until the point they had entered the shelter, with women being able to control and edit their transcriptions (Mies, 1983). Mies and her research group wanted to discuss with the women common themes they found among the life stories and as they wanted to avoid the possibility of a discussion dominated by only a few voices; they suggested the creation of a play based on the common themes (1983). The women participants wrote and performed the play and all women in the shelter were invited to see the performance and participate in the discussion that occurred after, both of which were recorded (Mies, 1983). My research project has adopted and expanded Mies' research methodology to account for the specificities of doing research as an Indigenous feminist woman and doing research with Indigenous women who have been harmed by men.

Decolonizing and Indigenous Research Methodologies

My research and my work are grounded in feminist methodologies because feminism is the only theory, practice, and social political movement that prioritizes women. Other research methodologies, theories, and movements may include the experiences and interests of women, but this is optional and when included, always secondary to the male-defined actually important issues at hand, whatever these issues may be. In Indigenous research and activism, issues of land, culture, and sovereignty continue to be defined by male leadership as our most important issues—these are the 'real' issues (McIvor, 2004).

Māori scholar Linda Smith's *Decolonizing Methodologies* and Margaret Kovach's *Indigenous Methodologies: Characteristics, Conversations, and Contexts* offer groundbreaking critiques of traditional methods and methodologies used by academic researchers and what these processes have done to Indigenous peoples and knowledges. The power hidden behind and within academic research and the power that academic research creates is made undeniably visible in these texts. Smith describes a decolonizing research methodology as oriented toward dismantling research as a colonizing agent. She states:

> Research is one of the ways in which the underlying code of imperialism and colonialism is both regulated and realized. It is regulated through the formal rules of individual scholarly disciplines and scientific paradigms, and the institutions that support them (including the state). It is realized in the myriad of representations and ideological constructions of the Other in scholarly and 'popular' works, and in the principles which help to select and recontextualize those constructions in such things as the media, official histories and school curricula (Smith, 2012, p. 8).

Smith argues, however, that research can be useful. She encourages Indigenous peoples and their allies not to abandon research itself, thus accepting the colonial academic lies told about us, but instead to use it as a way to 'talk back' and further, as a way to work towards Indigenous sovereignty and social justice: "in a decolonizing framework, deconstruction is part of a much larger intent" (2012, p. 3). Kovach, while similarly recognizing the contested spaces Indigenous scholars occupy in the academy, defines Indigenous methodologies as "… the theory and method of conducting research that flows from an Indigenous epistemology" (2010, p. 21). Indigenous methodologies offer ways in which to bring place-based and culturally-specific Indigenous processes, knowledge, and worldviews as research. As Kovach states, an Indigenous research methodology considers knowing "… a process of self-in-relation" and encourages an honest, collective (outside myself), and self-reflexive (within myself) approach that focuses on positionality and relationships as part of an interconnected natural world (qtd. in Kovach, 2010, p. 14).

While offering incredibly useful and important insights, neither of these methodologies adequately and consistently acknowledge the realities of patriarchy and the different impacts of colonization on Indigenous women from Indigenous men. This makes sense, given that the methodologies presented are not grounded in feminism and as a result, don't centre women. In turn, this affirms that feminism is the only theory, practice, and social political movement that consistently prioritizes women and establishes the need for an explicitly decolonizing feminist methodology:

> *The first step* in articulating a new method is to understand that one's personally experienced dissatisfaction with conventional methods is not an intrapsychic, private problem but derives from structural inconsistencies and skewed assumptions underpinning the methods themselves. Thus one begins to sense that there is a gap between the 'experience of the world … and the theoretical schemes available to think about it in (qtd. in Reinharz, 1983, p. 166).

Today, patriarchy, wherever we are, whoever we are, is our default ideology and without intentional grounding in feminist methodology, theory, and practice, women are at best, unimportant and at worst, actively harmed in the research process.

My Struggle, Our Struggles: Conscious Partiality

> 'Giving back' … sounds more akin to standing on two sides of a boundary that parties view as pretty much set. We good-intentioned liberal individuals in the broader imperialistic academy agree to negotiate and sign treaties—with individual subjects and sometimes with collectives—across that boundary. We do this in good faith and we figure out ways to do service or help build capacity in the communities in which we work (Tallbear, 2014, para. 3).

Mies proposes the use of conscious partiality; that is, a partial identification that

> … not only conceives of the research objects as parts of a bigger social whole but also of the research subjects, i.e. the researchers themselves … it enables the correction of distortions of perception on both sides and widens the consciousness of both, the researcher and the 'researched' (1983, p. 123).

A conscious partiality is about connections and relationships we make between ourselves as researchers with women participating in our research and figuring out how we fit, beyond that relationship, as women in our larger social and political world. It's an intentional feminist process and one that's useful in other relationships as well. Fay Blaney, a mentor of mine and member of the WAC for this research project, shared her experiences of doing a Master of Arts degree as an Indigenous woman activist:

> In this state, I am incapable of attending any of my meetings or other responsibilities. I resent this and feel worse. It is all so hopeless. I can't even save myself, let alone the world. I want to get my thesis done, but there is never any time. Every single waking moment is filled. In addition to parenting two children, working towards a Master of Arts degree, struggling to maintain my cultural identity, dealing with emotional scars, and work as a part-time college instructor, I volunteer my time to the Aboriginal Women's Action Network (AWAN) and represent our women in feminist groups, participate actively in the Native sobriety movement at cultural and political gatherings, and draw attention to the First Nations presence in universities. I am spread too thin. I am drowning. The only thing that saves me is the drive to prevent this suffering from happening to my children. Usually I just brush back the tears and run off to my meeting, but this time I just can't. I have fallen into that dreaded black hole, the site of the worst self-loathing imaginable. I am again that unwanted orphan who has no value and is a burden to those into whose care she has fallen—someone who should never have been born (Blaney, 1996, pp. 29–30).

Blaney's words echo my own experiences and the experiences of other Indigenous women in academia. Our struggles go far beyond the conventional academic struggles regarding representation and production of knowledge and our marginalized locations in these, and other, manstitutions. It's important that Blaney shared about her struggles in academia as her struggles are our struggles and they contextualize our work. Maybe our struggles as women are to a greater or lesser extent and to a greater or lesser consistency, but we are feminist scholars in an institution that wasn't made for us or made for us to succeed in. Recognition of this commonality allows us an opportunity to explore questions not just about the research and research outcomes, but about the research process as well. Applying the idea of conscious partiality throughout my research process, I have developed principles that build on Mies' work. These methodological principles can be used in feminist or Indigenous research and when working with Indigenous women who have been harmed by male violence. These principles also serve as a beginning outline in the construction of a decolonizing feminist methodology; they centre and prioritize Indigenous women, consider the specificities of oppression that confront Indigenous women, and provide a way for researchers to consider these issues before, during, and after the research process.

Ethics of Prostitution Research

Throughout this entire research process, I've been honest and upfront about who I am, the feminist work I've done, the politics I hold, and that I understand prostitution as a form of male violence against women. This honesty continued as I sought participants to speak with as part of the research process. As I've been a part of the Women's Liberation Movement and working with Indigenous women's communities for over a decade, I relied on the networks I formed over the years, as well as the networks of the WAC members to identify possible participants. Many, although not all, of the participants were women I had pre-existing relationships with. The importance of relationships and relationship-building remained foundational throughout the project.

When thinking through the ethics of this project, members of the WAC and I were very aware of the potential to cause harm to participants and this remained an ongoing concern and conversation over the course of the project. I didn't actively seek interviews with individual women who had survived male violence or with women who were currently in prostitution. Instead, to ensure participants had support, I asked an organization that helps women to exit the sex trade to identify women who may want to take part in a group interview. It was important that I clearly communicated to potential participants that their participation, withdrawal, or any statements made would have no bearing or influence on the support services they receive or could receive from the organization they are currently connected to or the organizations I provided to them as possible sources of support. The WAC recommended I seek women who were at least three years out of 'the life' (prostitution) so that she had an opportunity to put some distance between herself and prostitution and had some time to heal with the support of others. The risk to currently prostituted women's safety, income, and wellbeing was too great if I interviewed them for this project. This was not a decision made lightly.

Interviewing women who have survived male violence requires feminist training; this is not something we automatically know how to do. In fact, because of patriarchy, we're more likely to have internalized woman-hating and woman-blaming lies when it comes to cases of rape, sexual assault, woman abuse in the home, and other forms of male violence against women. I have training and experience working directly with women who have been victims of male violence. For example, I have worked with survivors of rape and sexual assault, prostitution, incest, and woman-battering. This work included providing women with support, information, and advocacy by, for example, accompanying victims of male violence to the hospital or police station, co-facilitating small group peer-counselling sessions, and finding appropriate resources to refer women to when the centre I worked at was unable to provide what the women needed. The importance of learning how to respond non-judgmentally and empathetically to both historical and immediate crisis situations women might find themselves in cannot be overstated. In this research project, understanding and practising confidentiality was also very important, as was ensuring the anonymity of women participants who requested it. Ensuring confidentiality was important for participant's wellbeing and safety. Lastly, I was reminded by both the WAC and my academic committee that it was critical I identify possible risks to myself during the research process and have a plan in place to manage those risks. As a survivor of male violence and an Indigenous woman myself, I had to make sure my physical and emotional health remained as good as possible for the duration of the project. I am grateful to have a strong support network, made up of professionals and peers, that I check in with regularly to ensure my own well-being and this continues after the project.

As a feminist researcher who has been active in the Women's Liberation Movement for the last decade and who has worked primarily on controversial issues such as prostitution, I'm very aware of the debates and hostilities around such topics. I'm also very aware of the importance of confidentiality and anonymity when addressing such issues, as there has and can be professional and other consequences for feminist women who understand prostitution as a form of male violence against women. The communities of women I work with have historically and presently been marginalized, socially and politically, within and outside of Indigenous communities. Providing a supportive and confidential or anonymous environment in which women can express any doubts they may have about 'sex work' is important as the dominant (i.e. patriarchal) way of thinking describes sex work as a largely harmless and legitimate occupation for women. Critical views of prostitution are often hidden among academics and advocates in Canada, New Zealand, and Australia and as a result, it was necessary to provide a way for women to share their thoughts and analyzes directly, securely, and anonymously. Although some of the methodological challenges of this research project were unique to this particular project, many apply to other research contexts as well. As a result, I began to build a decolonizing feminist methodology that took into account these challenges, other challenges, and what I learned during the research process.

(Not) Making the Documentary: An Anti-Machiavellian Upside-Down Inside-Out Research-Creation Unmovie-Making Adventure

November 9, 2018

Dear Diary,

Ok, I was talking about my friend, my friend who I was going to interview for the documentary. She had to go because her sister was just assaulted, brutally assaulted and she had to have surgery on her brain. It'll take a few weeks for them to figure out if she's going to have permanent brain damage or not. She says that she can move and stuff but when her sister talks, her words are garbled, she doesn't make sense and apparently, she can't open her eyes because of the swelling from the attack. Yeah, I guess I was just saying that ... it's ... because it's one thing to hear about it, and I think people hear about it and people like to talk about it, especially at university, the professors and the students ... I don't know, it's weird. it's almost like it's ... you know, it's not our fault. I think that it's not our fault that this happened, but you know, so many women did so much work for so many years to get people to pay attention to this issue of male violence against Indigenous women. And now it's almost everywhere and it's nowhere at the same time, because it's almost become ... I don't know what you call it. It's like a lipservice thing or like a trendy thing, or maybe that's not the right term, but where people are like, "oh, yes, we're going to address this. We're going to address this, you know, yes, we're going to do research and talk about this, this is important."

But rallies and marches and memorials and all this kind of stuff, um ... I think most of those people, unless, you know, unless you're an Aboriginal woman or you're very close to Aboriginal women, it's like, yeah, we're going to do all this! But then there's the actual reality of it. I don't know, maybe it's not possible to explain, I don't know, maybe it just isn't because ... either it's happening to you or it's happening to somebody around you, there's never a time when it's not happening. It just makes it really hard; I think ... it's a hard issue to research or to learn about and read about and think about, but it's that much harder when you're doing it at the same time that it's happening around you.

So just between my Masters and my Ph.D.— just in those school years—I was sexually assaulted four times by five different men just in the last couple of years. I think what I'm trying to say is that's really messed up. I mean, there's a lot of things that are really messed up. But I think one of the things is that you almost become ... how do I explain it, like numb, numb to it or like that becomes normal. And so I think for others it becomes something that they watch happen in the movies. I don't know, maybe that has something to do with it. Like hey, watch this! Maybe that's what it's like; actually, maybe that's what's happened: Canada is watching a movie about murdered and disappeared Indigenous women, about male violence against Indigenous women. I think that's what's happening because when you watch a movie, like you care, but, you know, the movie ends and you go on with your life, you don't ... it doesn't touch your life.

It's kind of a spectacle, it's something you watch, but it's not something that you ... you know ... that becomes close to you in any kind of way, you know what I mean? I think that's what's happening here—just watching—everybody's just watching. Well, not everybody, but the work that so many Indigenous women did for so long, for so many years, has got people paying attention but—and this is through no fault of theirs, obviously—but that's all people are doing, is paying attention. They're just watching. And that's the problem, I think, or one of the problems anyways.

But to actually, yeah, I don't know if it's possible actually ... to explain what that does to a woman, how it impacts everything and you don't even realize it, and you're just living your life like doo-doo-dee-doo. I mean, obviously, you're ... you know, you're upset. Oh, you know, my friend's sister possibly has permanent brain damage and my other friend is or whatever family member is ... you know, had her throat slit or, you know, somebody was choked unconscious or, you know, somebody was, you know, gang raped or ... you accumulate all these things in your head ... and yeah, I mean, most of the stories, they stick with you, but some of them for one reason or another, just stand out. But you know, I just ... so I just really think we've come into this moment where people are watching, but it's all they're doing is watching. And we haven't gotten to the action part yet, like anything that's actually meaningful, there's kind of, you know ... a lot of talk about it and maybe some programs and some stuff like that, but I guess it's because people are just watching and there's very little room to actually talk about what the actual problem is. It just makes it that much more difficult to try and do this, and I mean, it's not just the research, I mean, obviously that's what I'm doing right now, but it's like I do all these other things all the time that are in a similar kind of … same kind of things, and so it's just around me all the time. And then it's inside of you too, because you have all of these … your own memories and then all these other stories that you've collected over the years and you're sitting here and it's like around you and it's inside of you and it's in front of you and … you're like … I'm tired. And how could you not be, right? It's hard and I think … I think the university doesn't … they're not even on the same chapter, in the same book, they're not on the same page, I think about … yeah, it's one thing to watch it and do the research. It's another thing to live it and, you know, you can't just turn off your TV when you're tired of it.

I think the priorities are mixed up, you know, when it becomes about … I'm always trying to make sure that it's not all about me. This is a tough balance between being a part of the film and, yeah, not making it all about me, because it isn't but it's also important for me to be like I'm the one telling the story so you should know who I am. And I'm not pretending that … I'm not pretending that the women I'm interviewing are telling the story because they're not. I guess as all this has been going, this has been happening, it's like it's all about … recognizing the relationships, the importance of the relationships.

It all boils down to that, to the relationship, and that's for everything. That's for the research, the you and me, um, my relationship to my family, their relationships to each other. And, you know, I guess that's at the end of the day, too, that's why I'm not … I can't just walk away from what's going on with my family because it's about the relationship and because I can't abandon my sister. You know, she's in a situation where she is so consumed by the everyday: get up, take care of grandma and grandpa, grocery shopping, go to an appointment, make them lunch, clean up, like this every day. Her whole day is consumed by, you know, helping them. She can't, you know, she can't imagine being able to get respite care or even being able to imagine and then take the steps to do something different for herself, and not that it's the same, of course, with prostitution, but there's parallels there right, that you're so in the *everyday, just getting through the day that how can you even begin to imagine taking steps to make it different? It's kind of what Erin was saying where you need to be, like, stuck on somebody like flypaper and I'm stuck on my sister like flypaper right now because ... we just don't have any ... people don't have the ability to do all of that at the same time, get through the everyday and imagine different and then do something different.*

So, yeah, OK, so I guess we should finish because we should get packing, but tomorrow I'll talk a bit about ... I want to talk a bit about Yuly and I'm gonna write about that tonight[25] so maybe we can make a video ... I woke up this morning and it was better, you know, like I was feeling a bit better than yesterday, um, I didn't cry in my sleep last night right?

As I gathered more equipment, planned the documentary, and started filming with help from trusted friends and allies who have training in audio and video documentary production, the purpose of filming—of recording sounds and images of women and rearranging these sounds and images into a story—became more clear:

February 1, 2019

Dear Diary,

So I wanted to talk a little bit about, well, I guess a lot about—I guess this would be method and methodology? I started out thinking: OK, I'm going to make this documentary about prostitution. I've never made a documentary before but that's OK, I'll figure it out. And we did. And we filmed in _____ and _____. It was, you know, it's fun, and I was really fortunate to have help from the Trudeau Foundation to buy the equipment that I needed, we had our tripods and our lighting stands and cameras and all of our stuff, and we're really ... it was good, you know, we're learning as we went and that's OK.

Just before I got here [New Zealand], of course, I was looking again through the footage that we took and what I saw was ... women and

---

25 I have expanded on this in my forthcoming essay, 'An Open Letter to the Left Regarding Silence' which will be included in '*Womynifesto: Decolonizing feminist essays* (2023).

some of them, that I know really well, they're so far away, I'm so far away because the … it was too slick. It was too … I mean, it's never real, but it really felt not real. It didn't feel like it was me, like it didn't feel like it was … you couldn't see, I couldn't see.

And I guess what I do with my still-camera, like a camera-camera, is that I use that camera thinking that I'm taking a picture of the relationship between myself and the person or the people I'm taking a picture of. That's why I took a lot of pictures of my family, because sometimes there's a good relationship there, sometimes a bad relationship, but there's something there. And so, you know, for example, with my grandma, the photos that I took … only I can take those photos. If somebody took another photo, there's a different relationship there so it's going to look different, it's going to feel different. I felt like with the fancy video cameras that we're using … they don't … they aren't taking that picture. They're taking a video of a person and that's different than taking a video that shows my relationship to that person and in that, also shows the relationship of the person to the issue that we're talking about, right. It was just like … they felt so far away.

And this is not what I wanted. So I decided, even just thinking in terms of equipment, when we were doing the interviews … because we had these big cameras and tripods that made a lot of physical distance between myself and the women I was talking to that's not … that's not good. That you know, that puts already one barrier in between us … so I decided OK, well, when I was there, what felt the most real to me? What felt the most real to me was the little footage I'd taken with my phone, and I've done a few kind of little videos at home and in other places, you know, with my phone. To me, that felt way more … I can see way more … I can see those relationships and, you know, it's not real because of course you're taking an image of something but it really … I think … I guess what I'm saying is I think sometimes, all the time, sometimes, we either put too much emphasis on the technical part and we gotta get it perfect so we have to use the best equipment, you know, and it's got to be like these super-slick looking movies. I think it's … I'm not saying it's wrong to do that, but I think that that's the expectation is that it will be the priority and that's kind of how things are. But why does it have to be that way? Like, who decided that? Why does it have to be like that?

I think that what's more important is the process and the content and showing those relationships and showing, you know, the feelings that are part of those relationships. For me, I can't really do that when I have, like, a big honkin' camera in between me and the person and ... why does it have to be like that anyways? I don't know, maybe for some people they're able to do that, I don't know but I can see a lot of barriers to making something with all this fancy, schmancy equipment and usually it's teams of people, you have a crew of people but you don't necessarily know those people, right? That's their job. They might be strangers to you. For me, it was really important that, you know, I had Alex, my partner, well, partly because you know what you're doing, you're a sound and video technician, but also because of the support, having somebody here that knows me is a whole ... I can't describe ... how important it is and you know, I know you, obviously I trust you. I know that you have an understanding of the issues. I know that you'll listen, you'll follow my direction. I know that you're not going to be trying to challenge the politics of it. And I ... yeah, I trust you. I trust that you, you know, when things are confidential, they're confidential and so for me, that's really important, too, because that's part of the process is this relationship too.

It's funny because I don't know if I told you this, I was talking to Fay and I was talking to her about this situation where I asked an organization to help me out with my research project with something and they were very formal with me and this is not ... I didn't think that that would have been the case, because I know them and they know me. I was really hurt and I was trying to figure out why I was so hurt by that. She said, well, of course you're upset it's about the relationship, that's what's important for you because that's what's important for us. She's said it's kind of about what they said but more that you thought you had one relationship with them and turns out you don't. I was like, ohhh yeah, about the relationship, I read that in a book that natives love relationships, like they're all about relationships and we laughed about that. It's weird how it presents itself ... like when I'm reading a book and it's not that I was reading it in a book and then, you know, began to apply that principle in my work and in my life, it's not that. It's weird when you read about yourself in a book, it's weird because you just do the things that you do and you don't necessarily label them or articulate them as being about this or that, because it just is … like when it's a part of your normal living and just part of how you function in the world, it can be hard to identify it as something that's distinct because it's just … it's just how you do things, right? Anyways …

So it was really important for me to just be like, OK, I'm going to change gears here. I'm going to pare down the equipment. I'm going to have the smallest equipment that we can have. So we're using our phones and we're using apps on our phones, we've got some little tripods, we've got some little ND filters, we've got, you know, little rigs for the phones, you know, all this kind of stuff. It's a learning curve. I guess I kind of pivoted, you know, halfway through the film but why not? Why can't I do that, why can't I decide that: OK, so this isn't working the way I wanted it to, it's not … it doesn't look the way I wanted it to look. It doesn't feel the way I wanted it to feel. So then make changes and why can't I put that different footage together? I don't know, there's all these rules, you have to do things this way, but why? We don't have to, you can do it any way you want and I think that's OK. I mean, it's honest. It's honest that I learned something new and isn't that the point of a PhD, is to learn? So my plan now is to basically just make videos with my phone and yeah, that's what I'm going to do.

An Outline for a Decolonizing Feminist Methodology

1. Recognize and Account for the Realities of Male Violence Against Indigenous Women

The realities of male violence against women must be acknowledged before, throughout, and after the research process (Bell and Nelson, 1989). This isn't easy to do because such an acknowledgment is not only material and procedural, but political as well. As a result, acknowledging and then accommodating for the historical and current context of male violence that Indigenous women live and die in requires the researcher to do two things: (1) Stop pretending they're neutral objective research observers; and (2) Stop prioritizing their careers over all else. To acknowledge and accommodate for the material realities of Indigenous women's lives is a political decision that means facing a truth that might not match the truth as you theorized it to be. It means deliberately and bravely getting off the fence and making some decisions that may hurt your career opportunities now or in the future. Acknowledging and accommodating the realities of Indigenous women's lives in research means making conscious feminist decisions to stand with women and this isn't a popular or easy position to take—it requires some serious self-reflection about research motivations and goals. However, it's the only methodological principle that actually works in the interests of women.

Cree and Saulteaux scholar and member of the Star Blanket Cree Nation, Dr Gina Starblanket, raises important concerns about de-gendered Indigenous research by troubling the idea of "accountability to Indigenous communities." She challenges the idea that Indigenous communities are made up of groups of similar individuals with similar experiences, beliefs and interests (Starblanket, 2018); these individuals, groups, and thus 'Indigenous communities' are assumed to be, by patriarchal default, men. Starblanket argues instead for acknowledgment of the differences and hierarchies that exist within communities, including Indigenous communities. As a result, she argues, researchers may unknowingly rely on methodological frameworks that

> ... account primarily for researcher responsibilities to those in positions of leadership and with powers of representation and voice within collectives. Furthermore, it overlooks questions of accountability to those whose existence belies bounded notions of the Indigenous community. Taken together, these tendencies run the risk of reinforcing normative orders and the assumptions they entail, while also containing or marginalizing difference within communities (Starblanket, 2018, p. 3).

Starblanket's criticisms are important and useful for researchers doing feminist and Indigenous research. Challenging the degendered and thus default male-centredness of 'Indigenous community' and instead acknowledging 'community' as something made up of both women and men and that isn't always fair, representative, inviting to, or safe for Indigenous women is essential and again, not easy to do. 'Community' can and does cause serious harm to women, as demonstrated by disproportionate rates of male violence against Indigenous women both in- and outside of Indigenous communities (Bell and Nelson, 1989; McIvor and Nahanee, 1998; Kuokkanen, 2015). The acknowledgment of potential constraints and particular harms that Indigenous women face from men in and outside of their families, communities, and Nations, is essential in constructing a decolonizing feminist methodology.

2. Distinct, not Different

A decolonizing feminist methodology acknowledges connections between male violence against Indigenous women and male violence against non-Indigenous women. While Indigenous women, due to their social location, are forced to contend with particular histories and circumstances that present often multiplied and distinct barriers and challenges, we share with non-Indigenous women the biological, social, and political realities of being born and raised female in patriarchy. The male violence that is committed against Indigenous women doesn't happen on some entirely different planet somewhere else, committed by unknown assailants for unknown reasons—we understand this male violence as a particular form of male violence that shares horrific commonalities with male violence as it is perpetrated against all women. To accommodate for the particularities confronting Indigenous women in patriarchy, here are two examples of action to take (or not take) in a research project:

a) *Don't Ask Her Specifically about the Male Violence She's Experienced. She'll Speak about It When She's Good and Ready*

This seems like common sense, but it isn't. Or perhaps it isn't 'common sense' because it only makes sense to women. At any rate, the idea that men are actually not sexually or otherwise entitled to women's bodies and the idea that men are not entitled to demand that women recount their horrific experiences of male violence doesn't make sense in academia, government, media, or in any other number of manstitutions we navigate every day. As a feminist Indigenous woman researcher and activist, I've participated in many different public events over the years in many different venues. There is an unspoken—and sometimes very loudly spoken—expectation that I will speak of the male violence I've personally experienced when speaking publicly. The media, in particular, seem very eager to extract and scoop up whatever horror story they can to regurgitate in spectacular ways to their viewers and listeners, I guess because it makes a good story (how terrible is this). This same expectation is not present for Indigenous or other men and it's not present in the same way or to the same extent for non-Indigenous women. As an Indigenous woman, it's already assumed, not just that you've been victimized by men (which is unfortunately true for all women to a greater or lesser extent), but that, as an Indigenous woman, you've been victimized by men *and that this victimization has confirmed what we already knew about you, you worthless disgusting piece of nothing garbage and maybe, just maybe, you actually liked it because you squaws are dirty like that.* The 'stigma' of victimhood applies in this way to women and demonstrates that the shame women feel after being attacked by a man or men is a continuation of the male violence women—and in this case—Indigenous women, experience.

Assuming then, that it's fine and dandy to ask an Indigenous woman to tell you specifically about the male violence she's suffered, even when she knows this is the topic at hand because she volunteered to be a part of this research project, is unethical. Start a conversation with her, like she's human,[26] and she'll get to the horror stories when she gets to them, or not. Maybe she's changed her mind and doesn't want to speak anymore about what's been done to her or maybe she wants some time to adjust to her environment and to the research people in her environment before she rips open

---

26 She is human.

her painful unhealed and sometimes infected wounds so you can get your PhD or write your book or make your documentary or whatever it is you're doing. It's a humiliating experience to be asked to talk about the most degrading things you can imagine being done to you and your loved ones and about all manner of things being stuck inside you and your loved ones against your and their will. Think about it. Think about this as if it were your own life and how you would like to be treated in this situation. When Indigenous women are given respect, we don't have to expend the extra energy to make sure that we, and our loved ones, are respected. Indigenous women will speak about the male violence we've experienced when we're ready to do so and we'll do it on our terms. Do not pressure, whether explicitly or implicitly, Indigenous women to speak on your terms.

b) Never Discourage Her Speaking About the Male Violence in Her Life

It's frustrating how often this happens and it's frustrating how often this behaviour is justified by academics and supastar well-known well-respected academics at that.

> I firmly believe in the feminist principle that 'the personal is political', by experience I know that it can be a double-edged sword: Yes, there is a freedom that comes from disclosing that I am a survivor of sexual abuse and family violence; but in the act of unloading this burden of shame, I contribute to the negative stereotype of my people as inferior (Blaney, 1996, p. 19).

Blaney, as so many other Indigenous women, knows that racism absolutely permeates manstitutions such as academia, the police, the criminal justice system, and the media. Indigenous women know that due to racism, Indigenous men are more likely to face harsher prison sentences than non-Indigenous men (Razack, 2015). We know that the media often focuses disproportionately on violence committed by Indigenous men and that this media coverage reinforces racist stereotypes about Indigenous men as violent, inherently criminal, and corrupt and as a result of this focused racist media coverage, violence committed by white men against women is often ignored and made invisible (Jiwani, 2006). Indigenous women absolutely know, from their own and others' experiences, that racism plays a role in our lives as Indigenous peoples that it shouldn't—racism has no role to play anywhere. However, we also know that Indigenous women who question or challenge patriarchy and the behaviour of Indigenous men within our own families and communities are often outcast as disrespectful 'feminists' (McIvor, 2004).

Members of the WAC were adamant that this project include not only an analysis of the prostitution of Indigenous women as a process of colonization, but also to look particularly at the violence committed against Indigenous women by Indigenous men. In addition to what I know experientially and what other women have told me, I did a quick google search and found numerous news articles related to violence against women committed by Indigenous men in leadership positions: in March 2016 Alexander First Nation Chief Kurt Burnstick was charged with sexual assault (Huncar, 2016a). Despite protest by Indigenous women, Burnstick went on to be re-elected as chief, although his election was eventually appealed and overturned (Huncar, 2016b). In October 2016, the former police chief and member of the Atikamekw community, Jean-Paul Néashish, was sentenced to years in prison after being found guilty on ten sexual assault charges that included rape, gross indecency, and sexual touching of a child under the age of 14. Former Wemotaci band council chief, Marcel Boivin, was also accused as a perpetrator with Néashish (Wheeler, 2016). In August 2017, Xeni Gwet'in Chief Roger William was charged with sexual interference of a person under the age of 16 (Toronto Sun, 2017). In September 2017, Onigaming First Nation member Wab Kinew, with wide support from many politicians, was elected as leader of the Manitoba NDP party after it was revealed he had been previously charged with two counts of physically assaulting his former partner. Former Judge and Chair of the Truth and Reconciliation Commission, Ojibway Senator Murray Sinclair, stated in defense of

Kinew that the accusations of woman-battering were turning into a 'witch hunt' (Malone, 2017). There are many, many more stories, told and untold, similar to these.

The reality of male violence against Indigenous women is that Indigenous men, like other men, are committing acts of violence against Indigenous women. How do the constant reminders about the potential for unfair racist treatment of Indigenous men by the police, the criminal justice system, the media, and other manstitutions impact Indigenous women? As Kuokkanen states in regard to a case where many young Sámi women were being sexually assaulted in their community by Sámi men:

> ... a fear of reviving and further reinforcing negative stereotypes played a role in the widespread inclination to conceal and ignore sexual abuse cases of young Sámi women in Kautokeino ... most common negative stereotypes portray Sámi men as uncivilized and dirty drunks. Hence, the fear of reviving negative stereotypes is a fear of casting Sámi men in a further detrimental light. Rather than the female victims of violence, it is Sámi men who need to be protected. As a result, the indirect assault of Sámi manhood through negative popular representations is considered an assault on the Sámi people, the direct assault on individual Sámi women is not ... (2015, p. 280).

The reminders about how unfair the world is *to him* due to racism and classism sends a message, loud and clear, to Indigenous women: the reputation of Indigenous men is more important than your bodily autonomy, safety, and well-being (Bell and Nelson, 1989; Kuokkanen, 2015). As a result, Indigenous women are further actively or passively discouraged from speaking out against male violence in their families, communities, and nations.

3. Everything is Political

Mies describes a methodology for feminist research that includes the replacement of uninvolved 'spectator knowledge' with "... active participation in actions, movements and struggles for women's emancipation" (1983, p. 124). She goes on to state that, "... participation in social actions and struggles, and the integration of research into these processes, further implies that the change of the status quo becomes the starting point for a scientific quest" (Mies, 1983, p. 125). Here, feminist, decolonizing, and Indigenous methodologies share a similar foundation in regard to the call for action-orientated research that 'does something' and a critical engagement with the (false) idea of neutral, objective, value-free positivist research that continues to dominate academia as the most legitimate form of research (Mies, 1983; Kovach, 2010; Smith, 2012). The thing is, whether we're purposefully engaging in explicitly political research or not, we're doing politics. In an article written by Maddy Coy, Meagan Tyler, and myself, we quote Karen Boyle, who states that "Feminist researchers have long argued that 'the appearance of objectivity' is precisely that: an appearance … [t]o declare oneself 'neutral' on this issue is a politicized position in itself" (qtd in. Coy et al., 2019, p. 1932). We go on to argue, here in the context of prostitution research, that

> [I]t is impossible, even disingenuous, to claim that an epistemological starting point (even if unacknowledged) does not influence research design, sampling strategies, construction of interview guides, coding frameworks for analysis, and how data are presented in terms of the language used to describe the prostitution system and people involved in it (e.g., prostitution/ sex work, prostituted women/sex workers, pimps/managers) (Coy et al., 2019, p. 1932).

In other words, even if you say your research is not political, it is, and even if you say your research is value-free and objective, it isn't, and unless your research explicitly challenges the status quo (i.e. patriarchy), it accepts and works within it.

4. Not Everyone Is an Expert (But They Can Be)

"Listen to Indigenous women!," "Listen to family members!," "Listen to sex workers!"—"No, only listen to those Indigenous women/family members/sex workers over there, the ones who agree with us!" I'm sure many of us have heard or even made these kinds of statements before—except for the last one, that one usually goes unsaid. Feminist standpoint theory provides a way to engage with differences in women's analysis of their experiences. As Alison Jagger states,

> ... while women's experience of subordination puts them in a uniquely advantageous position for reinterpreting reality, it also imposes on them certain psychological difficulties which must themselves be the focus of the self-conscious struggle. Simply to a be a woman, then, is not sufficient to guarantee a clear understanding of the world as it appears from the standpoint of women ... the standpoint of women is not discovered by surveying the beliefs and attitudes of women under conditions of male dominance ... in the end, an adequate representation of the world from the standpoint of women requires the material overthrow of male domination (2004, p. 61).

In other words, a woman is not a feminist simply because she's a woman. In fact, it's probably more accurate to say that most women are not feminist theorists and activists. Patriarchy needs the majority of women to acquiesce to its ideologies and conditions and needs the majority of men to adopt its ideologies and conditions in order for the system of male dominance to sustain itself. As I have stated many times, there is a difference between an experience and an analysis of an experience:

> Feminist scholars who are critical of prostitution recognize that, as a result of many factors, women will have a wide variety of analyses of their experiences, and while it is not possible to critique a woman's individual experience, it is possible to disagree and debate with a woman's analysis of her experience. Being willing to challenge women's analyses presumes that she is intelligent, capable, and articulate as opposed to a patronizing presumption of women as only capable of sharing experiences and/or unable to develop or further develop an analysis through discussion, debate, and disagreement (Coy et al., 2019, p. 1933).

When doing research, the woman I'm working with knows things I don't know, but I also know things she doesn't know. In order to build a relationship that works toward the goal of Women's Liberation, we need to share what we know with each other. This could mean, for example, that I share what I know of feminist standpoint theory with research participants as a theoretical option to analyze their own, and other women's, experiences.

5. Honesty and Intentions

You are a participant in your own research project even if you don't think that you are. You're learning as part of the process, that's kind of the point. It was important for me, as a researcher, to take part in my own research methods. This meant, for example, that I participated in the group activities we did and that I appeared on-camera and shared my experiences, thoughts, feelings, and analyzes throughout the course of this project with the women I was working with. It's not easy to make yourself vulnerable in that way and I felt strongly that I didn't want to ask women who were participating to do things I wasn't willing to do myself. Additionally, the insight that I gained from participating in my own research project helped me to continually self-reflect on my own research process and goals and on my position as an 'outsider-within', a social location that

> has provided a special standpoint on self, family, and society for Afro-American women ... Black intellectuals, especially those in touch with the marginality in academic settings, tap this standpoint in producing distinctive analyzes of race, class, and gender (Hill Collins, 1985, pp. S14–S15).

In a decolonizing feminist methodology, as in feminist, decolonizing, and Indigenous methodologies, the subjectivity of the researcher is considered an asset as opposed to a liability. The acknowledgment of the researcher's biases, context, and intentions informs the research questions, methodologies, and goals, ultimately strengthening the research process by creating opportunities to explore roots, threads, and connections that may otherwise have gone unnoticed.

6. Culture and Women

Feminist Indigenous women have long cautioned against the uncritical acceptance of traditional cultural practices that oppress or discriminate against women (LaRocque, 1994; Bear, 2007). This is a very difficult position for an Indigenous woman to take, as she's (falsely) accused of attacking Indigenous (men's) sovereignty when in reality, she's critical of a cultural practice that limits or discriminates against her and other women. Particular to Indigenous communities though, while feminism encourages white women to think critically and to challenge their own patriarchal cultural practices, Indigenous women aren't allowed—let alone encouraged—to critique or challenge cultural practices and traditions within our own cultures that we believe to be patriarchal. There are different reasons why this happens but fundamentally it's because Indigenous men are seen to be, by outsiders, and believe themselves to be, more important than Indigenous women and also because of the external race and class oppressions that Indigenous women encounter.

When doing research with Indigenous women there can, might, and will be moments where the interests of the male-defined and male-constructed nation in terms of 'culture' or 'tradition' contradicts the interests of women. These are the difficult situations mentioned earlier where a researcher must make a political decision to stand with women or not.

7. Research Results

The presentation of research—how, where, when, and to whom, for example—is incredibly important but unfortunately too often overlooked. Instead of viewing the sharing of research as equally important to other parts of the research process, the results—the research 'outcomes'—are treated as largely unnecessary beyond publication in an academic journal or some other CV-building method of academic circulation.

Context matters. When it comes to research, we generally consider the context of the people we're doing research with such as, for example, what was her childhood like or what is her highest level of education? This context, both current and historical, is very important to consider. For example, does the Indian Residential School (IRS) system impact her life today, and if so, how? The context of the researcher, though, is just as important, as is the context of those reading or viewing the results of the research: What are their histories? What are their beliefs? These contexts are considered less, if at all, during research projects but are just as important. The default social organization and political ideology and practice of our world is patriarchy. This means that unless researchers and readers or viewers have intentionally sought out feminist theory and are intentionally and constantly unlearning the patriarchy, their foundational beliefs and vision for the future will be shaped and limited by patriarchal ideology:

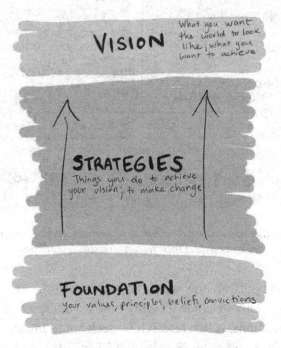

VISION — What you want the world to look like; what you want to achieve

STRATEGIES — Things you do to achieve your vision; to make change

FOUNDATION — Your values, principles, beliefs, convictions

Figure 5: A magnificent drawing demonstrating how research outcomes are limited by a researcher's foundational ideologies.

For example, the following image illustrates the ways in which feminist research compares to sex work research when examining foundational values and intended goals (either feminist or patriarchal) and the different strategies that accompany each of those very different contexts:

Figure 6: Glorious drawing demonstrating how 'sex work' vs 'prostitution' ideologies impact their respective research outcomes.

Research is political: how we come to focus on the area we focus on, the questions we come up with, how we interpret the answers to these questions, which research we seek out to inform ourselves about an issue, and so on (Bowles and Klein, 1983) and as Spender states,

> It is a political choice on the part of feminists to find in favour of
> women but this is no different from non-feminist researchers who
> have exercised their political choice by almost always finding in
> favour of men. The difference is that feminism acknowledges its
> politics (1980, p. 8).

Over the years, I, and other feminists, have been repeatedly told
that the feminist abolitionist position on prostitution, as described
in Chapter 5, and the liberal sex work position that seeks to
normalize 'sex work', as described in Chapter 4, have more in
common than we think and why not put differences aside and work
together? Of course, there are areas where our proposed strategies
may be the same or similar—for example, both feminists and sex
work advocates want all people selling sex acts in prostitution to
be decriminalized—but our foundational values differ and more
importantly, so do our goals. It's ok not to work together and in
this case, it wouldn't make strategic sense that two ideologically-
opposed political groups would work together; it would be a waste
of each other's energy, time, and resources. As yet another example
of patriarchy in action, we don't see the same types of 'why don't
you two just get along' statements about other issues—I doubt
anyone has asked why oil industry advocates and Indigenous land
defenders don't just put aside their differences and work together.
I suppose, though, unlike men, women in patriarchy aren't supposed to be disagreeable even when we passionately disagree with
each other.

An Example of a Decolonizing Feminist Method and Outcome

An example of the application of a decolonizing feminist
methodology is seen in what is known as the 'Bell debate' or the
'Bell/Huggins debate' in Australia. Indigenous feminist scholar
Megan Davis inaccurately describes the article at the centre of this
debate as follows:

In 1989, anthropologist Diane Bell, published an article, co-authored with an Aboriginal woman, Topsy Nelson, in *Women's Studies International Forum*, arguing that, unlike African-American women, Indigenous women had failed to adopt feminism to engage with the problem of intra-racial rape (2017, p. 147).

As is the case with too many of these stories, the source material is interpreted and re-interpreted and re-interpreted again and those re-interpreted reinterpretations become the end-all, be-all facts of the matter (which is not true) so it's always best to refer to the original document, if possible, which in this case is *Speaking About Rape is Everybody's Business* by Diane Bell and Topsy Napurrula Nelson.

I disagree with Davis that the crux of the article is that Indigenous women in Australia failed to adopt feminism. It is clear from their synopsis, that it is the profound silence regarding intra-racial rape that engaged Bell and Nelson (1989, p. 403):

> This paper interweaves anthropological and indigenous insights regarding the shifting contexts within which rape occurs and is analysed; the strategies women pursued in the past; and argues for the provision of services which take account of the needs of Aboriginal women. Socialist and radical feminists dispute whether it is class or gender that has primacy in their analyses of rape while black activists accuse both of being insensitive to issues of race.

Bell and Nelson were seeking an informed, respectful, productive discussion. The facts were irrefutable: attested by the Indigenous and non-Indigenous women Bell and Nelson cited, and manifest in the two Northern Territory cases Bell and Nelson summarized. As Nelson explained the situation facing Indigenous women in Indigenous communities, "No-one can take your body; that's her own thing" (1989, p. 404).

Bell, speaking about herself as a white woman, one with a long-standing commitment to social justice issues (Bell and Ditton, 1980), intimate knowledge of the communities of which she writes

(Bell, 1983), and a history of collaborative projects with Nelson (Bell, 1985), stated her responsibility thus:

> Although it could be said that this is "not my business," it is very much my business. I hold to the position that, no matter how unpleasant, feminist social scientists do have a responsibility to identify and analyse those factors which render women vulnerable to violence. The fact that this is happening to women of another ethnic or racial group cannot be a reason for ignoring the abuse. *But, it is cause to look carefully to the cultural context, to heed the silences.* Thus, my tack in now addressing this extremely sensitive topic, is to look again at the received wisdom regarding intra-racial rape; to interrogate anew the theoretical and practical pronouncements and hopefully, in so doing, to map the terrain on which informed discussion may occur and to create a space in which stories, like that told by Topsy, will reach a wider audience (Bell and Nelson, 1989, p. 404) (Emphasis added).

Responses to Bell and Nelson might have recognized that Indigenous men were relying on spurious legal defences regarding their customary rights and that courts were complicit with their less-severe sentences of Indigenous men who had committed violence; that Aboriginal Legal Aid represented the accused rapist and the victim was left without a cultural narrative or the resources to argue her right to be safe in her community; that Indigenous men were, in fact, taking her body, "her own thing." These were all matters that were, and are, on the feminist agenda. Sharon Payne (1990, p. 10) of the Law and Justice Department, Aboriginal and Torres Strait Islander Commission wrote of three types of law: "whites man's law, traditional law and bullshit law." Audrey Bolger's (1990, p. 52–53) research confirmed the findings of Bell and Ditton (1980, p. 17) a decade earlier that Legal Aid protected Aboriginal men charged with violent crimes against women. "More women have died from violent assaults in one town of the N.T. [Northern Territory] over the past five years than all the deaths in custody in the N.T. over the same period," wrote Aboriginal feminist Judy Atkinson (1990, p. 6).

Rather than address the substantive issue of intra-racial rape and flying in the face of facts, the response to Bell and Nelson was in a word (or three) absolutely fucking ridiculous. The 'debate' centred on who has the right to speak about and against particular forms of male violence against particular women and what is the 'correct' way to do so? Some Indigenous (Huggins et al., 1991; Moreton-Robinson, 2003) and non-Indigenous women (Hunter, 1996; Howe, 2009; Stringer, 2012) decided that Bell and Nelson (Bell in particular) were not the right women to speak out against rape and that they didn't go about it in the correct way. Rather than explore the case materials, or engage in deep listening, Stringer (2012, p. 27) and Cole (2000, p. 3) followed Aileen Moreton-Robinson (2003, p. 68) by 'cherry picking' Bell's statement of responsibility. They stopped mid paragraph, right before the sentence *'But, it is cause to look carefully to the cultural context, to heed the silences'.* Bell's cautions and approach were omitted (and even if Bell had not made this caution, her and Nelson's point—that Indigenous women deserve to be safe everywhere, even in their own homes and communities—still stands).

Is this a debate?

Bell and Nelson became the 'bad guys'. It was not their business. Huggins et al. (1991, p. 506) wrote:

> It is our business how we deal with rape and have done so for the last 202 years quite well. We don't need white anthropologists reporting business which can be abused and misinterpreted by racists in the wider community. They feed like parasites to this type of thing.

However, the feeding frenzy following the publication of Bell and Nelson was not based on a diet of racist reporting of Indigenous men, but rather a sustained attack on Bell, the feminist anthropologist who had supposedly not interrogated her whiteness and was brazenly claiming "she and everyone else had the *right* to speak about rape in *all* Aboriginal communities" (Moreton-Robinson 2003, p. 68; emphasis added). (Again, even if Bell had made this statement, I would argue that yes, she does have this right just as I, an Indigenous woman, have this right, to speak out against male violence against women and girls, wherever this violence may be occurring). Huggins et al. (1991, p. 506) depicted Nelson who, as "an older traditional Aboriginal woman who speaks English as a second language," could not possibly be a co-author of an academic paper and further her "quotations in the paper have little relevance to the chapter and nothing to do with rape at all." Nelson's (1991) letter clearly stating her position was ignored. Henceforth Huggins et al. (1991) and Moreton-Robinson (2003) were unfettered as they spoke for the 'we' of all Indigenous women.

The backlash that Bell and Nelson received for speaking about and against the rape of Indigenous women by Indigenous men was anti-feminist and anti-woman backlash. It fed the idea that feminists were imposing their agenda on Indigenous women, as if Indigenous women weren't feminist or even that Indigenous women were a 'different kind' of woman whose bodily violations required substantially 'different kinds' of responses to 'normal' women—an outright lie. It chilled the research environment on the complex underlying causes of male violence against women. The attack on Bell and Nelson also contributed to reducing

> ... opportunities of [Indigenous women's] alliance with the broader women's movement as white feminists, afraid of facing the same consequences as Bell, became even more reluctant to speak out on issues that disproportionately impact Indigenous women, such as the rape of Indigenous women by Indigenous men (Davis, 2017, p. 150).

This has resulted in the further political abandonment and isolation of Indigenous feminists in their politics and activism (Davis, 2017). Davis might note that Jackie Huggins (1998) does not claim to be a feminist and has written extensively on the irrelevance of the Women's Movement for Indigenous women.

Bell and Nelson conclude their article with some suggestions, the first of which states: "Acknowledge the facts: Aboriginal women are being raped by Aboriginal men" (1989, p. 415). This is what Bell and Nelson did and they did so with a woman-centred feminist analysis. They received incredible backlash for daring to speak out against rape and this backlash continues today, particularly in cases where Indigenous men are committing acts of violence against Indigenous women. It's in these moments that our commitment to a feminist methodology and to working for and with women is challenged as Bell and Nelson ask, "…who speaks of the anguish, shame and risk for the Aboriginal women victims?" (1989, p. 404). As Black feminist, lesbian, educator, and poet Audre Lorde stated:

> I was going to die, if not sooner than later, whether or not I had even spoken myself. My silences had not protected me. Your silences will not protect you …. What are the words you do not yet have? What are the tyrannies you swallow day by day and attempt to make your own, until you will sicken and die of them, still in silence? … We can learn to work and speak when we are afraid in the same way we have learned to work and speak when we are tired. For we have been socialized to respect fear more than our own needs for language and definition, and while we wait in silence for that final luxury of fearlessness, the weight of that silence will choke us (Lorde, 2019, pp. 30, 33).

Speaking out for women is frightening and sometimes it costs us: our lives, reputations, jobs, and friends. As Lorde acknowledges, on one hand, it's not easy to do but on the other, it's easier than the alternative. When we've imagined and articulated a vision for the world and taken stock of our principles and values, we can work towards that vision, despite the criticism and despite the backlash, as Bell and Nelson have so courageously done.

Conclusion: Toward a Decolonizing Feminist Methodology

The methodologies I've used and expanded on aren't new. Rather,

> … these methods already partially exist, but they have been so undervalued that they constantly need to be rediscovered. Also because they have been increasingly undervalued in our society, they have not had the benefit of much refinement. As each 'rediscovery' or

contribution is made, it appears new and gets its own name (Reinharz, 1983, p. 173).

I guess in this sense, I'm really talking about feminist methodology, as opposed to decolonizing feminist methodology. But I think in this case, it's important to point out the particular oppressions and barriers that Indigenous women face as researchers, as research participants, and as readers and viewers of research. In this way then, describing a decolonizing feminist methodology is less about identity and culture and more about the material realities of Indigenous women's lives and about the politics—acknowledged or unacknowledged—that accompany those realities.

CHAPTER 4

Sex Work

Sex work theory is anti-woman in similar ways that the Bell/ Huggins debate (or perhaps a better way to describe what happened would be the attack on Bell and Nelson) is anti-woman. Sex work advocates are very quick to point out that sex workers' experiences, feelings, thoughts, and analysis are incredibly varied (Doe, 2013; Graca et al., 2018); so incredibly varied in fact, that it's generally not possible[27] to generalize from any single or even group experience, feeling, thought, or analysis. This idea, that everyone has a unique experience of everything and as a result, we can't make any generalized statements about any group of people, demonstrates just how useless postmodern theory is to women. Because no experience can be representative of the 'sex worker experience', women's stories that very clearly communicate horrific treatment in prostitution are dismissed as being 'non-representative' while surprisingly,[28] sex workers who claim to love their jobs aren't dismissed in the same way. Instead, sex work researchers, in the interests of men, distract from the very serious and real issues being brought forward by women by stating that these weren't the right kind of sex workers to speak on this issue or that they had spoken about sex work in the wrong way or they had used the wrong language or any other

---

27 This is not true. It is possible.
28 This is not surprising.

number of similar statements. Instead of actually hearing what has been said and accepting that these 'unrepresentative' horror stories are actually some women's realities in prostitution, sex work researchers throw this 'discourse' right back into academia, the 'world of ideas' where debating complexities and nuance is more important than actually doing something to make the world a better place for someone other than yourself (Dworkin, 1993). As Bell and Nelson asked in their article about intra-racial rape, "… who speaks of the anguish, shame and risk for the Aboriginal women victims?" (1989, p. 404). Indeed, who speaks of the anguish, shame and risk for women brutalized in prostitution? Kwakwaka'wakw – Kwagu'ł, Dzawada'enuxw, Ukrainian, and English scholar Sarah Hunt clearly doesn't speak of the anguish, shame and risk for Indigenous women in prostitution in her article 'Decolonizing Sex Work':

> … Indigenous sex work has been conflated with sexual exploitation, domestic trafficking, intergenerational violence, and the disappearance or abduction of Indigenous girls and women. Interestingly, and problematically, girls and women are talked about together, as though they are a single category, which echoes colonial views of Indigenous people as children in need of paternalistic surveillance and control … many adult sex workers first became involved as youth, which undoubtedly has implications for their adult sex-working experiences; however, a nuanced exploration of this issue has yet to be initiated. Instead, children, youth, and women are conjoined as victims, and their varying degrees of agency and choice remain unexamined (Hunt, 2013, p. 90).

Here, the author dismisses the horrific realities of some women in prostitution to instead criticize the use of the term 'women and girls'. Her interpretation of why feminists often use the term 'women and girls' is incorrect. Firstly, using 'women and girls' doesn't collapse 'women' and 'girls' into a single category because it acknowledges both 'women *and* girls'. The term 'sex worker', arguably, does put 'women', 'girls', 'Indigenous women', 'Black women', 'refugee women', and so on, into a single category. In fact, because 'sex worker' is also a degendered term, it also lumps 'men', 'boys', 'Indigenous men', 'men who identify as transgender', 'women who identify as non-binary', and so on, into the single category of 'sex worker' as well. Some sex work advocates (Youthline, n.d.; Henne and Moseley, 2005; Rubenson et al., 2005; De Leeuw, 2016; Thorburn, 2018; Shoji and Tsubota, 2021) and popular news media (CBC News, 2010; Marwaha, 2017; CBC News, 2018) even collapse sexually exploited children into the category of 'sex worker' ('child sex worker', 'youth sex worker', 'underage sex worker'). Secondly, the reason feminist women use the term 'women and girls' is to make visible the particular ways patriarchy impacts girls because they are girls and not women. Due to their status as dependents and ideas about the role and value of girl children in particular, girls require different and/or particular supports and potential solutions to ending male violence against them than that of adult women.

What Does 'Sex Work Is Work' Mean?

> We recognize consensual sex work as an occupation that involves the exchange of labour for socio-material returns, examples of which include escorting, massage, dancing, street encounters, domination, and digital interactions (Orchard, 2021, n.p.).

Sex work advocates view sex work, a term coined by Carol Leigh (1997) aka Scarlot Harlot, as a form of labour that can and should be made safer for those participating in the industry. In this view, the stigma of engaging in sex work and any laws that criminalize any aspect of sex work are the primary sources of harm for those in the industry as they impede the ability of sex workers to access human rights, basic needs and social services when in need due to misinformation and negative judgement of their occupation (van der Meulen, 2013). Those who frame 'sex as work' advocate for either a legalized model, under which the sex industry (including sex workers who provide sexual services, sex buyers, managers, drivers, receptionists, bodyguards, and all others who profit from the sex industry) is fully decriminalized and regulated by government legislation, or a fully decriminalized model, in which the sex industry is fully decriminalized and regulation is provided in the form of municipal bylaws and workplace health and safety guidelines (van der Meulen, 2013). Under full decriminalization:

> ... workplace harms and grievances can be judged under more appropriate federal, provincial, or municipal policies. For example, there are existing federal provisions that protect against extortion, sexual assault, forcible confinement, and threat with a weapon— crimes that prohibitionists [abolitionists] claim are inherent to sex work (van der Meulen et al. 2013, p. 16).

According to this perspective, sex workers would be eligible for employment insurance, worker's compensation, health insurance, and all other benefits afforded to other workers, and could organize into unions to further protect their rights (van der Meulen, 2013).

The sex-as-work perspective dominates public, news, and academic discourse. Overwhelmingly, prostitution is normalized in popular culture and presented as light-hearted entertainment and an empowering choice for women (Coy et al., 2011). Examples of these representations include Hollywood films like *Pretty Woman* and *The Girlfriend Experience* and television shows like *Cathouse*, *The Client List*, and *Secret Diary of a Call Girl*. The language of prostitution has also become increasingly normalized, demonstrated by the expression 'pimp my ...', which refers to the process of making something better—the television show *Pimp My Ride* restored vehicles that were in poor condition into expensive customized vehicles that were tailored to the car owner's personalities and interests, and I remember seeing a 'pimp my poutine' section in a Montréal restaurant that offered patrons the ability to add a wide variety of toppings in addition to the traditional gravy and cheese curds. Dominant pop culture representations of prostitution obscure the violence that is perpetrated against prostituted women by men as johns and pimps, such as verbal assault in the form of racist and/or sexist slurs, beatings with or without the use of weapons, or the inherent violence of engaging in unwanted sex acts (Coy et al., 2011). These glamorized representations exist in stark contrast to the commonly-held misogynist beliefs of pimps, johns, and other men. For example, the study *Men Who Buy Sex: Who They Buy and What They Know*, found that out of the 103 johns interviewed:

> An adversarial stance toward women was evident in many of these men's responses. For example, 33% reported that most women are basically liars. Nearly one-half (46%) felt that most women get pleasure in putting men down. Thirty-one per cent felt that they 'get a raw deal' from women in their life (Farley et al., 2009, p. 13).

Additionally, the study found that the more accepting men were of prostitution, the more likely they were to accept rape myths as truth: 47 per cent of the johns surveyed believed that rape happened because men got carried away; 16 per cent stated they would rape if they knew they would get away with it; and 54 per cent believed the false idea that the existence of prostitution reduces incidences of rape (Farley et al., 2009).

The dominance of the sex work perspective is also evident in contemporary news media, even when the story contains sensationalized accounts of violence and victimization. The framing of sex-as-work is now being applied to news stories about children and teenage girls, as evidenced in recent headlines: 'Girl, 16, threatened with knives, pellet gun to work in sex trade: Toronto police' (Shum, 2016), 'Edmonton kids sold as sex workers, as teen prostitution becomes more common' (Bell and McConnell, 2016), and 'Montréal Grand Prix: Local teens recruited to work in sex trade, experts say' (Feith, 2016). The framing of sex-as-work is also very common and widely accepted in academia, even in reference to teenage girls. For example, in the book *Being Heard: The Experiences of Young Women in Prostitution*, the authors state:

> … not examining work-related issues, such as how youth sex-trade workers manage their work and risk, and the way they cope with stressful demands, may unintentionally harm the health and safety of youth sex-trade workers. By casting the net in terms of victimization, one runs the risk of entrenching stigma and pushing girls further and

further away from supports. Thus, viewing youth prostitutes solely as victims both legislatively and theoretically may be problematic (Gorkoff and Runner, 2003, p. 15).

In the article, 'Tender Grounds: Intimate visceral violence and British Columbia's colonial geographies', the author writes, "... as a teenager, Sheri spent more than five years as a survival sex trade worker in Prince George, British Columbia, a city on the edge of the Highway of Tears ..." (De Leeuw, 2016, p. 14). 'Sheri' is eventually revealed in the article to be one of the Indigenous teenage victims of Judge Ramsey, a white Prince George judge who sexually assaulted numerous Indigenous teenage girls he presided over (De Leeuw, 2016). The framing of an Indigenous teenage girl who is being sexually exploited by the judge presiding over her case as a 'sex worker' is problematic as it removes any responsibility from the adult men, including Judge Ramsey, for soliciting sex acts from a teenage girl. Rather, 'sex worker' frames this Indigenous girl as an active participant engaging with customers in the labour market and had Judge Ramsey not been presiding over her case (or perhaps even if he were), his solicitation of her is just another sex industry transaction. Ramsey's case also brings up some important questions about sex work and conflicts of interest: what happens when police officers, judges, and other men in positions of power hit up their favourite 'working girl' after a long day on the job? I was in Amsterdam, Netherlands a while back, a country that legalized prostitution in 1999,[29] and was told about a woman in prostitution who had appeared in court before a judge who also happened to be a 'client' of hers. McClintock begins her article 'Screwing the System: Sexwork, Race, and the Law' stating, "a prostitute tells me that a magistrate who pays her to beat him confessed that he gets an erection every time he sentences a prostitute in court." (1992, p. 70).

---

29 The legalization of prostitution in the Netherlands has been a failure. See 'The Legalisation of Prostitution: A Failed Social Experiment' by Sheila Jeffreys (2003), and 'Why Prostitution Should Never Be Legalized' by Julie Bindel (2017) for more information on the situation in the Netherlands.

Sex work advocates present women's engagement in prostitution as a decontextualized, individual choice that is beyond critical examination while also making a distinction between forced and chosen involvement in the sex industry. Jill Nagle, in the crucial text *Whores and Other Feminists*, states:

> Like many of the contributors to this volume, my racial and economic privilege afforded me the opportunity to choose participation in the sex industry from among many other options. This is not true for perhaps the vast majority of sex workers worldwide, especially those who exchange sex to survive on the streets, who support an addiction, or who are forced into it by others. Yet most public discussions about sex work fails to distinguish between voluntary and coerced sexual exchange, a distinction every bit as salient (and problematic) as that between consensual sex and rape. Sex worker activists around the globe have been laboring for more than two decades to improve conditions for those who choose the profession, and to oppose all forms of coercion, in the process calling attention to the larger economic context that severely circumscribes the range of options for all women (and most men) (1997, p. 2).

In this text, Nagle acknowledges the lack of economic and occupational choices available to women from a global perspective yet insists on the foregrounding of women's agency to suck the dicks of men whose dicks they don't want to suck and ignores systems of patriarchy and men's choices as sex buyers and pimps when it comes to the sex industry.

The representation of prostitution as entertainment or empowerment hides the realities of women who are pushed into the sex trade by social and economic factors such as poverty, racism, or a history of sexual abuse, and who are then often trapped in 'the life' and cannot simply get out when they desire to do so (Coy et al., 2011). These representation also obscure men's misogynist attitudes, behaviours, and any accountability for their harmful beliefs and actions about and toward women, hiding them beneath a *Pretty Woman* white-washing of the sex industry.

Decolonizing Sex Work

It's not possible to 'decolonize sex work' and it's either ignorance, deeply-embedded liberal politics, or a purposeful misrepresentation of both 'decolonization' and 'prostitution' to suggest this might be possible. Sex work advocates who do believe it's possible, even desirable, to decolonize sex work are often researchers, professors, or students. In this context, threading these two academic buzz-words—'decolonize' and 'sex work'—together makes a bit more sense, given the pressure on scholars to deconstruct, complicate, and nuance the shit out of everything until it doesn't make any kind of sense. It's in this that we can clearly see just how invested the manstitution of academia is in maintaining the status quo. The fiction that it's possible to 'decolonize sex work' relies on a number of flawed arguments: (1) Decolonization means recognizing consent, agency and choice within a colonial system; (2) Some Indigenous peoples are not negatively impacted by colonization; and (3) Inclusivity is decolonizing.

Decolonization, Consent, Agency, and Choice

A discourse that focuses on consent, agency and choice within a system accepts the terms of that system. This kind of discourse isn't radical because (among other things) it can't imagine changing the system, only adjusting choices within that system. Discussions about sex work focus on the consent, agency and choice of Indigenous women in prostitution and not only that but focus specifically on the *recognition* of the consent, agency and choice of Indigenous women in prostitution as some kind of 'decolonizing' process (or something I guess). Instead of advocating for more options for Indigenous women, sex work advocacy remains focused on recognizing what agency and shitty options Indigenous women do have and leaving it at that. In order to reconcile the idea of sex work as a legitimate occupation chosen by many individuals with all of their agency *and* the overrepresentation of Indigenous women in prostitution, the patriarchal history of those choices in the process of colonization must be made invisible or ignored and Indigenous women must be constructed as 'squaws' who desire to engage in unwanted sex acts with numerous unknown and undesired men in far disproportionate numbers to white women. To reveal a more accurate history and the consequences of this history for Indigenous women today we need to critically examine Canada's history of prostitution.

Acknowledging and analyzing the historical patterns and contemporary context in which a choice occurs doesn't necessarily mean that all agency is denied or ignored and that the individual making the choice is now purely a helpless victim of history and contemporary circumstance (Farley, 2009). While some women are forced into prostitution with no other options available to them, many women do choose prostitution as the best option among a range of shitty options. What's hopeful about this is that prostitution is a choice insofar as many women can choose differently, recognizing of course, that some women simply cannot and will be killed if they try to do so. If individual choice plays no part in the role of many women's prostitution, prostitution has simply become their destiny—their fate—and what more could we expect from *those* women? Feminists know that prostitution is not all we can expect for *some* women, such as groups of racialized, Indigenous, or poor women, or for any women in fact and 'sex work' does just that:

> In the 1870s and 1880s, the women campaigning against the Contagious Diseases Acts in the Ladies National Association in Britain argued that prostitution was the best-paid industry for poor women (Pateman, 1988, pp. 194–195).

The lives of Indigenous women are far more complex than can be described in a simple either/or scenario of 'princess' or 'squaw', 'virgin' or 'whore', 'victim' or 'free agent'. Rather, Indigenous women have long been making difficult decisions in order to survive ongoing colonization. For example, after the 1885 Métis Rebellion and due to white men's perception of increased threat, Indigenous peoples were confined to reserves with deplorable living conditions (Carter, 1997). Indigenous peoples on reserve were subject to a pass system that only allowed them to leave the reserve if they obtained a pass from the Indian agent (Carter, 1997). The justification for this system was to keep 'squaws' out of towns and villages and away from corruptible white men and 'vulnerable' white women settlers (Carter, 1997, p. 187). Recognizing the desperate situation they'd created for Indigenous women, white male Indian agents and members of the Northwest Mounted Police demanded sex acts in exchange for food rations from starving Indigenous women:

> The police gave them hardtack biscuits and scraps ... there were no white ladies in those days. The policemen want wives so they go around and pick the ones they want. They give the starving families groceries to get the girls (qtd. in Carter, 1997, p. 180).

Sure, Indigenous women had 'choices' in this oppressive situation. Their options included a bunch of shitty choices within a range of shitty available options and as such, Indigenous women then, like today, were forced to make difficult decisions: Iteskawin, a Lakota woman,

> ... consented to marry [NWMP Superintendent] Jarvis at the height of the starvation of the Lakota on condition that if she married him, he would ensure that her brothers and sisters would have something to eat twice a day (Carter, 1997, pp. 180–181).

The idea of 'consent', indeed 'agency' and 'choice', for Iteskawin and other Indigenous women are complicated in such circumstances. There's a lot of factors to consider, some within Iteskawin's control and many outside of her control: If Iteskawin and her family weren't starving, would she have agreed to marry Jarvis? What other food-generating activities were available to Indigenous women at that time? What kind of obligation did Iteskawin feel toward her family? Was Iteskawin under any pressure from her family and community to provide food? Could Iteskawin and her family have left the reserve? Could Jarvis have ensured Iteskawin and her family had enough food to eat without demanding sex acts from her in exchange? Iteskawin's choice to marry Jarvis can be acknowledged here as a constrained choice made within a context of limited viable options under oppressive conditions. There are numerous other accounts of white men in positions of power at this time demanding or offering the exchange of sex acts from Indigenous women for food rations or other necessities (Carter, 1997).

At the time, as today, not all Indigenous women were in prostitution, but all Indigenous women were seen as 'squaws' aka 'prostitutes'. The correlation between Indigenous woman and 'squaw'/'prostitute' was so strong that prostitution legislation was initially embedded in the *Indian Act* (Backhouse, 1985; Carter, 1997; Mawani, 2002). Prostitution legislation primarily targeted Indigenous women for criminalization, although Indigenous men were also covered under the legislation from 1879 until it was absorbed into the *Criminal Code of Canada* in 1892, where "... the provision against Indians keeping, frequenting, or being found in disorderly houses was reintroduced, but restricted to unenfranchised Indian women only" (Backhouse, 1985). Canada's prostitution legislation didn't attempt to eradicate prostitution but instead control where and between whom it occurred:

in the case of interracial prostitution ... officials seemed more concerned about where these sexual transgressions took place, leaving white men outside of the discourse and beyond legal and nonlegal punishment (Mawani, 2002, p. 58).

The Department of Indian Affairs at the time interpreted the prostitution legislation very broadly when it came to Indigenous women:

'A woman who allows a man to whom she is not married to occupy the same bed with her must certainly be regarded as a prostitute herself and if he or she is already married, committing adultery also' ... in other words, the Department of Indian Affairs in Ottawa was suggesting that all aboriginal women who had intimate relations with Native or white men, and who were not married to them, were indeed prostitutes and were to be treated as such (Mawani, 2002, p. 56).

Patriarchy and racism constructed all Indigenous women as 'squaws' and 'prostitutes', whether or not they ever actually engaged in prostitution, a belief that continues today. I can't count how many times men have assumed I was 'working' when waiting for family members in town, enjoying sunshine in a park, walking down the street minding my own business, taking the bus, going to the grocery store, or keeping a friend company while he fixed a car in his driveway. In other words, all Indigenous women are seen as sexually available to men and men view themselves as sexually entitled to Indigenous women's bodies. This belief was widely accepted and supported by legislation at the time. Today, this belief (i.e. patriarchy) is widely accepted among Canadians, although current prostitution laws namely, *Protection of Communities and Exploited Persons* (PCEPA) have progressively criminalized men's sexual entitlement to women's bodies.

The 'choices' made by Indigenous women to engage in prostitution while living in poverty and the 'consent' granted by Indigenous women to sexual acts demanded by men in exchange for food rations or other necessities is more complicated than 'she chose it'. The entitlement of Indian agents, police, and other men in this exchange can't be overstated—we need to remember that 'her choice' to engage in prostitution is constrained first in that women are required to respond to a question ("do you date?", "how much?") that men shouldn't feel entitled to ask in the first place. Instead, we can ask questions that help us to understand the historical and contemporary contexts of shitty male-defined options available for women to choose from. We can ask: what has changed between then and now? Certainly not the entitlement and underlying ideologies held by men about the roles, purpose, and supposed character of Indigenous 'squaws' and certainly not the poor socio-economic conditions that Indigenous women face. But what happens when wealthy Indigenous women professors and lawyers quit their well-paying secure jobs to choose to suck the dicks of men whose dicks they don't want to suck to make a living?

A number of Indigenous women writers have spoken back to the stereotypes of squaw, Indian princess, and sexually available brown woman, as well as the violence justified by these images of us (see Acoose, 1995; Dumont, 1996; Maracle, 1996). But has Indigenous women's refusal of these sexual stereotypes resulted in simultaneously distancing ourselves from women who are working in the sex trade? We need to examine the moralistic stance against sex work, and the conflation of sex work with exploitation, to see how we have internalized both this stereotype and its opposite. Although resistance to degrading and dehumanizing stereotypes of Indigenous people is important, it is simultaneously essential to look at how our responses affect—or fail to affect—the material reality of violence ... we need to move away from positioning ourselves as advocates for, and saviours of, some disempowered sister-Other and instead facilitate a process that centres the voices of sex workers themselves. Otherwise we risk reproducing the discourses of colonialism that constitute Indigenous women as without agency (Hunt, 2013, pp. 87–88).

Hunt's criticism relies on the false idea that there's at least some truth to the idea of Indigenous 'squaws'; that there are, in fact, Indigenous women who just really love engaging in sex acts in ways they don't want to with men they don't want to engage in sex acts with and that these women just really love pleasing the man she's with and feeding his ego while completely ignoring her own sexual desires and satisfaction. Her sexual desires and sexual satisfaction are unimportant in sex work; only the *appearance* of her sexual desires and sexual satisfaction are important in order to feed men's egos to try and get repeat 'customers' (Norma and Tankard Reist, 2016). While Hunt seems to recognize that the 'squaw' and the 'princess' are harmful, often internalized, stereotypes and should be resisted as such, she suggests that maybe Indigenous 'princesses' not currently in prostitution and who criticize the sex industry are moralizing, agency-denying women who judge themselves superior to the disempowered actual sex-crazy 'squaws' in prostitution. This theory acquiesces to the system (i.e. patriarchy) and fails to imagine what consent, choice, and agency might look like for women outside of patriarchy and what Women's Liberation might look like so it works to make the best out of the currently available circumstances without challenging the system. Men's idea that squaws really do exist is a big fucking lie, and so is their idea that princesses exist too. Men haven't created equivalent categories for themselves because men get to be men; men get to be fully human. Indigenous women, on the other hand, whether we enjoy heterosexual or homosexual sex with one partner, with many partners, or many different partners at the same time for our own sexual enjoyment and satisfaction, or whether we prefer not to have any kind of sexual contact with others, are still squaws. This is the difference between the reality of Indigenous women and the lie of the 'squaw': There are Indigenous women who enjoy all kinds of sex with all kinds of people at all different times, just as there are non-Indigenous women who have a variety of different sexual preferences and desires and this is great. But because of patriarchy, women who enjoy sex are seen as dirty and disgusting and labelled 'squaws' or 'sluts' or 'whores' and men are not. Women who love having unsatisfying sex with men they don't want to have sex with don't exist—except when women are represented as such in pornography. 'Decolonizing sex work' sounds and looks suspiciously patriarchal. Additionally, men are the primary benefactors of ridiculous ideas like 'decolonizing sex work' and these two things should raise red flags for any critically thinking person.

Colonization Only Impacts Some Indigenous Peoples' Problems or the Problems with Trafficking

The use of the terms 'trafficking', 'sex trafficking', and 'trafficking for the purposes of sexual exploitation' are now more commonly used than they were in the past among governments, non-governmental organizations, the media, academia, and others (Hunt, 2013; Kaye, 2017). Sex work advocates criticize this change in language and also criticize anti-trafficking discourse and work itself, for a few different reasons that are coincidentally, all wrong: Sex work advocates argue that the discourse of trafficking (and really, any feminist criticism of prostitution) infantilizes Indigenous women and makes them all victims while denying them their agency and that anti-trafficking initiatives in Canada harm those who are trafficked by giving more power to the colonial state.

What's so wrong with being a victim? Or recognizing you have been victimized? Here, we see the double standard that Indigenous women are held to: Indigenous men are victims of colonization while Indigenous women are not. The Truth and Reconciliation Commission (TRC) was, and continues to be, a very important process in Canada that works to determine the truth of Canada's Indian Residential School System (IRS) and "... lay the foundation for the important question of reconciliation ..." (TRC, 2015, p. vi). The TRC was commissioned to study the impacts of Canada's IRS and stated in their final report:

Canada's residential school system for Aboriginal children was an education system in name only for much of its existence. These residential schools were created for the purpose of separating Aboriginal children from their families, in order to minimize and weaken family ties and cultural linkages, and to indoctrinate children into a new culture—the culture of the legally dominant Euro-Christian Canadian society, led by Canada's first prime minister, Sir John A. Macdonald. The schools were in existence for well over 100 years, and many successive generations of children from the same communities and families endured the experience of them. That experience was hidden for most of Canada's history, until Survivors of the system were finally able to find the strength, courage, and support to bring their experiences to light in several thousand court cases that ultimately led to the largest class-action lawsuit in Canada's history. The Truth and Reconciliation Commission of Canada was a commission like no other in Canada. Constituted and created by the Indian Residential Schools Settlement Agreement, which settled the class actions, the Commission spent six years travelling to all parts of Canada to hear from the Aboriginal people who had been taken from their families as children, forcibly if necessary, and placed for much of their child-hoods in residential schools (TRC, 2015, p. v).

Because the TRC was, and is, largely a degendered process, Indigenous men have been found to have been victimized by colonization, sometimes to the point of excusing Indigenous men's violence against women because of this victimization (Greer, 2008; Innes, 2015). Throughout the TRC Final Report, Indigenous peoples are recognized as victims of colonization and of the IRS:

> The courts continue to hear Aboriginal rights cases, and new litigation has been filed by Survivors of day schools not covered by the Indian Residential Schools Settlement Agreement, as well as by victims of the 'Sixties Scoop' ... Yet, the importance of truth telling in its own right should not be underestimated; it restores the human dignity of victims of violence and calls governments and citizens to account ... This pattern of disproportionate imprisonment and victimization of Aboriginal people continues to this day (TRC, 2015, p. 8, 12, 164).

The TRC final report rightfully recognizes that the system of the IRS was harmful to Indigenous peoples, even despite the fact that some IRS Survivors described having "... some good moments ..." at the schools, such as being able to play sports (TRC, 2015, p. 110). Imagine if we responded to Canada's IRS and TRC report as we respond to the prostitution of Indigenous women: Scholars would reduce the discussion to one of consent, choice, and agency of both the children taken into the schools and their families that 'chose' to send them there; we would be denying IRS Survivors their agency if we recognized them as victims and survivors, let's just call them 'students' instead; and look! Sure there were harmful things that happened, but the IRS system wasn't inherently harmful by itself; some students enjoyed their time there! It was mostly the sexual and physical abuse, the neglect, the starvation, and so on that caused the harm. Can you imagine? If you can't, you can look to the justifiably horrified reactions to former Senator Lynn Beyak's remarks that called for Canadians to not just look at the bad, but also to recognize the good of the IRS system (Carleton, 2017). There's a difference between those who created, ran, and supported the IRS and those Indigenous peoples who were victimized by the IRS. Criticizing the IRS as a harmful system steeped in patriarchal, racist, and classist ideologies while understanding that Indigenous peoples at that time, like today, were making incredibly difficult decisions from a range of incredibly shitty options available to them; the system, here the IRS, and those victimized by that system, Indigenous peoples, are not at all the same. Yet, this happens all the time when we talk about a system that disproportionately impacts Indigenous women: prostitution. Suddenly, when the system of prostitution is criticized, this means women who are in prostitution are also being criticized. This is simply not the case. As Pateman states:

> The perception of prostitution as a problem about women is so deep-seated that any criticism of prostitution is likely to provoke the accusation that contemporary contractarians bring against feminists, that criticism of prostitution shows contempt for the prostitutes. To argue that there is something wrong with prostitution does not necessarily imply an adverse judgement on the women who engage in the work. When socialists criticize capitalism and the employment contract they do not do so because they are contemptuous of workers, but because they are the workers' champions. Nevertheless, appeals to the idea of false consciousness, popular a few years ago, suggested that the problem about capitalism was a problem about workers. To reduce the question of capitalism to deficiencies in workers' consciousness diverts attention away from the capitalist, the other participants in the employment contract (1988, p. 193).

Just as with the IRS, there's a difference between those who create, run, and support the system of prostitution, such as men who buy sex acts and pimps, and those who are victimized by this woman-hating system: the women who are selling sex acts. Similar to Beyak, sex work advocates remind us that not everyone has a bad experience, some women feel empowered and enjoy their time in sex work! It's those pesky laws and stigma that cause men to beat women with crowbars, choke and stab them, and so on: that's what causes the harm, not sex work or men!

Indigenous women, since white men invaded, have struggled to make difficult decisions in very hostile territories with few options available to us. The idea that discourses and action around trafficking harms Indigenous peoples because it gives more power to the colonial state is something to talk about while recognizing the constrained circumstances we find ourselves in as women in contemporary patriarchy. What strategies we'll use as we work toward Women's Liberation involves making many difficult decisions often with few resources, making mistakes, correcting mistakes, trying something new, and evaluating past wins and losses to plan better for the future. Like other radical feminist women, I believe that government can change and that leadership and justice are not inherently bad. We can radically restructure the system and implement new forms of feminist leadership and justice; I do believe this is possible. Capitalism, on the other hand, cannot be radically restructured and made feminist—if so, it becomes something else, something's that's not capitalism. Greed, profit at all costs, and individualism are foundational to capitalism and I don't believe these things can be restructured to work for women. As such, I'd rather work toward a radical restructuring of leadership and justice than put my trust in capitalism to ensure women's rights, and that's exactly what someone does when they argue for a reduced role or removal of state mechanisms when it comes to profiting from male violence against women. This is essentially what's happened in the pornography industry and it's been disastrous for women.

While sex work advocates argue that using the language of 'trafficking' lumps 'sex workers' in with actual 'trafficking victims', this isn't what this change in language has achieved. Instead, referring to 'trafficking' brings up images of women in chains (which is reality for some women) and allows this form of male violence against women to be separated from 'sex work'. This shift in discourse has actually made it easier for people in Canada and elsewhere to differentiate between 'forced' prostitution (trafficking) and 'chosen' prostitution (sex work). Women who don't meet the criteria of the perfect 'trafficking victim' in chains, beaten and bloodied who very clearly state that they are victims of sex trafficking must then be sex workers (perhaps 'migrant sex workers') making sexy choices. Men who buy sex acts from women in prostitution also rely on this false distinction between 'forced trafficking victim' and 'free choice sex worker': 2007 research in London, England found that 43 per cent of the men who participated in the study thought that the majority of the women they used in prostitution were 'non-British' and most likely from Eastern Europe (qtd. in Farley et al., 2009, p. 16). While most of the men interviewed wouldn't say that they had used a woman who had been sex trafficked, some men "... simply presumed that so long as there was no incontrovertible, visible evidence of force, women were on equal footing with them" (qtd. In Farley et al., 2009, p. 16). This distinction between 'forced' and 'chosen' prostitution is in reality much less clear with less rigid boundaries and we can only see this when we recognize and consider the larger sex-based systems of oppression and privilege always at work in the lives of women and men. Relying on this false 'victim/free agent' dichotomy to understand prostitution allows for the continuation of the 'virgin/whore' or 'squaw/princess' myth that separates, categorizes, and ranks women; demonstrates a lack of understanding of male violence against women, how this type of violence functions, and what it looks like; and focuses the discussion on women in prostitution, letting the men who buy sex and pimp women evade criticism. Whether we make a false distinction between 'forced trafficking' and 'chosen sex work' or not, the same men are involved as buyers of sex acts and as pimps. For example, in a 2009 study of 103 men who bought sex in the United Kingdom, 53 per cent of the men interviewed said they had used a woman in prostitution knowing she was under the control of a pimp, 55 per cent of the 103 men believed that most women in prostitution were lured, tricked, or trafficked into the sex industry, and 35 per cent of the 103 men said they had used a woman in prostitution that they believe had been trafficked into the sex trade from another country (Farley et al., 2009, p. 16). In all of these cases, the men went ahead to receive the 'sexual services' they had paid for (Farley et al., 2009).

Inclusive Sex Work

'Decolonizing sex work' is also a way to make sex work more inclus-ive of Indigenous women, a process that surprisingly also ends up benefitting men and men's profits. For example, the all-Indigenous Vancouver-based burlesque troupe, Virago Nation

> … showcases Indigenous sexuality as expansive and multidimensional in order to dismantle the lethal 'colonial virgin-whore dichotomy' … Virago Nation rejects these colonial discourses and binaries by showcasing themselves and their sexualities as complex and therefore non-generalizable by holding self-determination over their sexual representations through a physical display of Sovereign Erotics (Burns, 2020, pp. 33–34).

Yet, Virago Nation's 'decolonized sexualities' look exactly like the sexuality prescribed to women by men in a patriarchy. Virago Nation's burlesque shows don't challenge the status quo (i.e. patriarchy) any more than non-Indigenous burlesque shows or other types of 'sex work', such as stripping, do. Simply because a woman 'chooses' to do something doesn't make this choice a feminist or even decolonizing one (Jagger, 2004). Similarly, a claim that an action is 'feminist' or 'decolonizing' doesn't make it automatically so either. Virago Nation's claims to be presenting their sexuality on their own terms but reality shows and tells us that they aren't, they're presenting Indigenous women's sexuality on patriarchy's terms just with underwear that has west coast Indigenous art on it. Nipple pasty workshops do not present a tool to combat colonization, a reclamation of sexuality, or a decolonization of Indigenous spaces, communities, or minds (Burns, 2020). Patriarchal practices are not, and cannot be, decolonizing practices, no matter how many dreamcatchers or totem poles are included. Another example of the myth of decolonizing sex work is the expansion of pornography to include Indigenous women as just as fuckable as white women. Pornography is an arm of the sex industry that helps to normalize men's woman-hating behaviour in popular culture. As Barry states, "[Pornography] is the media of misogyny" (1979, p. 207).

Sex Work Politics Are Anti-Feminist and Anti-Woman

The issue is not that sex work politics simply stand in opposition to feminist politics, although this is true. The issue is that sex work politics are actively anti-feminist in that they attempt to take away women's ability to name ourselves and our political positions and they work to discredit feminist research as a whole. Sex work politics are anti-woman in that they refuse to recognize the body of feminist knowledge on male violence against women as valid and valuable and blame women for male violence committed against them by promoting rape myths.

Sex work advocates attempt to reframe and rename feminists who are critical of prostitution. 'Prostitution abolitionists' generally come from the perspective that prostitution is a form of male violence against women and advocate for the practice to be abolished. Some individuals who think sex work is work rename 'abolitionists' as 'prohibitionists'. For example, the authors of the 2013 book *Selling Sex: Experience, Advocacy, and Research on Sex Work in Canada* state, "we have chosen to call this grouping [of prostitution abolitionists] 'prohibitionists', as the term 'abolitionist' often has a positive association with the movement to end slavery" (van der Meulen et al., 2013, p. 14). 'Abolition' and 'prohibition' mean different things, as van der Muelen et al. recognize; they just want to make sure that feminist arguments have a negative association (prohibition) instead of a positive one (abolition). This colonization of language is unfortunately effective and results in intentional confusion as to the feminist position on prostitution as a form of male violence against women that should be abolished. For critical thinkers, however, it begs the question: why not just counter the feminist arguments against prostitution instead of re-conceptualizing and re-naming those arguments and then responding to those (false) arguments?

The majority of sex work research occurs within the area of public health and is not coming from a feminist perspective (Graham, 2014). As a result, information is analyzed with a narrow and degendered medical focus (Graham, 2014). This type of research—that is, claiming to use a scientific, objective, empirical, evidence-based method, methodology, and analysis—is the kind of research Indigenous scholars have long-criticized for the harm it causes to Indigenous peoples (Smith, 2012; Burns, 2020), yet it's the kind of research methodology used most often when academics study Indigenous women in prostitution in Canada. Using this type of research, sex work researchers also work to actively disparage and discredit feminist and Indigenous methodologies. For example, a well-cited sex work researcher, quoting Gayle Rubin, claims that feminist research that understands prostitution as a form of male violence against women is sloppy, unsupported, and outlandish; that feminist researchers choose and focus on worst-case scenarios to bolster their arguments; that feminists present anecdotes as evidence; and evidence that doesn't fit with the researcher's ideologies is ignored (Weitzer, 2005, p. 937). These methodological failures, Weitzer argues, "violate[s] most of the criteria for meaningful, serious, systematic, scientific thinking" (Weitzer, 2005, p. 937). When feminist researchers understand prostitution as a form of male violence against women, they are biased, and "biased procedures beget foregone conclusions," making feminist research on prostitution simply unreliable. According to Weitzer and others, research that understands sex work to be work is the only scientific, objective, empirical, evidence-based research—the only 'real' research and the only research that should count. Weitzer's own biases, which appear to be coated in misogyny, fail to recognize that in feminist and decolonizing/Indigenous research traditions, bias, positionality, and researcher subjectivity are considered assets to the research process, not liabilities, and doesn't discredit research in the ways that men have told us (and continue to tell us) that it does. Additionally, because the research methods, methodology, and analysis are not feminist and arguably, anti-feminist, sex work researchers don't have—and don't appear to see any value in—a feminist understanding of male violence against women—how this particular type of violence functions, what it does, and how to work with women who have been impacted by it. This also reveals giant blind spots in pro-sex work research and politics.

The Mythology of Screening

The case for the full decriminalization of the sex industry relies on a number of myths, one of them being that women are able to tell which men may be violent by having 'enough time' to properly screen them:

> A central part of violence risk management on the street is the process of screening clients, since not all of those who approach sex workers on the street are indeed genuine clients (Armstrong, 2014, p. 210).

Screening strategies might include evaluating a man's body language to see if he appears fidgety or nervous (Armstrong, 2014) or checking to see if there are additional men participating in the 'date' (Armstrong, 2014). Sex work advocates argue that if the entire industry is decriminalized, sex workers will have more time to assess the men who are purchasing sex acts, can conduct a more thorough screening process, and thus have more ability to determine if their 'client' will commit additional acts of violence against the sex worker in addition to coercing her to engage in unwanted sex acts with him. In particular, Armstrong et al. argue, full decriminalization of the sex industry can make screening easier as fidgeting and nervous or pushy and impatient men are easier to identify because they're not fearful of arrest (Armstrong, 2014). Sex work advocates claim more screening time makes sex work safer for sex workers. The Canadian Alliance for Sex Work Law Reform made this claim, and others, in a suit they filed in the Ontario Superior Court of Justice in March 2021. I asked the Canadian Alliance for Sex Work Law Reform about these claims on Twitter, also in March 2021:

Cherry Smiley
@_cherrysmiley_
...

Hey @CDNSWAlliance, can u tell me more about the translators in #sexwork? Also, please share your screening strategies! I'm sure all #women want to know how to tell which man is a murderer! This info could stop #MMIWG! Why aren't you sharing it?

> **Sex Work Law Reform** @... · 2021-03-30
> #Sexworkers can't wait any longer for our human rights to be protected by this govt.
>
> Today we launched a constitutional challenge 2 #sexwork laws. sexworklawreform.com/se...

8:25 PM · 2021-03-30 · Twitter for iPhone

Sex Work Law Reform @CDNSWAlliance · Mar 31   ···
Replying to @_cherrysmiley_
Indigenous #sexworkers in our Alliance - and in the MMIW Inquiry - were
very clear that criminalization is a barrier to reporting violence.
Decriminalization would most definitely help to stop #MMIWG. Once you
start listening to Indigenous #sexworkers we can have real convo.

◯ 1   ↻   ♡   �🗹   ⤴   🖶

Cherry Smiley @_cherrysmiley_ · Mar 31   ···
Appreciate you taking the time to respond, but this doesn't answer my
question. What screening tools do #sexworkers have that can determine
which man will murder and which man won't, and why haven't you shared
this info with all #women?

◯ 1   ↻   ♡   ⌄   ⤴   🖶

Sex Work Law Reform @CDNSWAlliance · Mar 31   ···
Women moving through life - #sexworker or not - should act like all men
have potential 2B violent. You pretending that women don't screen or
mitigate that violence every day in our lives is disingenuous. #Sexworkers
do it as do all women in societies.

◯ 1   ↻   ♡ 2   ⌄   ⤴   🖶

Cherry Smiley @_cherrysmiley_ · Mar 31   ···
Yes, all #women screen. In 2020, 75% of #Femicides in Canada were
committed by men women knew, sometimes their whole lives–that's lots
of time to screen. How do sexworkers know which men will murder and
which men won't if a woman can be murdered by a husband of 20 years?

◯   ↻   ♡   ⌄   ⤴   🖶

And also in response to my original tweet:

Sex Work Law Reform @CDNSWAlliance · Mar 31 ···
Replying to @_cherrysmiley_
We can share this information, though your sarcasm makes clear you aren't actually interested in #sexworkers working conditions. Many migrant #sexworkers hire translators to help advertise & work in different locations, much the same way other migrant #sexworkers use translators.

♡ 1   ⟲   ♡   ⊽   ⬆   🖶

Cherry Smiley @_cherrysmiley_ · Mar 31 ···
I asked because I am interested. Translators work to translate ads and work to translate between #sexworkers and men who buy sex acts? Do they also translate between #sexworkers and #pimps? Does this translation happen in real time? Or am I misunderstanding what you've said?

♡ 1   ⟲   ♡   ⊽   ⬆   🖶

Sex Work Law Reform @CDNSWAlliance · Mar 31 ···
Translators are considered "pimps" or 3rd parties, under the law – they are criminalized in the same way that other 3rd parties are, for helping #sexworkers write & publish ads, communicate with other people...

♡ 1   ⟲   ♡ 1   ⊽   ⬆   🖶

Cherry Smiley @_cherrysmiley_ · Mar 31 ···
My Q is still how does this work in practice. Is the translator right there to translate #sexworkers' boundaries with the man who has purchased sex acts? Or before? How do #women ensure their ads are translated correctly? Do u have resources to suggest where I can learn more?

♡ 1   ⟲   ♡   ⊽   ⬆   🖶

Sex Work Law Reform @CDNSWAlliance · Mar 31 ···
This conversation is disingenuous and your questions are getting a little bit creepy & sensationalist. We know from your history/profile that you only intend to use this information to discredit us, not support #sexworkers in having our rights respected. Gonna end it here.

♡ 1   ⟲ 1   ♡ 1   ⊽   ⬆   🖶

Cherry Smiley @_cherrysmiley_ · Mar 31 ···
Ok, have a good day!

♡   ⟲   ♡   ⊽   ⬆   🖶

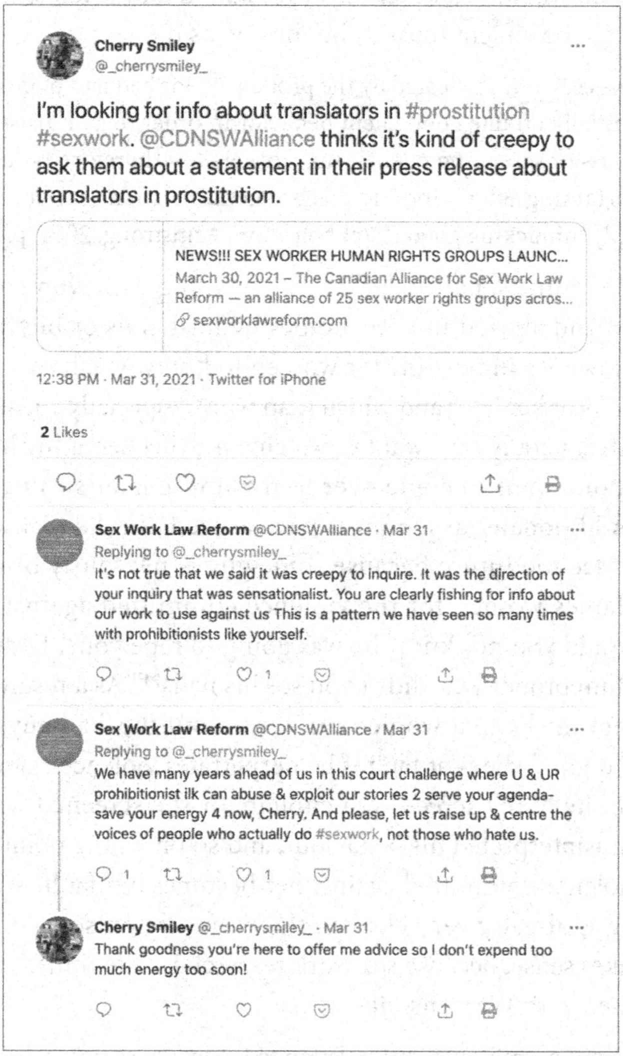

Cherry Smiley
@_cherrysmiley_
...

I'm looking for info about translators in #prostitution #sexwork. @CDNSWAlliance thinks it's kind of creepy to ask them about a statement in their press release about translators in prostitution.

> NEWS!!! SEX WORKER HUMAN RIGHTS GROUPS LAUNC...
> March 30, 2021 – The Canadian Alliance for Sex Work Law Reform — an alliance of 25 sex worker rights groups acros...
> *sexworklawreform.com*

12:38 PM · Mar 31, 2021 · Twitter for iPhone

2 Likes

Sex Work Law Reform @CDNSWAlliance · Mar 31   ...
Replying to @_cherrysmiley_
It's not true that we said it was creepy to inquire. It was the direction of your inquiry that was sensationalist. You are clearly fishing for info about our work to use against us This is a pattern we have seen so many times with prohibitionists like yourself.

Sex Work Law Reform @CDNSWAlliance · Mar 31   ...
Replying to @_cherrysmiley_
We have many years ahead of us in this court challenge where U & UR prohibitionist ilk can abuse & exploit our stories 2 serve your agenda- save your energy 4 now, Cherry. And please, let us raise up & centre the voices of people who actually do #sexwork, not those who hate us.

Cherry Smiley @_cherrysmiley_ · Mar 31   ...
Thank goodness you're here to offer me advice so I don't expend too much energy too soon!

Figure 7: Resplendent series of screenshots from Twitter of an exchange between myself, Cherry Smiley, and Sex Work Law Reform about their press release detailing a new constitutional challenge to Canada's prostitution laws.

More time to screen men makes sex work safer is a big honkin' lie, because no woman can ever know for sure if and when and how a man might be violent towards her or not, as the

> ... process is complicated by the propensity for bad and bogus clients to initially imitate good client behavior in order to gain trust. In the process of screening clients, sex workers are therefore tasked with ascertaining which individuals are genuine clients as opposed to simply mimicking good client behavior (Armstrong, 2014, p. 210).

Radical feminists, particularly those working with women being battered and abused in their homes by husbands or boyfriends, have known it's impossible for women to know which man might rape and beat her later and which man won't, especially considering men will generally say "want to watch a movie later at my house?" instead of, "want to come over to my house later so I can rape you?" Additionally, as feminists have argued, this lie that women can foresee the future because some guy is nervously biting his nails blames women for the violence committed against them: "How could you not know he was going to rape you?! Didn't you screen him properly ... didn't you see his nails?!" As a result, when we accept the lie that women can screen out the 'bad guys' from the 'good guys', she is at fault if he perpetrates violence against her because she didn't screen well enough, or she screened wrongly, or she misinterpreted his behaviour, and so on ... the point is that male violence committed against her becomes her fault. Woman-blaming is already very clear in the literature on sex work, and this makes sense, because sex work research isn't feminist and isn't concerned with Women's Liberation:

> Having a negative personal relation to the work is a risk factor for sex work which can lead to de-personalisation or burn-out ... But sex workers are not homogenous and those who have a positive outlook on their work are less likely to settle for uncomfortable working conditions, are more demanding and more inclined to safeguard themselves from negative experiences ... (Abel, 2011, p. 1180).

Those women who don't enjoy taking it in the ass from men they find disgusting need to get a more positive outlook because if you have a bad attitude at 'work', 'work' becomes more dangerous for you ... so, big smile! A politics of sex work blames women for the male violence committed against them and puts the responsibility to keep herself safe squarely on her shoulders without any state responsibility or any blame left over for the battering 'client' man. What happens when sex workers are having a slow night and rent is coming due or her kid's birthday is coming up? As sex work research shows, "... street workers talked about violating their personal rules and 'accepting risky tricks' when they had to make up for 'lost money'" (Lewis et al., 2005, p. 155). Indeed, this was the circumstances of some of the women in prostitution that Pickton murdered (Oppal, 2012). The only analysis that recognizes women's constrained options and situations in a patriarchy and the particular constraints women are subjected to in prostitution is a feminist analysis that sees prostitution as a form of male violence against women. All other frameworks, including a sex work analysis, ultimately blame women in prostitution for the fundamental and additional violence men perpetrate against them in a 'sex work transaction'.

Conclusion: Sex Work

Significantly, while violence against Indigenous peoples is central to settler colonial domination, so too is the denial and erasure of this violence (Bourgeois, 2018a, p. 68).

And this is what 'sex work' politics do, they deny and erase the inherent patriarchal violence of prostitution. And this makes sense, because sex work politics work very hard to maintain the status quo (i.e. patriarchy); they are anti-woman and anti-feminist. If we pretend that sex work is a bunch of very different people happily selling sexual services to other different satisfied customer-people, we can justify that prostitution isn't about women's oppression or Women's Liberation and actually has nothing to do with patriarchy or male entitlement or even colonization. What this does, however, is ignore the very clear patterns that are evident when it comes to prostitution: that women are overwhelmingly the sellers of sex acts and that men are overwhelmingly the buyers and pimps of women's sex acts; further, that women in prostitution globally are overwhelmingly poor, Indigenous, and of colour and that sex buyers and pimps can be any man and this is important information:

> ... it's very clear when you start to write about prostitution that you're using the oppressor's language, which is the male language. The institution is defined by the woman: prostitution; but it is the man who does the buying. There is no formal word to describe that man; we just have a couple of slang words like 'john,' 'trick,' that the prostitute uses. There is no formal word. Perhaps that's because it's all men, and men have never felt the need to use the specific word in the language that defines something that is their province (Brownmiller, 1973, p. 77).

This also helps us to see though the lie of 'screening'; that is, the idea that women are somehow able to determine, whether through their past experiences (Armstong, 2014), by assessing a man's behaviour and/or appearance (Armstrong, 2014), or by using intuition (Lewis et al., 2005) which man will be violent towards her and which man will not be violent towards her. While all women, in and outside of prostitution, use a variety of conscious and unconscious strategies in attempts to keep ourselves as safe as possible from male violence, the reality is that we're not able to predetermine which man will be violent, when and how, and pretending this is possible works to blame women when men do perpetrate violence against us.

It seems to be only when it comes to Indigenous women's issues that the recognition of consent, agency, and choice are the primary focus of decolonization strategies. This assumes that the primary focus of colonization is that Indigenous women's consent, agency, and choice are made invisible. Elsewhere, Indigenous men speak of a radical restructuring of the system in a decolonizing process while Indigenous women are only allowed to imagine decolonization as a recognition of our consent, agency, and choice to engage in sex acts with men we don't want to engage in sex acts with. The 'crime' of one woman 'denying an Indigenous woman's agency' becomes much worse than the sexualized male violence Indigenous women endure in the sex industry. Benedet describes the difference between prostitution and trafficking as follows:

> ... I think the other big misconception about the relationship between trafficking and prostitution is that trafficking is forced and prostitution is free, and that's when we rename it 'sex work'. That is not true. The reason these terms are not synonymous is because trafficking requires a third person. You can't traffic yourself, so it's true that not all prostitution is trafficking, but the reality is that plenty of women and girls are exploited in prostitution without a middleman or a trafficker. Their poverty, addiction, youth, indigeneity, or racialization is exploited directly by the men who buy them.
>
> The idea that trafficking is the bad prostitution and everything else is the okay prostitution is wrong. Once you have a third party involved, trafficking is simply the exercise of influence, coercion, threats, or pressure to get someone to participate in or to remain in prostitution. Given the nature of the prostitution industry, trafficking is not rare. It is, in fact, pervasive where third parties are involved (2018, pp. 8–9).

While feminist researchers are often accused of cherry-picking the most horrific stories of sex-trafficking in order to bolster our pre-determined conclusions (that prostitution is a form of male violence against women), the reality is that these stories are real; these things actually happened to a woman and she is bravely telling us what was done to her and how she survived. That she is more likely to be a poor woman and/or an Indigenous or woman of colour demonstrates how easily marginalized women can be dismissed in academia and in public policy when our realities don't match up with your queer and postmodern theories.

CHAPTER 5

Prostitution

The male demand for sexual access to the bodies of women is viewed as harmful and as a patriarchal practice rooted in male entitlement:

> ... the root question of an abolitionist approach to prostitution is not whether women 'choose' prostitution or not, but why men have the right to 'demand' that women's bodies are sold as commodities in the capitalist market (Miriam, 2005, p. 2).

In this view, the act of 'agreeing' to unwanted sexual acts for compensation is seen as the first source of harm for women in prostitution and to engage in the selling of sex acts is a result of limited choices available to women who are oppressed in a patriarchy (Carter and Giobbe, 1999). Trisha Baptie, an anti-prostitution activist and prostitution survivor, describes this act of agreeing to unwanted sex acts for compensation as the purchase of compliance from prostituted women as opposed to consent, an important distinction.[30] This list shows the major differences in analysis and beliefs between a position that advocates for a sex work model from one that advocates a prostitution one:

---

30 Personal communication; Baptie is in the process of expanding on the concept of 'compliance' in prostitution.

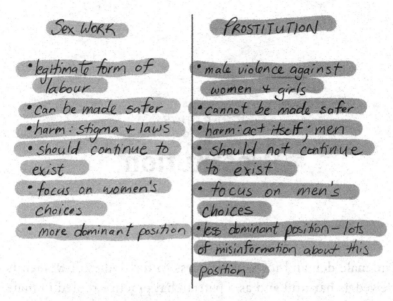

Figure 8: Majestic chart that shows some of the major differences in analysis and beliefs between a 'sex work' vs 'prostitution' position.

Prostitution, according to this perspective, cannot be reformed, regulated, or made safe and as a result, the practice should be abolished (Barry, 1979; Raymond, 2013). For radical feminists, the harm of prostitution originates in male entitlement to women's bodies for sexual purposes—the harm is that women are obligated, as per the duties of their 'employment', to engage in sex acts they don't want to engage in with multitudes of men they aren't sexually attracted to, again and again and again (Dworkin, 1996). It's men, as sex buyers, pimps, and sex industry supporters, who are the source of the harm in prostitution, not abstract stigma or laws.[31] In this way, prostitution can't be made 'safer' because that initial harm is inherent to the act of prostitution—this is what prostitution *is*. The Nordic Model approach is the policy most commonly supported by prostitution abolitionists (Mathieson et al., 2016). This policy was first adopted by Sweden in 1999 and is a three-pronged approach

---

31   Trisha Baptie has continually made this point, in a more articulate manner than I have, in numerous public talks since 2008.

including: (1) The decriminalization of prostituted persons and the criminalization of sex buyers and pimps; (2) Funding for comprehensive exiting and preventative services including, but not limited to: safe and affordable housing, a livable welfare rate, counselling, health care, and job training; and (3) A public education campaign that promotes the message that prostitution is a form of violence and that discourages men from purchasing sex acts (Mathieson et al., 2016). As McClintock states, "rape is not illegal, it is regulated" (1992, p. 77) and this can be clearly seen in the roles of women as wives and as women in prostitution.

Married Women and Prostituted Women

Until 1983, it was legal for a man in Canada to rape his wife (Koshan, 2010). Today, it isn't. However,

> ... the interpretation of these provisions by the courts, along with defence lawyer tactics and lingering assumptions about sex in spousal relationships, have made it difficult to obtain appropriate legal remedies for marital rape in light of issues related to consent, mistaken belief in consent, sexual history evidence and the production of personal records (Koshan, 2010, pp. 2-3).

Sexual assault in Canada is generally underreported by women for a variety of reasons related to sex-, class-, and race-based oppression in patriarchy. Marital rape is a crime that is particularly underreported due to women's perceived moral obligations to men and their families and keeping these families together at all costs; women's economic dependency on men in marriage; and the covert and sometimes still very overt idea that women, as wives, have a duty to provide 'sexual services' to their husbands (Koshan, 2010). Historically, men in patriarchy have viewed their wives as their property (Koshan, 2010); not property as in land-property, but as in women-property that they own; that belong to them, as Adrienne Rich explains:

> In the mystique of the overpowering, all-conquering male sex drive, the penis-with-a-life-of-its-own, is rooted in the law of male sex-

right to women, which justifies prostitution as a universal cultural assumption on the one hand, while defending sexual slavery within the family on the basis of 'family privacy and cultural uniqueness' on the other (1980, p. 645).

This idea was enshrined in law in Canada until 1983, that rape in certain circumstances—when a woman was legally married to a man, for example—was legally and socially acceptable. That idea —that rape in certain circumstances is legally and/or socially acceptable—remains embedded in our culture through prostitution: men are still entitled to sexually access the bodies of women against their will in certain circumstances and women are still obligated to provide sex acts to men against their will in certain circumstances, such as when a man pays a 'sex worker' to provide him with 'sexual services'. 'Sexual service' is another lie the sex industry tells to cover up what men actually do to women in prostitution and what they say to them as they're doing it and it assumes, like marriage, that men have 'sexual needs' (Whisnant, 2015, p. 194). Further, the idea of 'sexual services' means that a woman in prostitution (or in marriage) doesn't sell herself or even parts of herself, but that she is external to her 'product' (the 'sexual services') (Pateman, 1988; Pateman, 1999). In this view,

> there is no difference between a prostitute and any other worker or seller of services ... the body and the self of the prostitute are not offered in the market; she can contract out use of her services without detriment to herself (Pateman, 1988, p. 191).

This idea, that some women are able to endure unwanted sex acts day after day with men they don't want to be with socially or sexually and that this doesn't cause harm to 'these types' of women allows for the propagation of rape myths (that rape really isn't that bad, you're fine) in a complete rejection of feminist knowledge about male violence against women and also separates women into false dichotomous categories: 'squaw/princess', 'whore/virgin', deciding that women in prostitution are somehow fundamentally different than other women:

Many, perhaps most, women are repulsed and humiliated by (even the thought of) the physical touch of a strange man, but others obviously mind it far less (and this will depend in part on each's cultural and sexual history) ... the sexual history of prostitutes is often one of sexual molestation, incest and child-abuse—a state of affairs which must be battled on its own grounds. Nonetheless, this unpleasant face notwithstanding, it still remains the case that prostitutes frequently have a different relationship to their own bodies than many of the rest of us do, and surely women in different times, places, and cultures, have (Schwarzenbach, 2006, pp. 222–223).

In other words, Indigenous women are overrepresented in the sex industry because we like disgusting things that repulse other, civilized, respectable (white) women and we have a fundamentally 'different relationship to our bodies' than normal (white) women do. In this way, the false racist and sexist dichotomy of savage Indigenous woman/virtuous white woman is again reinforced by sex work advocates. Feminists, on the other hand, reject these lies about Indigenous and white women; Indeed, we reject lies about all women:

Now there is something else the male sex has always tried to do to cover up its crime: it has tried to separate the woman engaged in prostitution from the rest of the women in the culture. It calls her 'the other', it marks her the bad woman, it sends her to jail, and it tells the rest of us we are very good and virtuous and we have nothing in common with her (Brownmiller, 1973, pp. 73–74).

Susan Brownmiller, like other feminists, rejects this idea completely, stating that "... the feminist movement identifies itself with the female victim of the male-created institution known as prostitution" stating that she, like most other women, has considered prostitution for herself at some point (1973, p. 74).

In the past, until the introduction of PCEPA in 2014 in Canada, prostitution legislation focused on regulating where, when, and between whom prostitution happened—*the focus was not to eradicate prostitution but to regulate it*. The criminalization of the purchase of sex acts from women echoes the criminalization of rape within marriage—both laws send the message that men are not entitled to access sex acts from women in prostitution or in marriage and that women in prostitution and in marriage are not obligated to provide sex acts to men. This is why feminists fight for the Nordic Model of prostitution law: feminists believe that there are no circumstances where men's rape of women should be tolerated, accepted, regulated, sanctioned, or promoted. The reason why marital rape was made illegal and the reason why the purchase of sex acts from women by men was made illegal is because feminists recognized there are no circumstances where men are entitled to sex acts from women and no circumstances where women are obligated to provide sex acts to men. Feminists fought to change these laws and continue to fight for legal and social change towards Women's Liberation. Men, as a class, didn't fight for their legal right to rape their wives be abolished or that their legal right to rape a woman so long as they pay her be abolished. As Pateman explains in regard to the feminist fight to end marital rape:

> ... in the 1980s, this aspect of conjugal subjection lingers on in legal jurisdictions that still refuse to admit any limitation to a husband's access to his wife's body and so deny that rape is possible within marriage. A common response is to dismiss this matter as of no relevance to political theorists and political activists. The possibility that women's standing in marriage may reflect much deeper problems about women and contract ... the refusal to admit that marital domination is politically significant obviates the need to consider where there is any connection between the marriage contract and other contracts involving women (Pateman, 1988, p. 7).

This issue is not as complicated as it's often made out to be. Either men have an entitlement to sexually access women's bodies and women have an obligation to provide sex acts to men, or not. To allow exceptions in the form of marital rape or prostitution allows men the legal and social right to rape women in some circumstances and this is completely unacceptable to feminists.

Understanding Male Violence Against Women

Feminists understand male violence against women as existing on a continuum. The different types of male violence against women often intersect and overlap with each other, but all are grounded in male domination of women in a patriarchy. Barry defines female sexual slavery as

> ... situations where women and girls cannot change the immediate conditions of their existence; where regardless of how they got into those conditions they cannot get out; and where they are subject to sexual violence and exploitation (Barry, 1979, p. 162).

Female sexual slavery then, encompasses many different types of male violence against women such as prostitution, incest, marital rape, pornography, child marriage, and female genital mutilation (Barry, 1979). Male violence and the threat of male violence is one of the ways that men work to ensure women's subjugation in patriarchy as Barry states, "sexual terrorism is a way of life for women even if we are not its direct victims. It has resulted in many women living with it while trying not to see it or acknowledge it" (1979, p. 12). Women's subjugation by men is also ensured in patriarchy through the colonization of women's minds and the normalization of male violence against women. Barry refers to this as 'male identification':

> ... the act whereby women place men above women, including themselves, in credibility, status, and importance in most situations regardless of the comparative quality the women may bring to the situation. Through male identification, women automatically acknowledge men's authority, words, and actions. Interaction with women is seen as a lesser form of relating on every level. Rather, allegiance to men is automatic (1979, p. 202).

This is the status quo for women and men and helps us to understand the importance of feminist theory and action in undoing our colonization as women. Because this is the status quo (i.e. patriarchal) state of things, it's more difficult to see and more difficult to challenge, as Barry notes, "male identification is not just a series of specific acts. It is a way of life that permeates existence as much as the air we breathe ... surely the path of least resistance for women in patriarchy" (1979, p. 202).

Feminists and women who have been abused by their husbands or boyfriends have contributed incredible amounts of information that have increased the general public's understanding of woman abuse by men in the home (aka 'domestic violence' or 'intimate partner violence'). While patriarchy has, of course, fought back and continues to fight back against the woman-centred and feminist ways in which women understand male violence in their homes and while women are still blamed for men's violence toward them, feminists have worked to increase understanding of the insidious ways that male violence in the home functions, what the violence does, and how it impacts women. For example, feminists have revealed "... the mechanics whereby men can accomplish and maintain the captivity of women and children who, to the external world, appear 'free' to attend school, work, and live their lives" (Sheehy, 2014, p. 3). Abusive men use a wide variety of tactics in their relationships to ensure that women remain compliant, such as threats and/or acts of male violence to the woman, children, pets, or other loved ones, surveillance and control of the woman's activities including sometimes even her bodily functions, isolation of the woman from familial and social networks, control of finances and deprivation of life's necessities, and a wide variety of other strategies to keep women captive in a state of fear (Sheehy, 2014). These tactics are supplemented by promises to change (or promises to kill) if he thinks she might be getting ready to leave, gift-giving, displays of love and affection, and (empty) apologies (Sheehy, 2014). We also know, from the work of feminists and battered women, that "... simple compliance is often not enough ... an abusive man requires gratitude, admiration, and love ..." (Sheehy, 2014, p. 3). Rich's analysis of compulsory heterosexuality provides further understanding of the pressure women are under to 'find a man' and 'keep a man', still even today (Rich, 1980). Other manstitutions, such as police, the court system, and the welfare system, also work to maintain woman abuse in the home and male domination. They do this by directly or indirectly sanctioning male violence by failing to intervene or failing to intervene adequately (Schechter, 1982; Lakeman, 2005). We have today, generally, a better understanding of the reasons 'why women stay' in abusive relationships with men; or perhaps, to be more accurate, 'why men abuse their wives and girlfriends'. Yet, patriarchy ensures that battered wives are still often blamed for the violence men who claim to love them, perpetrate against them. Despite the knowledge we've gained about woman abuse in the home, this knowledge isn't applied to other instances of male violence against women, such as prostitution and pornography.

Stark and Hodgson, in their article 'A Comparison of Wife Beating and Prostitution', examine the similar ways in which battering of women and prostitution are deeply embedded in our culture (2003, p. 20). The article examines the intersections and similarities between woman abuse in the home, prostitution, and pornography, including that many women are battered and prostituted by their husbands and boyfriends who also make pornography of them;[32] the ways in which pornography is used as a 'training manual' for prostituted women and how it also serves as a record of sexualized male violence; the similar methods that batterers and pimps use to control women such as isolation, threats and intimidation, emotional, sexual and physical violence, and denial of her abuse; and the similar injuries that battered and prostituted women receive at the hands of men including lacerations, head injuries, burns, and miscarriages; the similar barriers these women encounter when seeking healthcare for their injuries; and the similar ways in which drugs and alcohol are used as coping mechanisms (Stark and Hodgson, 2003). The intersections between pornography and prostitution are also evidenced in a study of prostituted women in nine countries across

---

32   See for example, the stories by contributors to *"He Chose Porn over Me": Women Harmed by Men Who Use Porn*. Melinda Tankard Reist (Ed.) (2022).

five continents: "across countries, 47% were upset by attempts to make them do what others had seen in pornography and 49% reported pornography was made of them" (Farley et al., 2003, p. 44). The intersections between woman abuse in the home, prostitution, and pornography are multiple, and as a result, demonstrate that particular types of male violence and particularly, the male violence of prostitution and pornography, cannot be examined in isolation. These intersections between the different types of male violence that women experience also more clearly help us to understand the stigma that women experience as victims of male violence. Sex work advocates describe this stigma in prostitution and pornography as 'whorephobia', a false male-constructed concept that assumes some women are actually 'whores' when in reality, women are simply women who have a wide variety of interests, likes and dislikes and who engage in a wide variety of behaviours and actions for many different reasons. The 'whore', like the 'prude', doesn't exist. While stigma in prostitution has particular qualities to it and consequences for women because of it, the stigma is not because of the status of 'sex worker', but because she is a *woman* in prostitution. In this way, we can see that stigma is really just another term for woman-hating and woman-blaming and that it applies, in different ways and to different extents, to all women who have been attacked by a man or men, whether in her home by a battering husband or by a man who has paid her for sexual access to her body.

Prostitution Survey Results

As part of my dissertation, I conducted an online survey about prostitution. The idea to conduct an anonymous survey came about as a direct result of my experiences in New Zealand where I had difficulty finding anyone who was critical of prostitution to speak with me. An anonymous survey would give people more opportunity to express their thoughts without judgement or fear as one respondent confirmed in the survey comment option:

The pressure to believe prostitution is empowering is incredible. I can't say it out loud in my workplace or I'd be shunned or attacked. It's s[sic] weird issue that way-people can be respected for different beliefs on abortion, politics, and wind energy but not prostitution.

My survey received 217 anonymous responses. Participants were limited to individuals living in Canada, New Zealand, and Australia and who were 18 years of age or older. Except for the option to leave a comment, participants had to complete every question and no partially-completed surveys were accepted.

Eighty per cent (175) of participants lived in Canada, 14 per cent (32) lived in New Zealand, and four per cent (ten) lived in Australia. Eighty-seven per cent (190) of participants were female and 12 per cent (27) were male. Eighty per cent (175) of participants used the term 'prostitution' to describe the exchange of money or other benefit for sex acts; 15 per cent (33) used the term 'sex work'; and four per cent (nine) used another term 'other'.

Question	Yes	No
Do you think men are entitled to engage in sex acts with women whenever they want to?	3	214
Do you think men are entitled to engage in sex acts with women whenever they want to as long as they pay her?	8	209
Do you think it's physically, emotionally, and mentally harmful for a woman to engage in sex acts with somebody she does not desire to have sexual contact with?	211	6
Do you think it's physically, emotionally, and mentally harmful for a woman to engage in sex acts with somebody she does not desire to have sexual contact with if she is paid to do so?	206	11
Women are disproportionately the sellers of sex acts and men are disproportionately the buyers and profiteers. Indigenous women, women of colour, and poor women are overrepresented in prostitution. Do you think it is possible to eliminate sex, race, and class-based inequality from prostitution?	26	191

The survey results were generally expected, as I used word-of-mouth, social media, and a website to promote the survey. I also promoted the survey in public talks I gave during the period the survey was open. Due to my work as part of the Women's Liberation Movement advocating for the abolition of prostitution and that the survey was primarily shared amongst my network (to those who follow me on social media, my email contacts, listservs I am a part of, and so on) the results show that most women understand prostitution as a form of male violence against women that cannot be modified to benefit the most marginalized women in the sex trade.

Some of the survey results were troubling. For example, three out of 217 respondents believe that men are entitled to engage in sex acts with women whenever they desire to do so. This number more than doubles as eight respondents believe that men are entitled to engage in sex acts with women whenever they desire to do so as long as they can pay the woman. Additionally, six out of the 217 respondents believe that women aren't harmed when they participate in sex acts with men they don't want to engage in sex acts with. This number again almost doubles as 11 respondents believe that women are not harmed by engaging in unwanted sex acts as long as they are paid to do so. What this says is that five out of 217 respondents believe that money buys male entitlement to sex acts from women; otherwise, if he can't pay, he's not entitled and she's not obligated to provide sex. Five out of the 217 respondents similarly believe that payment of money negates any harm women experience from engaging in unwanted sex acts with men; otherwise, if he can't pay her, she's harmed mentally, emotionally, or physically by the experience of engaging in sex acts against her will. This demonstrates a lack of respect for women's bodily autonomy and a lack of recognition or knowledge about the very real impacts of male violence against women on women. It also speaks to the perceived power of money, of capital; that it can turn an unacceptable situation into an acceptable one. The survey received a number of comments. Some comments expressed gratitude for the survey questions, the research, or for the work I have done generally on prostitution; some comments detailed women's direct or indirect experiences of prostitution; and one comment questioned my intelligence: "These questions are exceptionally loaded and I find it hard to believe you are a PhD candidate who is unaware of nuance." Ah yes, nuance ...

Discussion About the Discussion

I hesitated to include any of the stories of the women I spoke with in this project. This is because I don't believe academia should be allowed to evaluate these stories as part of my worthiness or unworthiness of doctorhood and because I know there are academics who will read these stories, or other stories like these stories, and decide that these stories are not representative of women's experiences in prostitution and will decide that yup, sex work is still work. To dismiss these women's experiences is to dismiss Indigenous women. For example, a recent study found that out of a sample of 200 'sex workers', the majority of participants identified as Indigenous, Black, or otherwise racialized and 36 per cent had injected drugs and 54 per cent had inhaled meth or crack in the past year (Crago et al., 2021). Out of 200 'sex workers', 115 "... had experienced violence or confinement at work in the past 12 months" (Crago et al., 2021, p. 6). In this study, 'violence or confinement' meant that participants

> ... answered 'yes' to any of the following experiences: 'Abducted/ kidnapped/brought to a location against your will', 'Client broke condom on purpose/removed without consent', 'Sexual assault (sexual contact or service that was not consented to)', 'Strangled/stabbed/ shot with a gun', 'Physically assaulted/beaten', 'Locked/trapped in car', 'Confined/locked in space', 'Drugged', 'Forced to do sex work under threat of your safety or the safety of someone you know', or 'Forced not to work under threat to my safety or the safety of someone I know' (Crago et al., 2021, p. 11).

This information is, or should be, alarming. Instead, the sex work researchers made sure to let the reader know that "... this sample is not representative of all sex workers, and results may not be generalizable to other populations of sex workers or those in other settings" due, they suggest, in part to the disproportionately high number of marginalized 'sex workers' they sampled. As Graham has argued, this is very common in sex work research—that a methodological framework of quantitative 'public health' research has a very narrow focus that often discounts or ignores important information about the material conditions of women's lives (Graham, 2014). In this example, the purpose of the study was to examine Sex Workers' Access to Police Assistance in Safety Emergencies and Means of Escape from Situations of Violence and Confinement under an 'End Demand' Criminalization Model in five cities across Canada. The violence that the people (who were overwhelmingly women) described experiencing while in prostitution wasn't a focus of the study and even it if were, wouldn't have been examined with a feminist analysis. Instead, the male violence experienced in prostitution is blamed on the 'end demand' criminalization model with no comparative baseline, as is the reported low levels of access to police assistance by prostituted people in the study—it's all because Canada has criminalized the men who buy sex and the men who profit from women's prostitution as pimps that there's so much violence against 'sex worker' and that 'sex workers' can't report to the police in Canada and this is the opposite in New Zealand where 'sex workers' have a good relationship with the police and that's because they've decriminalized 'sex work'! (Crago et al., 2021). On a surface level, these findings might make sense but once we understand the narrow focus of the research and what information has been discounted or ignored and the fact that a feminist analysis was not used and instead an 'objective' quantitative methodology, often criticized by Indigenous peoples, was used to conduct research on a group of people who were disproportionately Indigenous, the findings don't quite make so much sense anymore. This is particularly true when we look at the publicly available statistics from the RCMP and police forces across Canada that demonstrate the 'end demand' criminalization model hasn't been vigorously or consistently enforced across the country.[33] At the least, questions arise about what the research is missing, or ignoring, or excluding in its methodology and analysis—one thing is for sure, that women are not centred in this research and that this research is not feminist and as such, doesn't have feminist goals such as working to increase the wellbeing of women.

The amount of courage it takes to speak up, as an Indigenous woman, to push all the shame and hurt aside for a minute, to say 'What happened to me was wrong', 'What happened to me was not my fault', 'I don't deserve to be raped and no woman does', is indescribable. What happens after too often breaks my heart. Sure, this isn't every woman's experience in prostitution, but this is her experience in prostitution. Her experience of prostitution is representative of herself and she absolutely matters, she is a whole world and she absolutely matters; nothing and no one matters more than she does. We can more clearly see how racism functions in and outside of the feminist movement in these scenarios. These stories, mostly of horror and terror with a few laughs and good times along the way, are overwhelmingly dismissed as non-representative of women's experiences in prostitution. Yet, they are overwhelmingly representative of Indigenous women's experiences in prostitution. In nearly every other injustice we face—whether it's high rates of incarceration, high rates of disability, or high rates of poverty— the impacts of colonization and other structural oppressions are considered and help to explain why Indigenous peoples are in the circumstances we find ourselves in as Indigenous peoples in contemporary Canada. When it comes to the prostitution of Indigenous women however, their marginalized social location

---

33   See Appendix B, compiled by Hilla Kerna on behalf of the Vancouver Rape Relief and Women's Shelter Collective, 2021.

in the hierarchy of 'sex work' is simply 'non-representative' and dismissed by sex work advocates.

Criticism of prostitution as a system of male domination and female subordination has arisen from radical feminist politics, and as a result, radical feminists generally support the abolition of prostitution. This makes sense, given that feminism is the only theory and practice that consistently prioritizes women and women's wellbeing as a class. Many feminist theorists, such as Adrienne Rich (1980), Kathleen Berry (1979, 1995), Carol Pateman (1988), and others have examined the ways that prostitution integrates into the lives of women as another form of male violence against women. Prostitution doesn't exist in a silo; it doesn't exist separate from the patriarchal world we all live in, no matter what anyone says. As a result, Indigenous women are overrepresented in prostitution where we are disproportionately harmed and then we are disproportionately dismissed when we speak out against prostitution as the source of that harm. Indigenous women matter and our realities aren't always what researchers want them to be— but we'll continue to speak out on issues that matter to us, as we've always done. Men, on the other hand, get (yet another) free pass when it comes to prostitution and it's their 'choices', their agency, their misogynist beliefs, and their woman-hating actions that we desperately need to hold to account. There are no circumstances where rape, paid or not, is acceptable.

Indigenous Women Who Survived Prostitution

I met with a group of seven Indigenous women who had survived prostitution in Canada. For one of the women, this was her first time ever speaking about her prostitution. I brought drinks and platters of snacks and we met together. We introduced ourselves, and several of the women were surprised that I was the researcher— they had expected someone more conventional and more formal, not someone who looked like them. We sat in a circle and I explained what we were going to do: we would each write out our stories of prostitution and survival using questions I had created as prompts for writing (or not). There would be no names attached to the stories and we would each then read out another woman's story. We would then pull out some common themes from the stories and have a discussion. The women decided that they wanted to read their own stories out loud for the group, so that's what we ended up doing instead. I audio recorded our discussion, except for the reading of the women's stories. I felt that recording these stories was voyeuristic and instead chose to allow women the space to say whatever they wanted about their stories knowing that these words wouldn't be captured.

The stories and statements made by the seven women in our group discussion embody everything that Indigenous women in Canada face in and because of prostitution: the anguish, male violence, the hurt, the racism, the shame, and the ongoing trauma that starts before, lasts during, and goes on for many years after they exit prostitution; the trauma lasts the rest of their lives. And sometimes the rest of their lives after they exit prostitution is not very long and this is absolutely connected to the horrors of sexual exploitation that don't confine themselves to one area but that can and do colonize women's bodies and minds and spirits full-force. One of the women in the group died before this research was completed. These women's words make crystal clear the deep and traumatic connections that exist throughout their lives and in their families, past and present and also make crystal clear the resilience of Indigenous women and our continued capacity to connect and to love, despite all odds. These seven women's voices contain everything there is to say about the prostitution of Indigenous women in Canada. Here is the transcript from our introductions and the discussion that followed the sharing of our stories:

Samantha: My mom and my grandparents were all alcoholics. My mom was a heroine addict. Unfortunately, she is passed away, it'll be __ years. It's because of her past ... I know the last __ years of her life that she tried to make amends and you know, be there for my children. She wasn't there for us when we were kids and stuff and

I think it really just caught up and ... it was done. I was sexually assaulted by my mom's best friend's husband at the age of seven then I was sexually assaulted by numerous boyfriends that my mom had, would bring into the house and I would be the one that would get sexually assaulted. Because I would take care of my sisters so I would be there so they wouldn't touch my sisters, which really fucks up your life (laughs) and your emotions and your brain and everything. We went from foster home to foster home so I've been in probably about 23 different foster homes from the age of three until the age of 16 when I took off and I became pregnant. I started hanging around with a couple of not-so-great people who introduced me to drugs and prostitution, and I was doing that for a long time. I am now this August, nine years clean of crack cocaine and ten years off the sex trade so it's a lot, the same thing as a cycle. I went through the same cycle my mom did. My kids went into care many times, went back. They went _____ and now as of _____ of next year they've been home for seven years. I got my ___ rescinded through the courts. I fought really, really hard. I went back to school, I have my social work diploma, and I'm going for my social work degree. Yeah so ...

Cherry: Awesome.

Sky: What's ___?

Samantha: _____ through Canada here in _____. So the government took my kids away from me permanently and then I fought back for them and then we rescinded it so ...

Cherry: And how many years to get them back?

Samantha: It took four years to get them back and they've been home for six years next _____ so ...

Cherry: That's amazing.

Samantha: Five years ago my kids came home. They knew the reason why they were gone is cause I did drugs. They didn't understand why I did the drugs and why or how it affected my life and how it affected them and when they came home I sat them all down. They're __, __ and __. My __-year-old still has a little bit of struggle. He's got a lot of mental health stuff like that but I mean, he understands ... I was terrified because they already knew about the drugs. What are they gonna think of me as a mom selling my body? [laughs] Providing for them and ya know, and they didn't understand that, ya know. Welfare wasn't a lot. It covered my rent, that was it, you know so I flat out just sat them down and I told them and I thought they were gonna judge me and that they weren't gonna love me as a mom anymore and ... but they do [laughs]. I think they're more protective now and it was a lot different than what I thought the outcome would be so cootos to you. You will know when the time is right for you to do that and I'm very grateful because like you said too, now it has this whole trust and freedom and my kids come to me when they're struggling with things like my son came to me, I smoke pot [laughs] like waiting for me to attack, ya know, like well, what else are you doing? Like, well I tried cigarettes I don't like it and I don't like alcohol. Ok, [laughs] like ya know what, if I didn't get that maybe I wouldn't know that he was smoking pot, ya know, or hanging out with the wrong crowd or anything like that, right, so I think it's good but you will know when you have that time and when that healing is gonna come so for me it's been really, really good and made us a lot closer and to me it shows that yes, they've seen the bad and they've seen how they've been taken away and they've seen what I was going through and now that I have them back and they've been back for six years they see the strength and the will and the strongness about that and I think they also understand other people. Like homelessness and other working girls on the street. They have a compassion to understand that they're not just looking at "oh, she's selling her body, ya know, for drugs." They're understanding there's more to that. There ... it's a person. It's, ya know, like, I'll give you an example. We were at the _____ just actually down here, me and my son. We went and got slurpees and we saw a working girl in the corner and my son went up there and gave her a bag of chips and five bucks and told her to eat and take care of herself and I've never seen him go up to a stranger at all (laughs) and this is __ year old, right, and he came in, he goes, "I had to mom. I had to make sure she had something to eat" and I was like "ok, let's go home" [laughs]. Ya know so it's been good. It's been a good experience.

Sky: I think I told you most of my background. I was in the foster care system from 12 and up. I grew up pretty ... from birth to 12 I was pretty upper middle class. My dad's an immigrant. My mom's, ya know, like _____ background but my dad's actually half ____ and half _____ from _____ so he lived _____, and he was just a very mean man. I think it was cause of how he was treated cause he lived in the ghetto right. Anyways so I just grew up with a lot of violence, a lot of addiction you know, and got apprehended at 12 and parents divorced at 11. I was apprehended at 12 and just decided I liked … not I liked … I felt safer prostituting than I did in the group homes I was in and got pregnant at 16 and yeah, I don't have schooling, I don't have an education. I don't, I've never had a job, never had resumes so I just supported my kids through prostitution and dope dealing and I did that yeah, until _____.

Jane Doe: I'm Jane Doe. This is one of my offices at the corner across the street. It's like a treadmill and I did the whole geological change from _____ to _____ to _____ to wherever the court system would take me. I'm usually a very happy, outgoing, positive caring person but I'm really struggling to figure out who I am and my identity because this last six years of my recovery has been so fast and there's been so many firsts and so many beautiful experiences, opportunities, but extreme ones, very highs and very lows and I just recently been to a really dark place. A dark place where years and years of core beliefs just came flooding in and it's always been … it's just been a break through in some ways cause I usually have to go deep or dark before I get to the light on the other side. So just holding on and doing what's in front of me has been keeping me going and just my PTSD has kicked in this last year and I really struggled to figure out where I belong or why I'm here or if I want to stay here. I feel like I'm stuck between two worlds sometimes, like I don't want to go forward, but I don't wanna go back. And I just feel like, sometimes I just feel like I get consumed in this world, in man's world and advertising and news, and the opportunity I get to work with other women and somewhere in there in trying to help others I stopped helping myself. So again, this is … I got scared because I feel myself putting back up walls that I thought were gone. And I'm being present right now, this moment but I'm back to that seven-year-old girl that just used to detach and I didn't need drugs for that cause she knew how to do that at seven and if I'm gonna survive I have to stay present but everything inside me doesn't want to because when I open that dark door I was reminded how comfortable it is there. I was reminded how that Jane Doe, she got me through a lot of ups and downs, hundreds and thousands of ups and downs and I miss her but now I'm trying to find a balance because she never really disappeared, she's just part of me. It's again, I don't know why … you said you're nervous and I wasn't when I came in here, I was fine [laughs and cries]. There's that four-letter word: fine. I'm ok and yeah, I'm just really, I guess, I feel safe here so … it feels like I'm able to breathe too even though it hurts right now. I feel like I can breathe and I'm not gonna be judged and I feel like I have to hide that part of me from most of the things I do in day-to-day stuff and I have to put on a different face. And it's like why did I come here to be clean, to just hide again? So yeah, I'm in a little bit of a battle right now but I know it's a good battle and I'll get through on the other side of it. And I should shut up. Sorry.

[Cherry thanks Jane Doe, tells her no need to shut up or be sorry, and says everyone is going to take some time to write down some answers to questions and can choose to write as much or as little of their story without identifying who they are. Then the stories will be shuffled so participants can read each others stories then debrief]

[Cherry offers a break to any woman who might need one. Talk of lunch being ordered. Women talk amongst themselves about healing and self-care and Cherry says we can talk more about a plan over food about what participants can do to be ok when they leave. Women talk about their personal lives. i.e. doing childcare and housework, laundry late at night and only getting three to three and a half hours of sleep a night. A woman asks where her writing will go and Cherry explains that they will go in a locked box for five years and she might include some voices into the film or decide later if we want to do an installation and offers women option to say no to using it]

[Group does exercise. Women decide to read their own stories]

[Cherry talks about consciousness-raising and feminist standpoint theory, "we need each other to analyze our experiences … when we're in it, it can be hard to see the bigger picture." Cherry asks if anyone notices any commonalities in the stories we read out loud?]

Jane Doe: There was a bunch of stuff I saw that was connecting but one of the ones that was shared was about that I knew that if he didn't know I was native that I would have to do dates for less really brought up a lot for me. My sister who is Blackfoot, she blended so if they were in Mexico, she would look Mexican and she was in Hawaii, she would look Hawaiian. She was quite beautiful but she didn't look like me, super native. I remember, I remember hating being brown cause I knew that's why everybody hated me and I remember, and this is something that came to light is, that even in the education system because she went to a less educated school down in the hood there's more, what's the word, multicultural people there where I was in a higher education school I was the only native in a white school, so I had to fight. And my adopted mother was white. I was native and my sister looked different and so I got called all the names in the book and I hated being Native so bad that I found out that when you bleach clothes it turns them white. So when I went home from detention, I bathed in bleach hoping that I could be white, hoping that then I would finally be accepted. Today I'm really glad that didn't work cause … I'd be proud, right. That was one of the … [woman in background "I think you're beautiful"] You are too. I'm glad I came.

Cherry: one of the things that I noticed was racism, like Jane Doe just mentioned and also sexual abuse in the home, the home didn't seem to be a very safe place for pretty much all of us.

[Cherry talks about her experience of white women not wanting her to talk about native men's violence]

Blue Sky: I think there was always family secrets. I believe the violence existed even before I was born so I was born into the violence and addiction and being, ya know … I shared in my story, writing about it, there was a lot of things that came to me afterwards and other women were sharing about, ya know, them being a young girl and being like a toddler and being neglected and being abused and then growing into a young girl and a young woman, being raped, being raped many times throughout my life and being abused by family members, being raped by family members. I remember being taken to the hospital a lot as a kid after a lot of the rapes and abuse happened and like still to this day I think that, ya know, I remember going to the hospital and having to get a needle in my butt and I still, to this day, I think was I given STDs and stuff like that as a child and, ya know, those kind of things and nobody ever really questioned it. I was taught to lie at a very young age, ya know and one of my sister's had shared this about living this lie and doing the work we do to help them, that we should be able to not only talk our talk but walk our talk [sobbing] and walking our talk is telling our truth and not hiding in the dark because that's what we learned to do, to hide in the dark and keep those secrets. And it doesn't feel good. It feels like you're going out there and being a fake or somewhat of a fake because you're not really sure in your soul and your heart to know where you came from and because the real guts, the real stuff from our life is what helps people. We share and talk about those things, because then we're being real, we're being true (crying) not just to everybody else but to ourselves. And ya know, like we talk about our home not being safe ya know, it wasn't a safe place. When I used to run away a lot, I used to run away and stay in the streets because it was safer. I felt like I was in control of my life. I could decide what I wanted to do with me, instead of everyone doing it to me. I didn't care that I had to sleep under the stairwells. I wasn't ashamed to take left over food off the tables in restaurants when I was hungry and ya know, go to turn tricks and it was fast money and it was easy money but you had to do gross things for it. I remember waking up times, places I was naked and just ashamed of myself and still to this day, I struggle with that. I struggle with my body image and depression and I don't really talk to people about my stuff because I learned at a young age not to trust people. Ya know, like I slowly started to come out of that ya know, trust my sister here to share, that's something that was huge for me to even talk about that to say "you know what? I used to work the streets." That's how I survived. I used to have to feed my family and I was only 13, 14 selling my body so that we could have food in the house but nobody ever knew where that money came from because I was lying, I always had these rich friends. These rich white friends that wanted to help me out and felt sorry for me. So I was always lying and lie after lie after lie and I still feel to this day that there's still part of my life that's still a lie because I haven't opened up about that and I think that's, ya know, I heard this saying that you're as sick as your secrets and I don't wanna have no more secrets. I used to wanna ... I could be at a place where I could, ya know, where I don't care what anyone thinks, where I don't care what anybody says and regardless of all the shit I went through in my life with my family it's like I still love them (sobbing). Ya know, love is really truly unconditional. The people that hurt us, ya know, but that's the creator put in me is to love but it's hard to forgive. Ya know it almost seems like two different things that how could you love somebody, but you can't forgive them and I struggle with that. I struggle with that. I struggle to get used to living in the skin that I showed up in. I don't like what I see everyday when I look in the mirror, I don't, I don't like that. Ya know, I'm learning to love that ... starting to learn, like when people say "well you gotta love yourself." Well, what the hell is fucking loving yourself?! Ya know, what does that even mean? What does that mean to love yourself? Is it accepting who you are? Because if that's what it is then I don't really truly love myself yet because I'm just slowly accepting things. I accept that I was raped by family members. When I was just seven years old, when I was raped by three men who were family members and they were men and then all the rapes that happened after that. Living on the streets and ya know, walking home drunk and getting dragged off the street and having a chain wrapped around my neck and being dragged and ya know, and the fear of not even ... trying to scream, but like there's no voice coming out. I'm so terrified and so many of those times I'm trying to run away from tricks because, ya know, they're trying to rip me off or, ya know, I'm trying to rip them off or, ya know, because I needed to survive and, ya know, so I think it's so important that we talk about those things because there's a lot of girls in my family. I have a lot of daughters. I have granddaughters and after I'm gone I'd like to think that the work I'm doing now is gonna somehow help them, protect them when they get older. Stop the violence and ya know, just stop that violence and keep speaking up about it and we always seem to be fighting against these big systems that continue to oppress us but we just keep trying to break those walls down and that's all we can keep doing, to make change, to stop the racism we deal with every single day. I see it every single day walking down the streets. When I see girls walking or guys walking and randomly getting stopped by the police, I make sure I make a point of stopping to record it or talk to those people who got questioned by the police to see what they were questioned about. They're just stopped because they're Aboriginal and that's hard. We live in that day and age where, ya know, it's a crime to be an Indigenous person in this country. It truly is, ya know ... thank you.

Samantha: You are right. I am Blackfoot too. My name is Samantha. and how you said if your sister went to Hawaii or anywhere in Mexico she can adapt. To this day, I am __ years old and people are shocked when I say that I am Aboriginal, they don't think I'm Aboriginal. They always thought I was Latin, Portuguese, Mexican, Italian [laughs] ya know, and they're quite shocked and then I like that though because when I see, I can see their expression change, ya know what I mean and I'm just like, so, yeah, I am Native, what's your problem? You obviously liked me before you knew that so what's the problem? Ya know so I like to do that. And you are right about our judicial system, everything. I work at _____ and I've had lots of dealings with police and lots of dealings with the paramedics and I had one individual who was higher than a kite and she didn't ... she trusted me ... she didn't want to go with anyone and I had to explain to her that I couldn't go with you but you do need to go get some medical help. They're here to help you, but those two paramedics that I dealt with were females and they were very rude to her because of her being Aboriginal and I got mad and I'm sitting there and I'm like you don't treat people like that and I'm like you came into this position and this profession to help people. That means people. That means human beings. It doesn't mean you only get to pick and choose who you want or because you've been on a 12-hour shift and you're tired, you don't have the right to choose and be rude to this person. Now you think this person wants to go with you to get help that they desperately need but they don't wanna go with you now because of the way you're treating them. Ya know what I mean, like I just get so angry (laughs) and I use my mouth a lot (laughs). So I hope there's some training or education, things like this that these professions should see this kind of stuff and how this knowledge and understanding of what it is to be Aboriginal or to be Indigenous and to be in this kind of environment, that we are humans too. Yes, we're on a healing journey and I mean I've been clean for nine years almost and I'm still, I'm still learning to love myself. I do it every day. I look in the mirror and I'm like I thank you Creator for another day here. I'm breathing. I thank you for being in my children's lives. What else can I do today to improve anything, whether it's helping another person, another human being, just being there to sit and listen and talk to someone. I'm not even halfway there to loving myself even though I'm clean. There's a lot that, like my friend here, Blue Sky said that I haven't opened up a lot and even though I have sobriety and I'm clean and free from addictions and the sex trade there's still stuff that's been bottled up because we are taught to lie and to keep secrets and we are invalidated, ya know, because we are young girls or we are women, we're not worth it. We don't have a voice and we need to have a voice.

Cherry: I remember one time I was in a line up at the pharmacy and there was like this little old white granny in front of me in the line up and we were waiting and she was like, "oh what are you?" I was like, well my father's Navajo, my mom is Thompson First Nation and she said to me, she was like "What?! No!" She's like, "You're too beautiful to be Native." I was like wow, that's a ... like what do you say to that? Yeah I find it hard too, to be in my body sometimes. it's like sometimes I wanna just like cut my body open and take all my skin off cause it feels gross.

Sky: I just wanna say one thing about loving ourselves cause I think it's really important. Once I figured out where the responsibilities lie in the systems that harmed me whether it was foster care system, whether it was patriarchy, whether, like whatever that system was, as soon as I could name it in my story I found it freed me to forgive myself and to not carry that blame around because that blame isn't mine, like I was twelve years old turning tricks. I have no blame in that. None, none. And once I was able to give up that blame, I found it a lot easier to love myself, right. Like, I'm awesome, like I just am, right? Like I have no, that's not something I personally struggle with now because once I was able to, like I looked at my life analytically and through the systems that were in place that harmed me I was yeah, able to find freedom in that and get to this place of not carrying what wasn't mine to ever carry in the first place.

[a few women speak at once]

Jane Doe: I think there was one of the common things was the abuse and I don't know in other's case, but I know in mine I remember … I just my mom, my biological mom, got a hold of me again. And ya know what, I still crave her love and I'm not gonna get it and I know that she's still sick and that I just have to … but I lead with love. Sometimes it feels like a burden but at the end of the day it feels like the right thing to do but I remember having … being … going out with her and when she picked us up and I have my daughter and my son with me and I remember feeling this is the perfect picture, everything is gonna be alright. I always dreamed about that it was always gonna be alright and I remember driving up and going to a pow wow, we're doing something traditional, we're actually being a family and then she started talking about my sisters, who are strangers to me and who get her love and I remember thinking, I feel fucking robbed. I feel like, you robbed me, and I didn't even get to hold that thought in my head for two seconds before I saw my daughter on the right hand side of me and I thought [sobbing] I bet she feels robbed. I know after talking to my mom again that she had abuse handed down, so we become the abuse to the abusers and it's come down generations. I look back now that I'm looking into it, it's come down five generations. Grateful I like to say, my daughter, she's breaking that chain. The other one that's from that whole moment of being robbed, I'm robbing her, is what happened is anger. When you talk about, [Sky], when you are, analytically you thought it out, and stuff like that the more further you went. The more further I come and the more further I see the bigger picture because back in the day I used to think it was just about control: I've got the money, I've got control, right. I'm in power and that was what it was about. I didn't know back then that this was just systematic, like I didn't have a chance (crying) from right from the get-go it feels like sometimes, but then again, I'm held with shame because I handed that down. I talked to you about this before. I don't … I'm angry. I'm at the point of being angry and I thought I don't wanna care, right, I wanna get out there but I feel there's more, almost shame, I'm right at that border of between, that anger and shame but do I dare get to be angry right? Because I hold onto the shame from what I'm passing on right, from all the crap that I did. When do I get to start again, and I don't? I will never because I have those memories in my head but I hang onto some power beautiful aspiring encouraging women who I mean … from where I was 6 years ago to where I am today is like night and day so I know that if I keep puttin' one foot in front of the other that love, that will come but I also find that as women we got such passions. I know myself I will easily love you before I will love me. Now in a relationship with a man I will easily give myself away to a man but what I have to do is fake it in early recovery because I told you not to get in a relationship and I really didn't want to but everybody was doing it and I was lonely and I remember seeing a guy and I remember having this moment where it was like, this guy was interested but the way he was treating me wasn't right and I knew that but the need to be loved surpassed that and it's gonna change because I'm a good person and I changed so he'll change too that kind of thinkin'. But then I had a moment where I thought I put my daughter there. Would you let your daughter date this guy? And it was like no, absolutely not and that's kinda what I had to do for a long time is put somebody I love in my place and eventually I hope it'll be me that I'll be able to put in that place and say no you don't, absolutely not … [several women talking-at once and laughter] right? That guy's bad news but I realize as women and we're involved in helping other people it's really like today I think it just felt like relief to come here and be able to talk and just be able to say whatever I could say and share that because I can't do that. The conversation you talked about, the difficulty of the conversation because it's sad and I sit back and I see so many, I mean even in the rooms I see horrible things that people passed on that can kill, literally kill us as addicts that we're passing on and there's this thing of "Ahh like ok" but with social media it's even worse right, because I can't actually put some of the things that are in my head on Facebook because I'm looked up to in the community. So, who do I get to talk to? I need to have those places and spaces where I can talk and I'm not gonna feel judged but there's not enough of those places to have those conversations or I find if I have those places with the conversations it's the same people and it's women. Where are the men? And I have a lot of people that work with women specifically women and yes, women need to help the women and stuff and raise them up but if you don't raise the men up, who are those women gonna be with? If the men are not standing present beside us, how is this gonna change?

Sky: So, I got to say two things to you because you're my friend. One is you get to be both. You get to be angry and you get to feel what you feel in relation to your daughter because they're two different relationships. So, you can have those simultaneous emotions because you're dealing with two different people and sometimes those simultaneous emotions happen with the same person, it doesn't mean that one emotion is bad or good. It doesn't mean that you need to feel one or feel the other one less. you just feel both of them and walk through. So you have a right to be angry and you have a right to wonder what your daughter is thinking about you, and that's ... you just sit in that place and you walk that through with the people who love you and the people ... like your daughter, ask her what she thinks, right. And I don't know what my second point was. I just really wanted you to know that you can feel all the feelings and all the feelings are ok because it's a journey we're on, it's not an end point goal. It's a journey.

Maria: This is Maria. Maria is actually a name that I used, one of my first out of many names but [voice in background: "same here"] ... I find what's really difficult is talking about the topic stuff without shaming my family, especially like some of them who are still like, living in vulnerability and I don't wanna trigger them but I feel like I'm only telling a portion of my story if I leave some of that shit out, but how do I get my family on board [crying] ... even when I exited, some of them I guess they thought I was too good ya know, and they stopped spending time with me and I can't just hand over money all the time and gifts and go on trips and I just ... I feel like even with my family my value went down cause I didn't have all of this money. But even with that, even with all that money, I have nothing to show for it now. I have nothing. and I was always living in survival mode. I could have like a few thousand dollars in a cereal box and I'm still looking over my shoulder worrying if I'm gonna get robbed by my pimp boyfriend or ya know ... I'm still like ... I have a regular, so called 'regular job' now, and still everyday worrying am I gonna end up in poverty again? Oh my god, what am I gonna do? I'm too old, those guys aren't gonna want me now. Even when I exited, I was already getting old for them. I was 28 and I was already noticing a decrease, they wanted younger. So like how, how do I get there, with my [sobbing] … my mom, like I carry a … like I love her but I don't really know her. I have a lot of pent up rage against her because of what she did. It wasn't until my daughter was a baby, she was probably about a year old and it just kinda dawned on me: I'm like, wait a minute, my mom left me when I was a one, like how did she do that? How, how did she … like I couldn't do that to my daughter and I'm not at all like a perfect parent. I yell at my daughter and I know that [crying] hurts her deeply but I always swore I would never hit my children. I would never abuse my children now I know the yelling isn't good either and I don't wanna scare her but I'm just … I feel like I'm just stuck in this rut, like it's like a tug of war. Either go all in or get the fuck out. Ya know, I keep living this lie and putting on this mask every day. I don't like who I see in the mirror [sobbing]. Even after the layers of makeup are on and …I just feel ugly inside. It doesn't matter, it doesn't matter what people say and to be completely honest a part of me misses the lifestyle. Just the … I just felt free like I was in control for once in my life and the people that were around me: the drug dealers, the pimps, the other girls—at least we had something in common, ya know. We could share our stories and not be shamed for it because I thought in the early years that if I shared my story with people I thought I could trust: family, boyfriends, that that would be healing and liberating but I would say probably 90 per cent of them use it against me somehow because they knew I wasn't ready to go public, "Oh I'm gonna call your employer cause I'm mad at you and tell them that," "No, you weren't actually doing that, that shit on your resume, that's bullshit," "Let's tell them, let's call up the massage parlour you used to work at." Shit like that ya know? And I'm in a rut and I fear all the time of relapsing and somehow I know I can't go back there though. I know … I know that the last trick I turned was on 107 Ave and if it wasn't for a very close friend of mine, he was like a father figure, he just happened to call me after the second guy. I was half cut and without me telling him what I was doing, he knew what I was doing, and he said go home. But yeah, I just … I don't know I can't seem to shake that thought like that what if … what if we end up in poverty again, how am I gonna support my children [crying]? Like will any man ever really love me the way I need to be loved or will they hate me for what I've done? Because I hate me for what I've done. Out of the thousands of men, I will never forget the first guy, who was in Saskatoon. He was a real pig and I could tell. He knew I was terrified and I'll never forget his face. I'll never forget that moment and a lot of them like it's just like, how can I possibly forget? But maybe that was part of the … my mind coping with it, is not remembering. But sometimes, ya know, I'm out in public, I'm like I never forget a face and I'm like, was that guy one of them? Cause there's literally probably thousands, right. What helped was one person told me to quit letting that fear … let that fear go because they themselves wouldn't want to be exposed, right. And I keep forgetting there's another side of the shame that they should be ashamed themselves too. But are they hurting like we are? Probably not, they're probably still exploiting someone somewhere. But man I just … I know the route of my experience is my childhood and the poverty and … I just don't want it to continue in my family. I think my sister is doing the same thing I used to do. She won't admit it, but I just know. Like you know right, when … ya just know. In a way I feel a bit responsible for that if she did make that choice because she was younger than me seeing me drive fancy cars, wearing fancy clothes, going shopping … Ya know, I can't imagine somebody hurting her like that and for some reason it was ok for me to be exploited and hurt, but my sisters, that … it was different. But I know now more, there's more awareness now about residential school effects and my mom was a product of that so as I get older, I'm ___ now, I'm trying to let go of some of that anger towards my mom and trying to understand where she came from. How she must have ended up in prostitution, the abuse that she suffered at home and then in residential school. I wish there was a place families could go to heal, ya know, and just get it all out, but anyway, thank you.

Jane Doe: I was detached at a young age and I knew that. I didn't need drugs and stuff to get detached because I had done that at a young age. It seems the more healthier I get or the more sober I get the more loss of memory I have. People, faces, names go out right away. I think I'm almost sometimes in some ways going backwards to … they didn't

want to know our name, I didn't wanna know their name. When I just
… this has come up lately, this lady called me out somewhere and I
got just like … there was my adopted mom and my adopted sister. My
adopted mom, she was an _____, very successful functioning
addict and I was the one who was the one who had the problem. I was
the one who was gonna die before I was 20, I knew that. Everybody
in our family knew that but my mom died of cirrhosis of the liver
like 12 years ago and my sister hung herself two years later. And I'm
here and it feels like I got wiped right away from that family. I feel like
with the family, with my own family, my blood, they're strangers and
I can't talk to them. I'm always, like they don't talk to … they were
taught by their Elders not to talk. Nobody wants to talk. So a lot of
my family is still sick so I feel like I have all these questions inside of
who am I? Where am I? This will help me know who I am today and
I'm … there's nothing. I get reminded about my sister, I don't even
remember her. I don't even remember her, I don't remember her face,
I don't remember her voice. I lived with her for ten years. How do you
forget somebody? I had a friend recently, she was murdered. I lived
with her for three years. How do you forget people that you've known
and were there as a kid and you don't remember them? And then
the one thing I see as the children taking on adult responsibilities. I
think that's a common thing is being adults, like I can't imagine my
grandson, he's eight, and I'm grateful that he's had this life I mean
… and I see other families and I went with my friend the other day
and her daughter was graduating with honors and grade nine, and in
my head I'll probably be in the probation office right now or in the
principal's office or just … this brings up a lot but at the same time
in six years, this today feels like the first day that I've been on a level
playing field. And I'm not a dirty Indian. I'm not a ho. That's not all
I'm gonna be [crying], I'm not a disaster. And I … it's always such
extreme emotions too, I don't know, I know this is not normal. I know
this is not normal by far and I live an extreme lifestyle so I understand
why those emotions … but I don't … sometimes I just feel like I'm
going in reverse for some things. Is it, am I losing those memories
because I don't need to know those memories because they're in the
past? I don't know. I too would like to have a place where people can
come together and as family, can heal. It pisses me off, it really pisses

me off [sobbing] when I know the amount of money ... I know that the top fucking 20 people in this world can feed and change this world, 20 fucking people. I'm really fighting to see the beauty in this world. I had this inner child, she woke up, that seven-year-old girl woke up in sobriety and it was like she literally woke up and I could see the beauty in this world that I hadn't seen before. And I used to have opportunities to fly into somewhere and I remember for the first year of flying and being so excited that I was even on a plane that I even got through customs that I even got off the block, and I would fly in and I would say "See the mountains," I would see the clouds, I would be in this moment of ahhh! and then you'd see the lights and it would be so beautiful and I would see beauty. And now when I fly into somewhere and I see buildings and I think, are there women in those lockers? Why are there gates up in that house when we're going by? Are there women in there? Are there children in there? This is the way my mind is starting to see, like I'm really fighting to see the beauty and then ... oh now, maybe I was meant to have those six years to get that beauty and that hope in. That's part of self-love is keeping that inner child, to see the beauty and I do. I do because I surround myself with people who are part of that, but it gets tiring. I remember once wanting to commit suicide by using and the other day I got tired [crying]. I thought, I'm tired. I'm tired. I'm tired of fighting, I'm tired of putting this face on, these masks. I'm tired of not being able to be in a place where I can just be me and breathe. I used to run to _____. [women chatting about quitting smoking] And that's the other thing, medication. Keeping you, keeping medicated or something, over working, giving back, being of service.

Samantha: I see another thing that's common ... and it's not very talked about too because we are women and the ones that hurt us are men, family members that are men, but we also have to realize in our group here the boy children. That abuse is always locked up, hidden and in secret and never spoke about either and we need to make that ok too, ya know. Like they need to be able to express how they feel and what they're going through. So, I see that in our own group that we don't, we don't have that. I couldn't speak, I have sisters. I found out later on in life when I was over 18 that I had three brothers from my real father, and I was told that this other guy was my father but he wasn't. I don't have that background but I do know that there's a lot of family, that they have a lot of children and they're boys and girls and it's not just girls that are getting abused, it's boys as well. So I just wanted to see that commonality cause it's not here either ya know and …

[Cherry speaks about men's responsibilities to end violence and Samantha talks about not trusting men except for her sons]

Samantha: I can't see myself in a relationship although I want one, it's not that I don't want one. I want to be happy. I want to have a life with another partner and enjoy things and stuff like that but anyone that gets close to me I'm just like [barking noise and women laugh]. I'm like a yappy chihuahua … cause that mentality comes back is, what do you want from me? What do I have to give to you? You know what I mean like that and I have to give you sex so you can talk to me? Am I giving you sex cause you can hug me? You know what I mean, like that's where my head is, that's where it's at. It's like I have to do something for you in order to accept me and like me for who I am, I have to engage in you and you don't have to engage in me, you know what I mean? I've been in a few relationships and those relationships have been bad [laughs] like, and I don't know if it's like tattooed on my forehead, like "abuse me." Take, ya know, take me, like for my whole entire life. I was dating this guy three years ago, we started dating in November, February, March comes around and I'm at the grocery store and a girl confronts me in a grocery store. Are you kidding me? Who does stuff like that? Who confronts another woman in a grocery store? I was flabbergasted, like I was like what the heck? And she's all like [growls] like in my face and I'm like, what is going on? And she's like "well, when did you know him?" I'm like November and then her whole face changes cause she just started seeing him in January and I'm like "yo bitch, it should be me who's mad at you" and I'm like sitting here like what the hell is going on? Like you're embarrassing me in a grocery store, ya know, this is my local grocery store. I'm here every other day, like [laughter in room] what the hell, right? And then things like that, like you think you found someone who was nice and then they go and do shit like this and god knows if it's not just her. What if there were other women ya know what I mean, like so and it just keeps building and it's like you men aren't giving yourselves any like [laughs] any anything to offer cause all you see is cheat, cheat, lie, lie, steal, steal, beat, beat. My whole, like my whole sexual life, it sucks [laughs]. But I don't ... I need something concrete. I need something real and I'm not seeing that and it just, it bothers me because I'm raising two boys, two young men and how am I to raise these two young men with a bunch of bad men, ya know. It's hard to try to see that equal side of that right, like, it's hard. It's hard to trust, it's hard to ... and as for family, that's a hard one, it took me a long time to forgive my mom and it still hurts [crying]. I wish I didn't lose her as much as I did. She was young, but like I said, I blamed it because of her history, her old drug use and stuff like that, and I used to hate it when she was so good to my kids because she wasn't good to us and I hated that. I hated that so much. Then I changed it because [sobbing] I thought well, if I'm changing and I'm being sober and I'm getting my kids back, I have to see that other side. My mom was white. She's a white woman and she didn't come from a very good home either. She was abused and raped when she was younger from family members. Both my grandparents were alcoholics and weren't very good with her and then she got pregnant when she was 15 and back in that day, she didn't have any rights so my grandparents took that child away and gave it up for adoption. Ya know what I mean, like she's from a white family ya know, you don't think white people do stuff like that too right. So I get where my mom's upbringing came and how she felt and stuff like that and how I'm trying to change my life and I'm grateful that I got to talk to my mom and tell her how I felt and it's like what you said, was how do you love someone and then forgive them? I don't forgive my mom. I don't think I ever will, but I love her because I wouldn't be here if it wasn't for her. I wouldn't be on this earth if it wasn't for her and I have to show her that respect so I'm grateful that I got to express how I felt to my mom, whether we still didn't have a great relationship but at least she knew how I felt and where I stood. I have no relationship with my sisters, and if it wasn't for me they wouldn't have such a cushy lifestyle right now because they were taken away at a young age because I went against my own mom in court telling her that she was an unfit mom, and my sisters got all adopted in the same foster home, a great foster home. My youngest sister's ___ and still lives with the foster mom, they only know her as mom. But we don't have a relationship because, we just don't and it's hard because one thing that hurts the most is I'm not gonna be here forever. I'm gonna die at some point [crying], who are my kids gonna rely on? Who are my children gonna look up to? They only have them, the only three of them will have to look after each other cause I have no family. No family, no family on their side, on their dad's side. No family on my side that even care. That's what hurts the most, but in the same sense I always say this because it's my life, I live it the way I want to and no one gets to choose that. And if you wanna judge me, you can judge me all you want because it's the way I live. They don't live my life, so … and I think I'm doing a pretty good job right now, and so if it's only me and my kids then it's only me and my kids. But if you want to have some kind of relationship with your mom, it may not be with your sisters, but I know it's hard with parents and I always say that if you don't have that, if you don't have that conversation, you're gonna regret it, whether the outcomes a negative or a positive. I would just make sure you try to say something. But it's hard, it is hard not to have family. But I have family, and it's me and my children and that's who I'm sticking up for [laughs]. It sucks though, it sucks. It's hard. Memory too, I've lost lots of memory. I don't remember faces. I don't remember people's names. I think it has to do with the drugs, I really do [laughs]. I do think it has something to do with all that, all the drugs and everything and just like, not just getting older and stuff like that. But yeah, that's how I feel is we have that … boys aren't, young men aren't looked at because you're men, they're not supposed to talk. But it seems it's just us girls all time. It's the women that are the ones that, we fight with everything, our family, work, being in the public ya know like back in the day when we weren't even allowed to vote, ya know what I mean so … it's been a long, long, long time. We need to start sticking up, having a voice.

[Cherry checks in and asks, what do you want people to know about prostitution? what would help women in prostitution?]

Jane Doe: Nobody should have the right to buy and sell another person. I really was thinking about this the other day as far as what to do and again, it may be coming off the drugs and I've opened myself to such a bigger picture and I'm wondering where my purpose is, which direction do I go? Do I still stay in sexual exploitation, social justice? Do I be a front face, do I be a back base? Is that even where I'm supposed to be? I'm like, I guess you would say coming out of college, and now you're supposed to go live your life but I'm doing it at ___, and I see ads and posts and stuff because, like I said, a lot of my friends work in sexual exploitation and human trafficking and I was thinking about that. Thinking about what can we do? I mean I know some of the things that I've been involved in and what we've done. How do you stay hopeful? Because I just … I don't know, I just see this social media now, it's like, you're giving a wheel with no guidelines, this generation. It's so massively easy to groom somebody and not just young women, young people, period, into all different kind of sorts, so much evil right, so I think … I had to stop like at least once every couple of days but can … like never mind what the world can do, what about, what can I do? And today, some days it's just holding on. Like lately it's just holding on and keep going, putting one foot in front of the other and do what's in front of me. Dress up, show up, right, like today, yesterday, the last few days. It's like dress up, show up. I don't wanna be a downer and like, but I do, I'm curious as to what to go to … the next … how do you help everyone in prostitution? Because when you say prostitution, it's not just the prostitute, it's their family. It's their … the people that they are in community with, or not. Yeah, this is perfect timing because this to me is hope. This to me is change. This to me is you freakin' came all the way from Montréal to _____ of all places, so I don't know it's just … I know there's ideas. I know I'm gonna hear about some of them hopefully.

Maria: I know I mentioned it earlier, but I think if I knew back when I was 18, 19, what I know now like, the effects prostitution has had on my life, maybe I would have tried something different. I suffer a lot like my self-esteem ya know, it's like I wanna … I don't know like, I'm really not comfortable in my own skin and I feel like I try to, I try to think about what I think men are thinking about and I don't know why I do that but I just think like the way I look at men, I just think they must have some kind of deviant mind in some way, whether it's towards a child or a vulnerable woman or man like, I just think like every … not everybody but there's a lot of perverts out there and it's not just men, it's some women too and I just hate obsessing about stuff like that but I feel like I'm trying to think about it so I'm aware of it so I can protect myself and my family from it. But I hate thinking that way all the time cause it's gross. Like I don't wanna, ya know, like my daughter's been dancing pow wow since she was two and she's been asking me for years now, "mom, when are you gonna dance with me?" And I there's something blocking me, like I wanna learn women's traditional. I wanna learn that I think it's … I just love it when I see it. I just feel connected to the ancestors and … but it's like something's blocking me, and it's probably the shame that I carry, because when I was a teenager I had dreams of being a professional dancer [crying], ya know, that was my dream. I was gonna be a dancer on MTV or some kind of dancer somewhere, somehow. But that dance ended up turning into something that also became exploited, stripping. I just … I gotta like … man, like I can't live with regret, but I think back to when I was training as a ballroom dancer and I was kind of, ya know, living in two different worlds. I did try but I just, at some point, I gave up on those dreams and I just got fully entrenched in that lifestyle and it's fucking hard to get out of. It is hard and it can be dangerous to get out of. I don't think sometimes people are thinking maybe, maybe I should, ya know, respond to this ad, make a few quick hundred bucks, I'll only do it a month. They don't realize that that month can turn into years and years turn into decades. Ya know, it's really hard to get out of and it's addictive. I don't know. I just … and I see that too with social media. Everything's like hyper sexualized and you see like eleven year old's looking like they're made up to be like nineteen and striking sexy poses, even my own daughter. One day I caught her looking in the mirror and she was doing that duck lip thing you see all the time, and I said to my daughter "what are you doing my girl?," and she's like, "oh, ya know," she got shy and I said "who did you see doing that?" and then I just start worrying again, like oh my god I don't want her to think that she has to be sexy, ya know. Where is she learning this stuff from? I don't know I just … that's gotta change somehow, like, you're right there's no … it's like the frikkin, it's all … what do they call it, there's no limits with it on there, on social media.

Samantha: Social media should be used for awareness and stuff like that. This is how we're going to help people in prostitution, whether it's a male or female, and so a lot of education and a lot of awareness. And that lies too, with the police, the EMS, and stuff like that, when you're dealing with someone that vulnerable on the corner of the street. Instead of going up there and already having that bias against that person because they're on the street working it, you know, they should have education on how to approach people in that because you don't know what their situation is, you don't know if they're forced up there because they have a pimp or if they're doing it for survival or stuff like that. I think education and awareness is one way to go, to learn about prostitution. They should be putting stuff like that in education and I'm not talking about grade school [laughs] or elementary, I'm talking about college and stuff like that, more real-life things that are imperative people understand, especially in college when you're naive and young and vulnerable. I think education and awareness needs to be brought up a notch or two on that.

Cherry: In college, I can tell you, it's "sex work is empowering," "sex work, sex work, sex work, it's great." That's what they're teaching in colleges.

[a woman asks "who's teaching that!?," another woman responds "white people," a few women speak at once]

Sky: So I'm gonna fess up on the sins of my ... by and large it's ... we have this problem in _____. Aboriginal women take advantage of drop-in centres, whatever, for women involved in prostitution and there's educated white women who are running these centres and they say they're representing Aboriginal women and girls and it goes to higher education cause ya know, white people talk to white people. I talked to an Aboriginal person, and in that the truth is grotesquely distorted because Aboriginal ... well, like myself included, like yes, we want harm reduction. I want a condom to make sure I'm not gonna catch something in this moment but do I want prostitution as a system to continue? No. I'd like to see prostitution ended in my lifetime right and so the argument gets distorted that what women are asking for is for safety or for, ya know, that it's stigma that is killing women, and it's like no actually it's men that are killing women, right. And so there's this distortion that happens at a higher level and the women on the ground, their voices are completely taken out of the equation, unless you're usually a privileged white woman who chose to enter prostitution in college or something like that, right. So they're kind of held up as these shining examples of how empowering and how freeing prostitution can be and it erases everybody else's story because we live in a colonial racist country, right and in that by privileging that one story it erases the commonality that we're talking about in this room right now, right, and I think the lynch pin to all of this is men. I understand men as boys go through abuse like we do but they're still privileged in society cause they're men. And so they don't … they don't suffer the same way women do, and they're not exploited by and large in the same way women are, right, and I think in these conversations, it needs to just be ok that we're focusing on women and women only cause we have a lot of hurt to heal and we need to be able to say "yeah, it was men." I mean, I was involved in prostitution for 15 years and I was never bought by a woman, right, like it was men. And I think it's ok to acknowledge that and to say to them you need to be doing this on your own, you need to find your own space and you need to do it on your own and I'm not gonna do it for you. You need to … women have somehow figured it out right, like we pulled it together and feminism started and all these different amazing women figured out how our lives intersect with each other, right, and men need to do that for themselves. Cause I'm quite honestly too emotionally exhausted trying to help our women, but I'm not willing to waste my energy and my resources … not waste … but I'm not willing to put my resources and energy into helping men because they need to learn how to do the emotional work themselves. They are not good at it and they need to learn it. I mean, I'm raising 3 boys right and I just wanted to say as well, for your daughter, for everyone that's realizing how hyper sexualized culture is nowadays and raising children there's an amazing resource online called culturereframed. org and all it is about is the hyper sexualization of children and youth and how to fight against that and how to help raise your children questioning the norm.

CHAPTER 6

Shut Up Squaw: The Silencing of Indigenous Women

I'm a feminist, not the fun kind (Dworkin, qtd. in Bart, 1996, p. 272).

Radical feminists have never been embraced and celebrated by the dominant (i.e. patriarchal) culture. In this chapter, I describe what I learned about the realities of prostitution while in New Zealand and about the academic hostilities and barriers to Indigenous feminist research and analysis and the ways in which Indigenous and other women who engage in public scholarship are silenced and/or punished for their feminist perspectives.

I Went to Aotearoa and All I Got Was This Lousy PhD

As in Canada, there's no evidence that prostitution existed in Aotearoa/New Zealand before the arrival of white male settlers (Belich, 1996; Donne, 1927; Wilton and Slavick, 2018). You'd think, given this history and the current overrepresentation of Indigenous women in prostitution, that the violently misogynist, racist and capitalist roots of prostitution would be glaringly obvious. And I guess they are obvious? The issue I suppose is instead of outrage, we get apathy; instead of accountability, we get justification; instead of challenging the status quo (i.e. patriarchy), we feed it.

When we're looking at issues that so severely impact women in our patriarchal world, we need to evaluate our own worldviews before we start asking questions of others and of the world around us. If we don't, what we end up doing is starting our research halfway in by recklessly accepting the conscious or unconscious patriarchal assumptions we hold by default. For example, some questions we should ask ourselves, as researchers, before we begin prostitution research include: Do I think men are entitled to engage in sex acts with women whenever they want to? Do I think men are entitled to engage in sex acts with women whenever they want to as long as they pay her? Do I think it's physically, emotionally, and mentally harmful for a woman to engage in sex acts with somebody she does not desire to have sexual contact with? Do I think it's physically, emotionally, and mentally harmful for a woman to engage in sex acts with somebody she does not desire to have sexual contact with if she is paid to do so?

While feminist researchers have asked and continue to ask these and other important questions of themselves and of the world around them, 'sex work' researchers have failed to do so. As a result, 'sex work' theory provides contradictory or insufficient answers to critical feminist questions about sex, race, and class oppression in prostitution, sometimes dismissing these questions entirely when answers are politically inconvenient. Despite these lingering questions, or perhaps because of them, New Zealand decriminalized prostitution and designated the practice as a form of labour ('sex work') since the passing of the 2003 *Prostitution Reform Act* (PRA). The PRA fully decriminalized the sex industry and 'sex work' is commonly accepted as a form of service work by governments, organizations, businesses, and the media across New Zealand (Brunton et al., 2010). New Zealand was the first, and so far has been the only country, to fully decriminalize prostitution and differs from other approaches in that it demonstrates, according to sex work researchers, "… a shift from regulating sex work from a moral perspective to acknowledging the human rights of this section of the population" (Abel et al., 2010, p. 1). I spent nearly three months in New Zealand researching prostitution. Using experiential analysis (Mies, 1983; Reinharz, 1983), I reflect on my time doing prostitution research and advocacy in Aotearoa and share what I learned about prostitution and about doing feminist research on prostitution.

Prostitution in New Zealand

I want to bring us back to basics. Prostitution: what is it? It is the use of a woman's body for sex by a man, he pays money, he does what he wants. The minute you move away from what it really is, you move away from prostitution into the world of ideas. You will feel better; you will have a better time; it is more fun; there is plenty to discuss, but you will be discussing ideas, not prostitution. Prostitution is not an idea. It is the mouth, the vagina, the rectum, penetrated usually by a penis, sometimes hands, sometimes objects, by one man and then another and then another and then another and then another. That's what it is. I ask you to think about your own bodies—if you can do so outside the world that the pornographers have created in your minds, the flat, dead, floating mouths and vaginas and anuses of women. I ask you to think concretely about your own bodies used that way. How sexy is it? Is it fun? The people who defend prostitution and pornography want you to feel a kinky little thrill every time you think of something being stuck in a woman. I want you to feel the delicate tissues in her body that are being misused. I want you to feel what it feels like when it happens over and over and over and over and over and over and over again: because that is what prostitution is (Dworkin, 1993, p. 2).

The most important thing that I learned about prostitution in New Zealand is that 'sex work' works: it works to uphold male domination and female subordination—it works for men because prostitution is a patriarchal practice and patriarchy benefits men and it doesn't work for women because prostitution is a patriarchal practice and patriarchy disadvantages and hurts women. So, if you're looking for a legal framework that shamelessly encourages men to exploit and profit from women's inequality in patriarchy, the New Zealand model of prostitution decriminalization is the model for you!

I also learned that prostitution is so embedded in the culture and landscape of Aotearoa that it's a non-issue. In New Zealand, the battle is essentially over and 'sex work' is most certainly work. Governments, organizations, universities, and media work to silence any criticism of prostitution that may arise within and outside of the country, but given how deeply normalized the idea of 'sex work' is, these are uncommon occurrences that don't require large investments of time, energy, or resources to squash. Now, don't get me wrong. I didn't travel to New Zealand naively; I chose these territories precisely because of their policies that decriminalized prostitution and also because of the parallel histories and experiences of Indigenous women in Aotearoa and Canada. As a feminist, I'm aware of, and experienced with, the politics that accompany prostitution and the hostilities that arise from those politics, most often aimed at feminist and other women who challenge the status quo (i.e. patriarchy). I was however, unpleasantly surprised to see and experience just how totally Aotearoa has been colonized by 'sex work' ideology:

January 20, 2019

Dear Diary,

I'm tired right now, which I think I say that every time. I slept last night, it was the best night I had in a long time. I was up for an hour around 3:00 a.m., I was up again at 6:00 for a while and then I went back to sleep. But I had to take a sleeping pill ... I don't ... I've got nothing left, but I'm ... just got nothing left. I haven't been sleeping. So I guess I'm going to talk a little bit about the project and everything and what's going on with that. And then I'll talk a little bit about other things.

So I think I've said this in so many other videos, but I'm going to say this again, which is that I didn't realize ... I knew it was going to be bad. Like I knew it was not easy to come to New Zealand and do research that's critical of prostitution because in 2003, they decriminalized the pimps and the johns and brothel keeping and women in prostitution. And so it's been that way for 15 years like that, 15 years for that legislation to really take hold, which it has. So I knew, you know, I knew there was going to be challenges, but I didn't know. And I don't know if

I could have known until I got here, you know, just how bad it is, how hard it is.

And I think ... I mean, it's with [prostitution], but it's also with gender identity ... but what I see is that the gender identity issue seems to be something that's very much at the forefront. There's lots of talk about it online, there's events, it seems like there's a lot of organizations that are working on that issue, it's very visible and not much debate. But those who are questioning the idea of gender identity are just getting smacked down basically by these organizations, by individuals, but also by members of parliament. So members of the government are singling out individuals who are critical or questioning this idea and criticizing them, which to me, that's a bit scary to be trying to stop discussion in that way by a government. I find with prostitution and these two things [prostitution and gender identity] are linked in some way.

I find with prostitution, and I think it's because it's been 15 years of this legislation, that they don't even need to have a discussion about it. It's like it's a non-issue now. It's become so embedded and so just a normal part of everyday culture that ... there's no need almost for pro sex work organizations like the New Zealand Prostitutes Collective, for example, who receive a lot of stable funding from the New Zealand government, they don't need to be actively promoting their agenda because it's just accepted.

So there's just not a lot of discussion about it. And I ... it's scary here, but it's scary in a really quiet way. I think that if you were a visitor and you were to come here—I'm a visitor, I came here—spending some time here, you wouldn't really know it, like you wouldn't. There's not ... I haven't seen giant advertisements. You don't see, you know, brothels with giant signage or anything. It just kind of blends in like a grocery store or a post office or whatever. I don't think that's any better or any worse than, say, for example, in the Netherlands, where it's very much you can see it, it's very visible and you know, you can see women in the windows and you see the pimps on the street and you see the men, you know, going to pay a woman to do sexual acts with him, you see it—in Canada, you can see it, too. You don't necessarily see brothels, although you see plenty of massage parlours that everybody knows are brothels and you'll see women on the street sometimes ... I don't know, it's not invisible, but it's not like hyper visible at the same time, depending on where you are in certain areas ... Here, you just don't see it, and that's not any better or any worse, it's just different. It means that the discussions that need to happen or that should be happening are different because it's very much a cultural acceptance with very, very, very, very little resistance. And those that do resist are often ... there have been, you know, individuals making claims about them and it can get really hostile. So because it's just kind of how things are here in some ways, it's a different challenge to challenging [prostitution].

It would be like, OK, we need to get rid of ... I don't know, think about what type of store—clothing stores—we need to get rid of clothing stores in New Zealand. People are like, what! That's crazy! What do you mean get rid of clothing stores in New Zealand!? So it's at that level where people can't even imagine that there could be something else.

January 22, 2019

Dear Diary,

In New Zealand, like outside of New Zealand, everything that we hear coming out of New Zealand is good, [prostitution is] great, it's working, everybody loves it here, like everybody, you know. And you would think ... you know, as somebody who's maybe not involved in the issue, that that would mean that it's working right because everything is good that comes out of here. But once you're here and you see the ways that those who are critical are stopped from speaking or those who might be critical ... there's no venue, there's no place they can go where you can even ask questions and further those questions and think about those questions and talk to others. Women are afraid here to even speak to their co-workers that maybe they're having questions about [prostitution]. There's nowhere to start that, to even start the conversation. So that it doesn't mean that it's great here and it's all good, it just means that those who are critical or who are actually being harmed by [prostitution] don't have a place where they can begin to talk about that. The universities here are very much controlled by pro sex work ideology, researchers [are] able to access funding and then do research that legitimizes the pimps and stuff.

New Zealand, as the rest of our world, believes patriarchy to be natural and inevitable. As a result, prostitution is also believed to be natural and inevitable. As Gillian Abel acknowledges, this misogynist assumption has long-existed in Aotearoa and was not challenged in public discussion of New Zealand's prostitution policy change in 2003: "… the argument that prostitution is a form of violence against women did not feature heavily in the debate leading up to the passing of the PRA and was marginalized on the basis that it offered nothing to protect and empower those working in the sex industry" (Armstrong, 2020). Understanding that this is simply untrue that a feminist analysis of prostitution offers nothing to women in prostitution and that feminist perspectives were not actually heard or taken into account in the debates leading up to New Zealand's celebrated and historic total decriminalization of prostitution gives more context to the present-day silence surrounding prostitution in the country. As Armstrong notes, "since the PRA has passed, the neo-abolitionist [feminist] perspective has remained marginalised" (Armstrong, 2020, p. 4). This is, or should certainly be, cause for great concern, as women's sex-based equality concerns were, and are, dismissed as 'non-issues' when it comes to prostitution in New Zealand and the current regime of decriminalized prostitution in New Zealand reflects these blind spots. For example, some scholars (Nagle, 1997; Smith and Mac, 2018) claim that the decriminalization of prostitution is a feminist framework that works to empower all sex workers, regardless of gender but that, at the same time, the sex-based inequalities evident in prostitution are not the only or most important or even important at all to analyze against the backdrop of global patriarchy, capitalism, and racism. This position, that decriminalizing men who buy sex and men who pimp women, is a feminist position while at the same time criticizing feminist methodologies and analysis doesn't make sense. What also doesn't make sense is that some sex work researchers, such as Gillian Abel, have recognized the short-sightedness of the full decriminalization of prostitution, acknowledging that this position actually doesn't work to reduce sex-based or other social inequalities:

> … I instead see … the integrative policy [full decriminalization] response [rising] out of a concern to address the human rights of sex workers. Policies on sex work are not redistributive policies, which would be the best way to address social inequalities. They instead tend to focus on the outcomes of social inequality, rather like the ambulance at the bottom of the cliff (to use a popular public health complaint) (Abel, 2019, p. 1925).

Policies that work to further normalize and embed prostitution are not revolutionary and are not feminist. In fact, they work to slap bandaids on gaping bloody wounds—they are insufficient to address women's material realities and needs in the present and they work to keep women in prostitution by refusing to challenge patriarchy and the male sex right. Short-term and long-term, a decriminalized prostitution regime hurts women.

Māori scholar Jade Kake and feminist scholar Fern Eyles take up these questions and more in regard to Māori women and prostitution in the chapter entitled 'Te Tiriti o Waitangi and Prostitution Reform in Aotearoa New Zealand: An Overview' in the edited book, *Decolonizing Futures: Collaborations for New Indigenous Horizons* (Maryuama, 2022):

> The lead up to, and passing of, the 2003 prostitution law reform in New Zealand has received considerable controversy. Most criticism has focused on the composition and features of the industry, with little consideration given to the configuration of the working group informing the law review. Under Te Tiriti o Waitangi, the Crown has a duty to consult with Māori regarding issues that impact them. Whilst the composition of the working group was largely predictable, the authors contend that the exclusion of representatives for tangata whenua (Indigenous) and wāhine (women) interests (and, arguably, the inclusion and weighting of others), and failure to appropriately consult tangata whenua in the development and review of legislation is a breach of Article Two … did the Crown meet its obligations under Te Tiriti o Waitangi in the development and review of the

Prostitution Reform Act 2003? Furthermore, how were the interests of Māori—in particular, Māori women—considered in determining the configuration of the Prostitution Law Review Committee? Possible outcomes include recommendations for Treaty compliant legislative reform, which could include reconfiguration of the Prostitution Law Review Committee and a full review of the Act (Zaman, 2020).

Doing Prostitution Research in New Zealand

It's difficult to do ethical research in New Zealand on prostitution and nearly impossible to do feminist research in New Zealand on prostitution. This is because in Aotearoa, prostitution is not believed to be harmful to women and is seen as a type of service work. As a result, there are no women's groups, such as women's refuges or rape crisis centres, that understand or respond to prostitution *as a form of male violence* or that offer exiting services that understand or respond to prostitution *as a form of male violence* to assist those who want to leave the sex industry. Instead, prostitution is treated as *an occupation* with *workplace hazards*. This means that I wasn't able to follow through with my research plan of speaking with women who had exited prostitution supported by an organization because there weren't any organizations that offered this kind of support.

December 15, 2018

Dear Diary,

So I came here [New Zealand] hoping to do what I did in Canada, which was go through an organization to find women, to do a version of consciousness-raising essentially, a focus group with. And I knew that there wouldn't be any exiting services, there's no dedicated organization to help women who want to leave prostitution. But I don't know, I guess I had thought maybe if I reach out to a rape crisis centre or transition house or, you know, that there might be room to work with those kinds of groups. No, no. The women that are in those organizations are very, very pro sex work. Those organizations are very, very pro sex work. So there's not even this kind of ... there's zero linkage between male violence against women and prostitution right, because it's not prostitution, it's a job. It's totally separate. So it's not possible for me to go through an exiting service, first of all, because there is none. And secondly, because others who are working on issues of male violence against women don't recognize prostitution as a form of male violence.

Attempted Silencing

Critiques of prostitution within New Zealand are silenced by individuals, organizations, academic institutions and even government agencies. I experienced this first-hand while in New Zealand when I rented a room at the Auckland Institute of Technology (AIT) to give a presentation about the harms prostitution causes to women, particularly Indigenous women, in Canada. When meeting with a representative of AIT to book the room, I was told that while the AIT promotes events that are booked by outside parties, the AIT would not promote my event because it was critical of prostitution. The AIT compared my event to other events the university would rent space to but not promote, such as a pro-life presentation on the issue of abortion. Even though I paid the same fees as others to rent space to give a presentation at the AIT, I was denied promotional services offered to others because the university firmly believed that 'sex work' was work.

The event went ahead but, unfortunately, didn't go as planned. Turns out I had listed the wrong location on my own promotional materials. There are two universities very close to each other in Auckland and being unfamiliar with the territory, I got the locations confused and was only told this by an individual who showed up to the presentation late. Another issue that occurred was the room I had rented was not prepared for my presentation as promised. There was a table with a dirty tablecloth and various utensils left over from a previous event right in the middle of the room when I arrived. My soundperson and some individuals who came to see the presentation moved these items out of the room while I prepared for the presentation I was about to give. A third issue that occurred during the event was the doors to the university building I was presenting in were locked when they were supposed to be open. The university told me this was a mistake on their part as they miscommunicated with university security. At any rate, I'm not sure how many people came intending to come to the event and left once they discovered the locked doors and no easy or direct way to contact anyone to open the doors to the building. I did contact the university afterwards requesting a fifty per cent refund. The university agreed to provide me with a refund, but this never happened as they were requesting banking information that Canada, as a country, does not subscribe to and were not willing to work with me to provide an alternative route for a refund.

The Silence Is So Loud

Experiencing first-hand the silence of prostitution in Aotearoa was painful. It did, however, give me some insights into questions I had before going to New Zealand. Nearly all, if not all, academic research that originates in New Zealand or that is done in New Zealand on prostitution presents the New Zealand Model as progressive and successful in supporting sex workers rights as workers. This is strange—how is it that nearly all the academic literature about the New Zealand Model of prostitution policy is overwhelmingly positive? Maybe this is definitive evidence that the full decriminalization of the sex industry is actually the best model and is the policy approach to follow regarding this issue? Given my experiences and knowledge as a feminist working on the issue of prostitution for over a decade and my social location as an Indigenous feminist scholar and all the experiences and knowledge that goes along with that (Smith, 2012) however, I knew better than to assume that just because academia (or any other manstitution—but especially academia) says something is true, it must be true. I thought the buckets of research coming out of New Zealand reigning praise on the New Zealand Model might raise some suspicions or at the very least, raise some questions, given that the model is considered so beneficial to sex workers, who are overwhelmingly female, in the contemporary patriarchal, capitalist, racist culture of New Zealand. Using my experiences in New Zealand, I describe three ways that Indigenous and other woman are silenced and/or punished for their feminist politics: (1) the New Zealand Model as *THE* MODEL; (2) a lack of understanding of male violence against women by sex work advocates, and; (3) the confusion of queer theory.

THE NEW ZEALAND MODEL IS *THE* MODEL
(Just Ignore the Bad Parts)

Nearly all research that comes out of New Zealand sings the praises of the New Zealand model (Raymond, 2018). It's absolutely critical, especially on controversial issues that disproportionately and so severely impact women such as prostitution, that we not only evaluate our own biases (that we all have) before we begin learning about the issue but that we continually ask whose voices are missing and why as we do our research. There are many different factors that stop women in prostitution and stop women who have survived prostitution from speaking including a) histories or experiences of sexualized male violence and the normalization of that violence; b) shame and stigma; and c) the values, beliefs, and intentions of non-feminist researchers who select, interpret, and distort women's words.

Assuming that silence means consent, or worse, that silence represents contentment, even happiness, has proved disastrous for women who are beaten and abused in their homes by their husbands or boyfriends or for Indigenous girls and young women in Canada's residential school system. In both cases, some individuals were able to speak out but consequently punished for their actions. The material conditions of women's lives—that included the threat of murder or physical torture and starvation—ensured, and continue to ensure, that the majority of women are unable to speak freely about their experiences of male violence against women, their analyses, and their hopes for the future without consequence. These conditions, as well, are imposed on women as girls so that we learn not to speak from the get-go with a greater or lesser threat of consequence:

> Then, on a deeper level, one of the things I've learned in the last fifteen years is how much women are silenced through sexual abuse. The simple experience of being abused, whether as a child or as an adult, has an incredible impact on everything about the way you see the world around you, so that either you don't feel you can speak because you're frightened of what the retaliation will be, or you don't trust your experience of reality enough to speak—that happens to a lot of incest victims. Or you are actually physically kept from being able to speak, battered women do not have freedom of speech. So it operates on that level (Dworkin, 1996, p. 203).

If male violence is all you've known, how do you know you deserve anything different—anything better?

Another factor that stops women from speaking about their experiences in prostitution is the often life-long shame and stigma that follows women who are in and who have survived their time in the industry. Women who have traded sex acts to men for money, housing, something to eat, new clothes, drugs, a slurpee or for anything else they needed or wanted have done absolutely nothing wrong. Yet it's these women, and other women whose bodies have been violated by men, who are weighed down and silenced by the unwarranted shame of their own actions. That's messed up. Why would a woman feel ashamed if she's done nothing wrong? Patriarchy, that's why. The men who buy sex acts from women and the men who sell women to other men, in addition to men who use pornography and men who harm women outside the sex industry, don't carry this shame—why would they? They've done nothing wrong! Male dominance and the entitlement that men believe they have, not only to women's lives, women's physical and emotional labour, time, attention, physical bodies—but even to *the insides of women's bodies*—is a foundational Canadian value. Cree prostitution survivor, Taanis Bellarose, made a critical point to understanding the silencing of women in prostitution: she stated that one of the reasons we don't actually know how many women have been in prostitution is because many women, for various reasons but reasons often related to shame, will never speak about being in prostitution to another person.[34] As Bellarose noted, maybe some women were in the life for a short while; maybe some women don't describe what happened to them as prostitution; or maybe some women just want to try and forget that it happened and move on with their lives the best they can—for these reasons and more, there are so many women out there who have been in prostitution who will never share their stories with academic researchers, film crews, or journalists;[35] a point that I also made while testifying, under what I would describe as hostile conditions, as an expert witness in an Ontario court about a prostitution-related case:

> **JL (James Lockyer), counsel for the defense:** Now, I refer you as well, this is a common theme through—you're familiar with the literature in this area, it's a common theme that when they ask, they actually interview real, live, breathing sex workers, they typically say why did you get into the industry? And the large majority, 80 plus, say they're in it for the money. They may have other reasons for it but that's the primary motive, is that right?
>
> **CS (Cherry Smiley), expert witness:** Yeah, many women say that they are, yes, that they're doing it for the money, yes.
>
> **JL:** Yes, so they made that choice?
>
> **CS:** I think it's important that you talked about real, living, breathing sex workers, because it is very difficult to interview women who have passed, and this includes murdered and disappeared Indigenous women. And so in this issue, we hear many voices, but there's many voices that we don't hear and I think that if we follow that she's just choosing to engage in it, without considering the context and history of that choice for Indigenous women, we would end up in a situation where Indigenous women are 'savage sexualized squaws' and they

---

34 Personal communication.
35 Personal communication.

just happened to choose prostitution more often in disproportionate numbers to other women.

JL: But that's your characterization, correct?

CS: Yes?

JL: Yeah.

CS: This is my research and work that I do and the perspective that I take (*R v Anwar and Harvey*, 2018).

And the thing is, women should not have to reveal their experiences in prostitution in order to have a say about prostitution, and this is true for all other forms of male violence against women as well. We are women and prostitution impacts all women, to a greater or lesser extent, closer or further away, and this alone is reason enough to have a say on this issue.

A third factor that stops women in prostitution from speaking about the male violence done to them is determined by what questions researchers ask and how the researchers interpret and present their research findings. Feminism is the only analytical tool that consistently prioritizes women and opposes patriarchy. Most prostitution research is done from a public health perspective (Graham, 2014), a perspective that is decidedly not feminist and that some argue is anti-feminist. As a result, most prostitution research fails to centre the collective experiences and needs of women and to analyze these experiences and needs in the context of patriarchy. For example, a woman in prostitution stated in an article about sex workers' responses to sex work stigma:

> [W]hen clients come, they do because of my attitude, and because of the way I look, and because of the service I give, that's, that's very positive, that way. My thoughts, like, yes, it has made me feel more positive about myself ... (Benoit et al., 2020, p. 90).

This woman's response is not considered at all within the context of patriarchy. Instead, it's presented as active resistance to stigmatization through the use of reframing which the authors describe as a technique some women in prostitution use to "... describe their work in positive terms, such a making connections between sex work and empowering outcomes in their lives or point to the elements of sex work that are useful for society at large" (Benoit et al., 2020, p. 83). The consequences for women due to a lack of a feminist analysis in research is thunderous here. Instead of the women's comments being analyzed in the context of sexualized male violence against women that might bring up subsequent questions about women's self-esteem and sources of self-esteem available to women in patriarchy, her comments are 'objectively' analyzed by the researchers as only a positive way to reframe stigma.

The New Zealand Prostitutes Collective

The New Zealand Prostitutes Collective (NZPC), founded in 1987 by 'sex workers' and funded primarily by the New Zealand government since 1988 (New Zealand Prostitute's Collective, n.d., a), often guides, partners, and works with researchers to help facilitate research on sex work in New Zealand. The NZPC understands 'sex work' to be work and advocates for the human rights, health, and wellbeing of all sex workers:

> We are committed to working for the empowerment of sex workers, so that sex workers can have control over all aspects of their work and lives. Our services focus on workers rights, HIV and STI prevention, and education … NZPC has long been at the forefront of reforming the law for sex workers. We helped draft the Prostitution Reform Act which decriminalised sex work in New Zealand, and built support for it as it passed into law. NZPC provides expert advice to those with an interest in law and policy surrounding sex work in New Zealand. We are also a crucial point of liaison between government and non-government civil society, and the sex industry (n.d.,b).

The NZPC is New Zealand's national and government-funded prostitution organization and "… was instrumental in designing, advocating for, and—in many ways—assisting in the implementation of the change in law that resulted in the decriminalization of sex work in 2003" (Healy et al., 2017, p. 50). As feminist researcher

Janice Raymond notes, the NZPC was also heavily involved in the 2008 Prostitution Law Review Committee and influential in the *Report of the Prostitution Law Review Committee on the Operation of the Prostitution Reform Act 2003* (2018). The 'outsized' influence Raymond claims the NZPC has over the sex work narrative coming out of New Zealand is accurate and has very real consequences for women in Aotearoa and elsewhere. This also brings up concerns about the academic research on prostitution that has come out of New Zealand, given that the NZPC are considered the authority on prostitution but also have very real interests, economic and otherwise, in the continuation and promotion of the sex industry in New Zealand. These conflicts and conflicts of interest are real and in some cases, have resulted in the cover up of additional male violence in prostitution by reframing and renaming the male violence of prostitution as 'something else'.

No Child Rape Here, Only 'Family Abuse': Consequences of the Lack of Feminist Knowledge about Male Violence against Women

A second way that feminist women, particularly women who have survived prostitution, are silenced is by a lack of feminist knowledge and analysis of male violence against women by sex work advocates. For example, according to the NZPC and the New Zealand government, sex trafficking and/or sexual exploitation of children and young people under 18 years old doesn't really happen in New Zealand (Newshub, 2017; US State Department, 2021). This is despite research demonstrating otherwise by New Zealand sex work researcher Natalie Thorburn (Thorburn and de Haan, 2014; Thorburn, 2016a; Thorburn, 2016b; Thorburn, 2017; Thorburn, 2018; Thorburn, 2019) and others (ECPAT, n.d.; Saphira and Oliver, 2002; ECPAT Child Alert, 2018; US State Department, 2019), despite stories I was given in informal and formal conversations in Aotearoa and Australia, and despite the plain ridiculousness of such a claim in our patriarchal world. One of the reasons sex trafficking and the sexual exploitation of children and teenagers doesn't happen in New Zealand is because of the way male violence against women is defined, categorized and re-categorized and the ways in which language is manipulated by sex work researchers and advocates. For example, the NZPC publicly challenged Thorburn's research into the prevalence of the sexual exploitation of children claiming that this exploitation was actually family abuse, not sex trafficking: "Let's not conflate it with sex work and say 'oh they've been trafficked into sex work' when actually they're being abused by family members" (Newshub, 2017). Reclassifying child sexual exploitation and sex trafficking of children as solely 'family abuse' means that statistics are skewed (ECPAT Child Alert, 2018), that sexually exploited children are not receiving the support they need, that men who rape children are not being held accountable, and that the reality of male violence against women, including that of prostitution, is being actively concealed in New Zealand by men and other parties with something immediate and tangible to lose. Another example of the NZPC's lack of knowledge about male violence against women is evident in the following statement made by Catherine Healy on behalf of the NZPC:

> While their individual situations and conditions of work vary, access to these sex workers by NZPC is direct, and it is usually immediately apparent that they are free to talk and seek support, and usually control their own phone numbers and advertising. In discussions, they make it clear that they chose to work as sex workers. By listening to what these sex workers themselves say about their lives, we therefore conclude they are not victims of trafficking (Healy et al., 2017, p. 54).

This statement demonstrates what I consider an offensive lack of feminist knowledge about male violence against women and lack of knowledge about how patriarchy shapes the material conditions of women's lives. As mentioned in Chapter 5, many women who are victims of male violence will not immediately or readily identify themselves as victims of male violence, for a variety of valid (and patriarchal) reasons; some women will find ways to excuse the male violence or minimize the male violence out of fear; and many women will blame themselves for the male violence that has been perpetrated against them (Barry, 1979). The commonality of these actions tells us much more about the woman-hating culture we live in and the ways that women are able to respond to male violence against women in this culture than they do about individual women's supposed 'failings' to keep themselves safe or their supposed deeply-held desire to be abused.[36] Similarly, female victims of sex trafficking may not acknowledge themselves as trafficking victims, just as women who have been beaten and raped by their husbands may not identify themselves as abused women or victims of wife battery—but they are. Renate Klein, referencing Mies' research project with the battered women at Women's House in Germany, noted that there were instances where the women being interviewed didn't tell the truth about their experiences and that this was discovered when their children gave a different account of what had happened (Klein, 1983). Klein states:

> ... the researchers realized that they should not dismiss their method of openness and honesty, but, on the contrary, that they should acknowledge the obvious need of these women to 'fake' as an important part of their strategy to survive. As Mies comments 'we then realized that the truth of a person cannot be asked for, is not static, but grows and develops during the course of a lifetime' (1983, p. 95).

Klein speaks to a feminist methodology that functions in an interactive way, as opposed to a linear way; that is, that women researchers take into account theirs and others' intuition, emotions, and feelings as part of the research process (Klein, 1983). This approach:

> ... in combination with [the researcher's] intellectual capacities for analysing and interpreting our observations ... might produce a kind

---

36   Despite what pornography and other manstitutions tells us, no woman desires to be abused by a man or men.

of scholarship that encompasses the complexity of reality better than the usual fragmented approach to knowledge (Klein, 1983, p. 95).

Additionally, attempting to draw a distinct line, as Healy has done, between forms of male violence against women demonstrates a lack of feminist knowledge about male violence against women— what it is, how it functions, and how to provide a feminist response to women who have been attacked by men. A lack of feminist knowledge or application of feminist knowledge in day-to-day interactions with women, many of whom are struggling due to the material conditions created by patriarchy, is deeply troubling due to the patriarchal lies we learn about male violence against women as default.

Male violence against women doesn't easily fit into neatly segmented and singular boxes. Instead, instances of male violence bleed—figuratively and literally—onto and into one another on a continuum of male violence against women (Kelly, 1988; Sheehy, 2014). This kind of feminist knowledge doesn't just happen one day, out of the blue; in fact, it's quite the opposite. In our patriarchal culture, feminist knowledge must be purposefully sought out and takes a great deal of practice and skill to implement in relation to ourselves and to other women. This is one of the reasons that it's especially concerning that bias isn't recognized among sex work researchers because our default bias, everywhere—when doing research, when working with women who have been attacked by men, when going about our everyday lives—is misogynist and woman-hating because, well, patriarchy. Feminist theory, practice, action, and organizing is always intentional. This is because we must first acknowledge and learn about our supposedly 'natural and inevitable' patriarchal culture, unlearn the lies this culture has taught us about ourselves, other women, and men, and relearn a woman-centred and feminist way of relating to ourselves, to each other, and to the world.

NZPC Interview

I met with two workers from the NZPC while in New Zealand: I was hosted at the Auckland centre and we were joined by Catherine Healy remotely from Wellington. I had many questions to ask the NZPC but focused my interview on what exiting services the NZPC offers to women in prostitution in New Zealand as they state on their website, as of September 25, 2021, that "NZPC runs community centres where you can drop in for: ... Support for people who want to change direction, either inside or outside of sex work" (New Zealand Prostitute's Collective, n.d., b). As Healy stated in the interview in regard to exiting prostitution:

> We certainly promote the idea that if people want to move on and be it in the context of sex work, move on to different circumstances that they're experiencing in the context of sex work or quit sex work completely, then we are there to support them. And we were just reflecting actually on our most recent contact with people. And it's not a frequent request I have to flag. And, you know, mostly people do say, oh, yeah, I stopped working three months ago and have had a long break and I'm coming back, etc ... it's our experience that a lot of people just worked and stopped. It's honestly not a request [help exiting] that comes along (2018).

During the interview, the NZPC discussed the supports they offer to help women leave the sex industry. These supports included: government representatives will come to the NZPC centre to receive women's applications for unemployment so they don't have to go to the government office; they help to build women's confidence as leaving prostitution will mean changes in their lives such as leaving their friends and changing their habits; help with resumes; assistance in finding women housing as some women live in brothels and once they leave prostitution, they have nowhere to live—Healy noted that sometimes 'clients' will take in homeless women who are trying to leave prostitution; peer support by workers at the NZPC; and a Māori flag as a recognition of Māori people and as a symbol of welcome.

Given the NZPC's lack of feminist knowledge about male violence against women, it's not surprising that the 'exiting supports' the NZPC offers are completely inadequate. This was also confirmed in informal conversations I had with women in or formerly in prostitution in New Zealand who had sought out help to exit and didn't receive the help they needed from the NZPC or from any other organization in New Zealand. With no other options, they continued in or returned to prostitution. Using a feminist analysis, we can start to see why the NZPC doesn't receive many requests from women to help exit prostitution: they don't have a feminist understanding of what male violence against women is, what it looks like, and how it functions and as a result, they don't have a feminist understanding of how to support women who have experienced male violence. Additionally, because the NZPC is absolutely convinced that sex work is work, women who have not experienced prostitution as sex work but as a form of male violence may be hesitant to seek support from the NZPC or may not receive the support they need to make the desired changes in their lives. This is again, partially why a feminist analysis is so important: to make the simple assumption that women don't request exiting help from the NZPC is because they don't need help exiting prostitution demonstrates a lack of understanding of male violence in women's lives and the ways that patriarchy shapes women's thinking and material conditions.

The Collusion of Queer Theory, Sex Work, and Transgender Politics

A third way that women with feminist anti-prostitution politics are silenced is through the academy's near-wholesale adoption of queer theory to examine sex work. Examining prostitution as a sexuality, or as gender resistance, or as a legitimate occupation for some people (i.e. women) and not others (i.e. men) is the dominant way that prostitution is analyzed in academia. With the exception of some individual feminist scholars, prostitution is not analyzed, or even thought about, as a form of male violence against women and within academia it's even considered 'violent' to do so.[37] Other politics, such as feminism that advocates for the abolition of gender, are also seen to be 'violent' and completely unacceptable to think, let alone say. While not universally true, most sex work advocates are also transgender advocates who use queer theory in their work; conversely, most feminist advocates who see prostitution as a form of male violence against women are also critical of gender or are gender abolitionists who use radical feminist theory in their work. The anti-woman and anti-feminist threads that run through transgender politics, queer theory, and sex work help us to see more clearly just how misogynist these theories and politics are and also help us to see how pro-woman and pro-feminist a radical feminist analysis that calls for the abolition of prostitution and gender is.

An example of the collusion of woman-hating transgender politics, queer theory, and sex work can be seen in the claims by some transgender and sex work advocates that a benefit of prostitution is that it helps to develop and/or affirm individual men's 'gender identity' as women (Nadal et al., 2012; Laidlaw, 2017; Youthline, n.d):

> Since others found that engagement in receptive anal intercourse is a gender affirming act ... it is possible that particular sexual acts themselves are gender affirming and that sex work is one means through which to consistently achieve this feeling. In this way, sex work may not only provide a financial advantage to trans women, but may also be emotionally beneficial (Laidlaw, 2017, p. 31).

This statement is beyond offensive to women by assuming that to 'be a woman' is to be sexually penetrated, against your will, by men and pretending to like it so you can get paid—this is, or should be, troubling in academic and policy discussions about transgender politics and sex work, but it isn't; instead, it's either ignored or accepted at face value without any concern for the broader implications of the concept of 'gender' in law and policy.

---

37   Please see Appendix A for examples of these types of accusations.

Transgender politics, queer theory, and the idea of 'sex work' are linked in theory and in practice and one of the things this does is allow for more ways to call for the silencing of feminist women. For example, feminists who seek to abolish the sex industry, in addition to being told to shut up because they hate/exclude/kill 'sex workers', can also be accused of 'transphobia' and subsequently, told to shut up. Again. Conversely, feminists who seek to abolish gender can, in addition to being told to shut up because they hate/exclude/kill men who identify as women, also be accused of 'whorephobia' and hatred of sex workers and subsequently, told to shut up. Again. Queer theory accuses feminists of focusing on women as if it's a bad thing, constructing feminists as 'exclusionary' and 'mean' for having a focus they should not have (according to queer theory) and subsequently, told to shut up. Again. For the third time, at least.

Conclusion: The Silencing of Indigenous Women

Sex work advocates use a variety of tactics to silence criticism and dissent of prostitution including working to silence criticism of the New Zealand Model of prostitution policy within and outside of the country; by rejecting and attempting to discredit feminist knowledge about male violence against women including how it functions and how it impacts women in patriarchy, and by confusing everyone and working to maintain the status quo by adopting anti-woman and anti-feminist queer theory in relation to the sex industry.

The NZPC rigorously defends a sex work position to the detriment of women's wellbeing and safety but are seen as authorities and objective parties when they are far from that. As Sabrinna Vallisce, a former member of the NZPC now feminist activist, stated to me in an interview:

> They're [New Zealand government] saying if you just sort of ignore the abusive parts [about prostitution], it's fine, it's working well. I mean that's not their wording, they obviously use very careful

language around this. But it really was just saying turn a blind eye and look at the good stuff and it's fine (Pers. Com., 2019).

As an Indigenous woman in Aotearoa said:

When did humanity decide that Indigenous Women and children were not worth fighting for ... entering the trade is not an informed choice, it is not an empowered choice therefore it is not a choice, *it is something we do because we think this is all we are worth, because we think this is the best we will do, because we already think it is normal* [emphasis mine].

This woman matters and what she has to say matters. While 'sex work' may be a non-issue to many in New Zealand, it most certainly is an issue to the Māori and other Indigenous women overrepresented in prostitution, to the women who have tried to leave prostitution so many times they've given up, and to the women who think men have no right to sex on demand, prostitution is an issue for us and it is a political issue that deserves rigorous examination, discussion, and debate.

CHAPTER 7

In Conclusion

I recall a meeting with my supervisor toward the end of my PhD journey and I was tired, was I ever tired. A PhD is a long-haul journey and I had hauled longer than I wanted to already. Life kept getting in the way, life from before, life from now, and it was a lot to deal with—too much, sometimes, if I'm being honest. I almost gave up on a few different occasions, but here I am, I came out the other side. My supervisor and I were talking about my race to the PhD finish line and I said something along the lines of "I need to sprint to the finish because I need to get this done before someone else dies"; meaning, before someone else is taken by overdose or goes missing or gets hurt; before another crisis stops me in my tracks. The next day, it was announced that a mass unmarked grave containing the bodies of 215 children were found at the site of the former Kamloops Indian Residential school (House, 2021). I'm not from Kamloops but I'm from that area and again I slowed to a crawl. This is what universities can do to 'decolonize'—they can recognize and accommodate for the impacts of colonization on Indigenous women students that result in crisis after crisis after crisis in their lives, in the lives of their loved ones, and in the lives of Indigenous peoples generally. Dreamcatcher workshops and beading circles, all well and good, are an easy answer and an insufficient one to support Indigenous scholars, as are all the well-meaning statements of solidarity. In the end, I suppose, dead children are easier to respond to than live ones.

Indigenous Feminism Redefined: Depoliticize This

> We identify the agents of our oppression as men. Male supremacy is the oldest, most basic form of domination. All other forms of exploitation and oppression (racism, capitalism, imperialism, etc.) are extensions of male supremacy: men dominate women, a few men dominate the rest. All power structures throughout history have been male-dominated and male-oriented. Men have controlled all political, economic and cultural institutions and backed up this control with physical force. They have used their power to keep women in an inferior position. All men receive economic, sexual, and psychological benefits from male supremacy. All men have oppressed women (Redstockings, 2000, p. 223; first published 1968).

> Feminism is an analysis of women's subordination *for the purpose of figuring out how to change it* [emphasis mine] (Gordon, 1979, p. 107).

Decolonizing feminism is a courageous, political, action-oriented women-centred theory and practice that is part of the historical and contemporary revolutionary work of the Women's Liberation Movement. Decolonizing feminism recognizes the hierarchies of race, class, and sexuality that divide women from each other as rooted in male domination and the importance of a holistic and inter-related analysis. Decolonizing feminism celebrates cultural differences but rejects the woman-hating idea of 'cultural relativism' and refuses any cultural practice that restricts, limits, or discriminates against women and girls because of their sex; all cultures and traditions are open for criticism and change. Decolonizing feminism always prioritizes the collective liberation of Indigenous and other women and names patriarchy as the central component of women's oppression.

Decolonizing Feminism

A. Woman-centred Theory

Women define who women are. We name ourselves and our realities as we see and experience them. We recognize the very real impacts patriarchy has on women's lives, including the colonization of our minds that results in false consciousness. As Mary Daly states:

> The exploitative sexual caste system could not be perpetuated without the consent of the victims as well as of the dominant sex, and such consent is obtained through sex role socialization—a conditioning process which begins to operate from the moment we are born, and which is enforced by most institutions. Parents, friends, teachers, textbook authors and illustrators, advertisers, those who control the mass media, toy and clothes manufacturers, professionals such as doctors and psychologists—all contribute to the socialization process. This happens through dynamics that are largely uncalculated and unconscious, yet which reinforce the assumptions, attitudes, stereotypes, customs, and arrangements of sexually hierarchical society (1985, p. 2).

This false consciousness can be undone with feminist thought and action. We construct feminist theory from our realities as we see and experience them and build on women's past feminist theorizing and action. Feminism is the only theory, practice, and movement that prioritizes women in a struggle for Women's Liberation. Feminists recognize that women's struggles aren't all the same, while also recognizing that women's differences don't negate our commonalities and that women's commonalities don't negate our differences. As Hill Collins explains:

> In the following passage, Ms. White assesses the difference between the controlling images applied to Afro-American and white women as being those of degree, and not of kind: 'My mother used to say that the black woman is the white man's mule and the white woman is his dog. Now, she said that to say this: we do the heavy work and get beat whether we do it well or not. But the white woman is closer to the master and he pats them on the head and lets them sleep in the house,

but he ain't gon' treat neither one like he was dealing with a person'
(qtd. in Hill Collins, 1985, p. 148).

As women, we recognize patriarchy as our primary oppression
while also recognizing we are oppressed by class, race, and sexuality.

B. Woman-centred Practice

It takes courage to put women-centred feminist theory into
practice. This is especially true among Indigenous and women of
colour, due to the pressure put upon us to prioritize race over sex.
Cultural relativism

> … asserts that the practice within a specific culture are unique to the
> values, systems, and practices within that culture. For the cultural
> relativist there are no universal standards and the morality and values
> of one national culture cannot be compared to that of any other.
> Cultural relativism dominates the social, political, and academic
> thought today and it serves as a justification for many inhuman
> social practices. If one questions the principles of cultural relativism,
> one is charged with ethnocentrism. Ethnocentrism assumes that the
> judgements made about another culture stem from the assumption of
> the superiority of one's own culture (Barry, 1979, pp. 162–163).

Examples of cultural relativism include, for example, the argument
that the hijab is empowering for Muslim women or that Indigenous
women are restricted in movement and behaviour during menstru-
ation because this is a seen as a powerful time for women in
Indigenous cultures. In each of these examples, women's freedom is
dictated and restricted by men.[38] As Barry states, "there is nothing
unique across cultures in the practices of the enslavement of women
except perhaps the diversity in the strategies men employ to carry
them out" (1979, p. 163). For Indigenous women, a reclamation and

---

38 (Mahmoudi, 2019); For earlier criticism of and action against the veiling
of women in Iran, see also work by Mohtaram Eskandari, Noor-ol-Hoda
Mangeneh, Mastoureh Afshar, and Jam'iyat-e Nesvan-e Vatankhah, (Patriotic
Women's League of Iran), Zandokht Shirazi and Majma'e Enghelabi e Nesvan (the
Revolutionary Society of Women), and Sediqeh Dowlatabadi and the publication
Zaban-e Zanan.

revitalization of traditional Indigenous cultures doesn't guarantee Women's Liberation as culture and women's rights are two separate things and can and do come into conflict with each other. Cultural relativism is not a pathway to women's liberation. For women, and particularly Indigenous women and women of colour, we endure immense amounts of pressure to stay silent about men's violence and men's discrimination in our own cultures. We are often punished for speaking out against male domination and female subordination in our own cultures and it takes great amounts of courage to do so: "... it is at this point a political action to tell it like it is, to say what I really believe about my life instead of what I've always been told to say" (Hanisch, 2000, p. 113). As feminists, we blame men when men are to blame.

C. Expressly Political

I am not speaking of all feminist agencies and positions, but the contradictions are in keeping with the fractures in feminism, where, for example, the Toronto Women's Bookstore carried pornography even while I witnessed other feminist groups march down Yonge Street, declaring that strip clubs exploited the women who worked in them. And, of course, they weren't talking about unfair labour practices, which would have been helpful. They were moralizing. Judging. Defining women's experiences for them and defining them as exploited but only in the guise of taking care of them—rescuing them (Doe, 2013, p. 185).

Firstly and contrary to Doe's analysis, disagreements within feminism are political and are not coming from a place of supposed moral superiority. Feminism is political and as such, there will be disagreements and differences:

The exercise of political freedom is difficult and demanding because it requires that we make judgments—hard, messy judgements. Claims about the relative value of different choices, claims about the justice or injustice of particular courses of action, are exercises in judgment. Without making judgments, politics becomes vacuous relativism: we have no reason to prefer one course of action over another. Yet making judgments is always potentially terrifying and demands a certain amount of courage because, when it comes to political matters, we have no objective set of standards for judging that could serve as a set of guidelines for us to follow. Political freedom requires that we make the best judgments that we can, without knowing for certain that the judgments we make are correct. Moreover, politics involves making our uncertain judgments public, submitting them to the scrutiny of others, and trying to persuade these others to share our views. However, there is no guarantee that when we share our judgments, other people will agree with them. Simply because I believe my judgment is the best does not mean that others will, too (Ferguson, 2010, p. 251).

Disagreements and differences actually work to strengthen the Women's Liberation Movement, not weaken it. However, feminism ceases to be feminism when it stops working toward Women's Liberation and when it stops prioritizing the needs and wellbeing of women as a sex class.

Secondly, feminists refuse to accept men's terms as the best and only terms. For example, we reject men's false separation and categorization of women as 'whores' or 'prudes'; 'squaws' or 'princesses' while recognizing that patriarchy has limited women's conceptualization of ourselves:

> In a sexist world, symbol systems and conceptual apparatuses have been male creations. These do not reflect the experience of women, but rather function to falsify our own self-image and experiences. Women have often resolved the problems this situation raises by simply not seeing the situation. That is, we have screened out experience and responded only to the questions considered meaningful and licit within the boundaries of prevailing thought structures, which reflect sexist social structures (Daly, 1985, p. 7).

We don't blame women for the ways that patriarchy has impacted them, but we assert our right to disagree politically with other women about the analyzes of ours and other women's experiences.

Third, save yer own damn selves. Feminists are not here to save anyone and the idea that we are is a purposeful misrepresentation of our political movement and political goals. Like many other women, I'm sure, I don't have the time, energy, or resources to change the material circumstances of a woman's life when she isn't also working to change the material circumstances of her life. I barely have enough time, energy, and resources to keep myself afloat somedays. This doesn't mean I don't care about other women, on the contrary, I very much care about other women but this does mean that everything isn't all about you, sex worker activist who refuses to be saved. Feminism is a political movement for Women's Liberation and this means that women, as individuals, can't get to the revolution by themselves. We need each other and feminists recognize that our struggles are tied together as women and that we share ideas, tools, strategies and resources in our shared struggle for women's collective liberation—do not mistake these politicized actions as charity.

D. Interconnected

> Women must learn to accept responsibility for fighting oppressions that may not directly affect us as individuals. Feminist movement, like other radical movements in our society, suffers when individual concerns and priorities are the only reason for participation. When we show our concern for the collective, we strengthen our solidarity (hooks, 1986, p. 137).

Dworkin also recognizes the importance of relationships and inter-connectivity in a criticism of lesbian feminist politics:

> I often feel that in a funny way, parts of the lesbian community are equally corrupt in that they are totally self-referential. Their idea of feminism has to do only with each other and not with women who are different from them and not with women who are in different situations than they are (1996, p. 212).

Patriarchy is everywhere. Patriarchy is normal. In order to construct and build on feminist theory, we need to recognize the many ways that male violence against women and other patriarchal practices are embedded in our lives—these woman-hating ideologies, traditions, and behaviour know no bounds. As a result, our feminist responses must be equally all encompassing in recognizing the interconnected ways out of patriarchy and toward Women's Liberation. Losing an overall feminist vision for liberation and revolution is a constant threat—it's easier, it's less radical, less dangerous to the patriarchy, less complicated, and men like you more. When we trade our larger feminist vision for single-issue politics—such as, for example, focusing only on a criticism of transgender politics or focusing only on the issue of men's 'free speech', we can end up working beside and with conservative, misogynist men who don't give a shit about women or about Women's Liberation and whose criticisms are fueled by homophobia or other forms of hatred. When we have a feminist vision for liberation, that becomes the goal and policy changes, social changes, and the like, are steps that we achieve on the way to that goal, not end points in themselves. This doesn't mean, however, that we need to try and take every issue on every single time as hooks states:

> Every woman can stand in political opposition to sexist, racist, heterosexist, and classist oppression. While she may choose to focus her work on a given political issue or a particular cause, if she is firmly opposed to all forms of group oppression, this broad perspective will be manifest in all her work irrespective of its particularity (hooks, 1986, p. 137).

Indigenous worldviews also emphasize the importance of inter-connectedness and relationship. When studying patriarchy in order to end it, we also need to identify and name its relations. As Russell states:

> There are no piecemeal solutions to rape, woman-battering, the murder of women by men, or the molestation of young girls by their fathers. All of these crimes against women are linked. They all involve the acting out of male power over, and often hatred, women (Russell, 1980, n.p.).

Feminism recognizes the importance of identifying patriarchy, how it interconnects with capitalism, racism, and processes of colonization, and how it works to keep women oppressed (Frye, 1983). Feminists as well recognize the importance of relationships between women and it's in these relationships that we're able to develop theory and action toward Women's Liberation.

And in The End

> If I had to name one quality as the genius of patriarchy, it would be compartmentalization, the capacity for institutionalizing disconnection ... The personal isolated from the political. Sex divorced from love. The material ruptured from the spiritual. The past parted from the present disjointed from the future. Law detached from justice, vision dissociated from reality (Morgan, 1989, p. 51).

There are many things we know and don't know about patriarchy. We don't know the exact origins of patriarchy, despite much theorizing, although like Lerner, I believe that the exact origins of patriarchy are "... far less significant than questions about the historical process by which patriarchy becomes established and institutionalized" (Lerner, 1986, p. 7). One of the things we do know is that patriarchy isn't natural or inevitable or biological, even though it pretends to be (Lerner, 1986). We also know how patriarchy works to separate and compartmentalize and disconnect (Morgan, 1989): patriarchy works to separate prostitution from murdered and disappeared Indigenous women and girls and separate murdered and disappeared Indigenous women and girls from male violence against all women and girls; it works to separate women from each other with bullshit woman-hating categories like 'sluts' vs 'prudes', 'squaws' vs 'princesses', 'good girls' vs 'bad girls', and pits Indigenous and non-Indigenous women against each other. These categories are so embedded in our culture that even in some feminist environments, women are separated from each other and classified as either 'survivors' or 'women', when, if talking about patriarchy, all women are both and all women live under the constant threat of male violence: she could easily be you and you could easily be her. We also know that patriarchy promotes single-issue research and analysis, even though our experiences as women and as Indigenous women are not at all 'single-issue'; rather, we experience our oppression as women as a birdcage with many connecting wires that work together to keep us trapped (Frye, 1983). We know that patriarchy works to separate the past from the present from the future by decontextualizing and ahistoricizing issues, like prostitution, that greatly impact women and we know that patriarchy works to normalize male violence against women and girls by trying to change and control the language women use to talk about ourselves and what matters to us—from battered women to battered spouse (Schechter, 1982), for example, or from woman in prostitution to 'sex worker', 'prostitution abolitionist' to 'prohibitionist', or even 'woman' to 'cis woman'—in each of these cases, women are erased, male violence against us is sanitized and normalized, and the language to describe ourselves and our realities are taken from us, confused, and colonized. We know that patriarchy works very hard to disconnect the individual from the collective and to privilege not only the needs, but the wants, of the individual who, surprise! happens to be male by default. We see this when someone says "but I have a friend and she likes doing sex work"[39] and because they know someone who likes something, that something must be good and they've just wholesale won the argument with their ridiculous point—guess what, rapists like raping too but that doesn't mean that rape is good. We also know that patriarchy is thriving in academia and continues to divorce action from theory through the lie of objective, neutral, 'evidence-based'[40] research. An area where patriarchy likes to

---

39 What is actually meant by this statement is "but I have a friend and she likes being penetrated orally, vaginally, maybe anally by the penises of multitudes of unknown men, sometimes at the same time, over and over and over again because she's just like that and likes performing sex acts with men she thinks are disgusting and does not desire sexually at all"—just FYI, friends don't tell woman-hating lies about friends.

40 Evidence-based research' is a term often used by sex work researchers in attempts to discredit feminist research on prostitution. It sounds good, but it's really just a new term for 'objective' research. So instead of doing 'objective' research, sex

smoosh things together is linking Indigenous cultures and women's rights together when in fact, these are two separate things. When we link Indigenous cultures and women's rights, it means that Indigenous and other feminists get stuck in the supposed 'sacredness' of Indigenous women and fear of being called 'racist' stops women from disagreeing and debating with Indigenous women on issues that impact and matter to women. It's the opposite trap of 'the squaw' where Indigenous women are seen as too stupid and too savage to disagree and debate with respectfully, so their ideas are either completely dismissed or go unchallenged and consequently, aren't given an opportunity to further develop. As LaRoque has stated:

> We have all experienced colonization, which is to say 'invasion', but we have not all experienced it in the same way or to the same degree. As an individual, I cannot entertain racist, sexist or ideological injunctions that I must be a carbon copy of other colonized persons and colleagues. It is imperative that we treat with respect other people's works upon which we build our 'dialogics', not to mention, our degrees; it is also important to maintain our right(s) to disagree. Writers owe much to each other, and I acknowledge my debt to all these writers I use, but I must also retain my right to debate and to question. My goal is not to settle for politically-correct or kitsch notions, as I have been pressured to do by both White and Native camps; my objective is to offer valuable criticism and my own thinking (1999, pp. 70–71).

There are many things we know and don't know about women's lives, Indigenous women's lives, cultures, traditions, feminism, feminist theory, and so on. One of the things we do know about feminism is that it is *always* woman-centred, *always* political, and *always* looks at the ways the world is interconnected and what this means for women. Feminism works in a holistic way to bring

---

work researchers do 'evidence-based research' where they pretend they have no bias and no agenda and so their pro-dick-sucking-for-other-women-research is correct while feminists have bias and an agenda so their anti-prostitution for all women research is worthless.

together, build bridges, and connect. We also know, that like any other social and political movement, feminism has particular theoretical and material foundations, goals, and strategies to achieve those goals. Like any other movement, feminism has a definition and boundaries. A redefinition of colonization as a hierarchical sex-based process allows for a woman-centred definition of decolonizing feminism that prioritizes women's sex-based oppression while also recognizing and challenging women's oppression based on class, race, and sexuality.

Appendix A

I wrote and published an article on *Medium* that I titled, 'Transwomen are Women. Or Else'. One of the main points of the article is that Indigenous women, pre-colonization, knew where babies came from. Many people, including many prominent Indigenous academics, activists, and others, seemed to be deeply upset about me and my article and accused me of transphobia (and other things) in the comments section of the *Medium* article and on Twitter. Some individuals who participated in this Twitter pile-on, by making comments, sharing, or liking vicious tweets about me (I have included a small sample in this appendix) were from my own university, including Métis/Saulteaux/Polish artist Dayna Danger and Inuk scholar Dr Heather Igloliorte. Other supastar names that participated include: Chippewa and Potawatomi artist, Chief Lady Bird; Métis scholar and podcaster, Molly Swain; Mniconjou Lakota and citizen of the Cheyenne River Sioux Tribe storyteller, Taté Walker; McMaster University Assistant Professor and Kanien'keha:ka scholar, Kaitlin Debicki; Ryerson Assistant Professor and Cree-Métis-Saulteaux writer, curator, and researcher, Jas M. Morgan; Associate Professor and Canada Research Chair of Indigenous Methodologies with Youth and Communities at the University of Toronto, Unangax̂ scholar, Eve Tuck; Managing editor for *Room* magazine and co-organizer of the Indigenous Brilliance reading series, Nehiyaw writer Jessica Johns; Aboriginal Outreach and Retention Coordinator at the Aboriginal Education

Centre at the University of Windsor, Kat Pasquach; Former City of Fredericton Poet Laureate and member of the editorial board of *The Fiddlehead*, Jenna Lynn Albert; Assistant Professor at Ryerson University in the School of Social Work and Tk̓emlúps te Secwepemc First Nation member, Jeffrey McNeil-Seymour; and so many other writers, editors, artists, scholars, podcasters, filmmakers, musicians, and so on.

Here is a very small sample of social media responses to me and my article, 'Transwomen are Women. Or Else':

DaynaDanger
@DaynaDanger

She's tried to join Missing Justice lol NOPE

I did tell Indigneous Directions of Concordia about her and how's she a swerf and terf and her views are literally killing our trans indigikin

Unfortunately the Ivory tower really protects this shit. Enough is enough!!

11:41 PM · 2020-07-19 · Twitter for iPhone

4 Likes

Yakogay ✿ @PastelNerd23 · 1d ﹀
Replying to @_cherrysmiley_

You're right, you are the wrong kind of
ndn. You're a colonized TERF. You're an
insult to the community. How dare you
hide behind traditions as a reason to
spread hateful lies about trans kin.

💬 1   🔁   ♡ 10   ⬆️

 ◁Ṵ‖ᵈᐠ 🏳️‍🌈 🔥 🍵 awas simâkanis · 1d ﹀
cw: swerf bullshit

wow so i googled **ch*rry sm*ley** & found
an article where she doesn't apologize
for saying prostitution should be
abolished, b/c it's a form of male
violence. her PhD studies are based on
this. what a mess.

💬 1   🔁   ♡ 5   ⬆️

 Angelina Rose @Angelinarrose · 16h ﹀
Replying to @_cherrysmiley_

this is the most disgusting, transphobic
thing i've read in a long time, and coming
from an Interior Salish woman? you ought
to be ashamed of yourself. not to
mention that it's almost
incomprehensible. I'm very unimpressed
@Medium published this

💬 1   🔁   ♡ 8   ⬆️

Appendix B

The following chart was compiled by Hilla Kerner on behalf of the collective of Vancouver Rape Relief and Women's Shelter. The chart shows publicly available statistics from the RCMP and police forces across Canada (via Statistics Canada) between the years of 2015–2018 that demonstrate charges laid in response to the current prostitution legislation (Protection of Communities and Exploited Persons Act, PCEPA):

2015–2018	BC	Alberta	Sask	Man.
Obtaining sexual services for consideration	5	659	367	383
Obtaining sexual services for consideration from person under 18 years	13	14	9	4
Receive material benefit from sexual services	1	20	0	3
Receive material benefit from sexual services provided by a person under 18 years	1	2	1	2
Procuring 1731+3120	13	44+9	3	4
Procuring – person under 18 years	7	8	0	2
Advertising sexual services	0	1	0	0
Trafficking in persons (NOT only sex trafficking)	15	47	5	22
Bawdy house	0	0	0	0
Living off the avails of prostitution of a person under age 18	1	0	0	0
Obtains or communicates with a person under age 18 for purpose of sex	0	1	0	0
Communicating to provide sexual services for consideration	0	49	20	1
Stopping or impeding traffic for the purpose of offering, providing or obtaining sexual services for consideration	8 All in Van.	1	1	2

Ont.	Que.	N.B.	N.S.	P.E.I	NFLND & Lab.	Yukon	NWT	Nunavut
193	99	42	16	1	2	0	0	0
24	18	0	1	1	0	0	0	2
7	3	0	0	0	0	0	0	0
20	16	0	0	0	0	0	0	0
82+1	50+2	0+1	5	0	0	0	1	0
32	51	0	6	0	0	0	0	0
9	0	1	0	0	0	0	0	0
406	113	2	18	0	0	0	5	0
0	2	0	27	0	0	0	0	0
1	0	0	0	0	0	0	0	0
0	0	0	0	0	0	0	0	0
10	12	0	0	0	0	0	0	0
20	3	0	1	0	0	0	0	0

References

Abel, Gillian. (2011). Different stage, different performance: The protective strategy of role play on emotional health in sex work. *Social Science and Medicine*, 72(7), 1177–1184. <https://doi.org/10.1016/j.socscimed.2011.01.021>.

Abel, Gillian. (2019). The problem with sex work policies. *Archives of Sexual Behavior: The Official Publication of the International Academy of Sex Research*, 48(7), 1925–1929. <https://doi.org/10.1007/s10508-018-1366-5>.

Acoose, Janice. (1995). *Iskwewak kah'ki yaw ni wahkomakanak: Neither Indian Princesses Nor Easy Squaws*. Toronto: Women's Press.

ajik. (2022, January 4). 31st annual women's memorial march. *Feb 14th Annual Women's Memorial March: Their Spirits Live Within Us*. <https://womensmemorialmarch.wordpress.com/>.

Altamirano-Jiménez, Isabel. (2012). Indigeneity and transnational routes and roads in North America. In J. Castro-Rea. (Ed.). *Our North America: Social and Political Issues Beyond NAFTA* (pp. 35–48). London: Ashgate Publishing Ltd.

Anderson, Kim. (2000). *A Recognition of Being: Reconstructing Native Womanhood*. Toronto: Second Story Press.

Anderson, Kim. (2011). Affirmations of an Indigenous feminist. In C. Suzack, S. M. Huhndorf, J. Perreault and J. Barman. (Eds.). *Indigenous Women and Feminism: Politics, Activism, Culture* (pp. 81–91). Vancouver: UBC Press.

Anderson, Kim. (2016). *A Recognition of Being: Reconstructing Native Womanhood* (2nd Ed.). Toronto: Women's Press.

Anderson, Kim, and Dawn Memee Lavell-Harvard. (Eds.). (2014). *Mothers of the Nations: Indigenous Mothering as Global Resistance, Reclaiming and Recovery*. Toronto: Demeter Press.

Anderson, Kim, Maria Campbell, and Christi Belcourt. (Eds.). (2018). *Keetsahnak: Our Missing and Murdered Indigenous Sisters*. Edmonton: University of Alberta Press.

Armstrong, Jeannette. (1996). Invocation: The real power of Aboriginal women. In Christine Miller and Patricia Chuchryk. (Eds.). *Women of the First Nations: Power, Wisdom, and Strength* (pp. x–xii). Winnipeg: University of Manitoba Press.

Armstrong, Louise. (1990). Making an issue of incest. In Dorchen Leidholdt and Janice Raymond. (Eds.). *The Sexual Liberals and the Attack on Feminism* (pp. 43–55). Oxford: Pergamon Press.

Armstrong, Lynzi. (2014). Screening clients in a decriminalised street-based sex industry: Insights into the experiences of New Zealand sex workers. *Australian and New Zealand Journal of Criminology*, 47(2), 207–222.

Armstrong, Lynzi. (2020). Decriminalisation of sex work in the post-truth era? Strategic storytelling in neo-abolitionist accounts of the New Zealand model. *Criminology* and *Criminal Justice*, 21(3), 369–386.

Arvin, Maile, Eve Tuck and Angie Morrill. (2013). Decolonizing feminism: Challenging connections between settler colonialism and heteropatriarchy. *Feminist Formations*, 25(1), 8–34.

Atkinson, Judy. (1990). Violence against Aboriginal women: Reconstitution of customary law—the way forward. *Aboriginal Law Bulletin*, 2(46), 6–9.

Backhouse, Constance. (1985). Nineteenth-century Canadian prostitution law reflection of a discriminatory society. *Histoire Sociale-Social History*, 18(36), 387–423.

Barry, Kathleen. (1979). *Female Sexual Slavery*. New York: New York University Press.

Barry, Kathleen. (1995). *The Prostitution of Sexuality*. New York: New York University Press.

Bart, Pauline. (1996). The banned professor: Or how radical feminism saved me from men trapped in men's bodies and female impersonators, with a little help from my friends. In Diane Bell and Renate Klein. (Eds.). *Radically Speaking: Feminism Reclaimed* (pp. 262–274). North Melbourne: Spinifex Press.

Bastarache, Michel. (2020). *Broken Dreams Broken Lives: The Devastating Effects of Sexual Harassment on Women in the RCMP*. Final Report on the Implementation of the Merlo-Davidson Settlement Agreement.

<https://www.rcmp-grc.gc.ca/wam/media/4773/original/8032a32ad5dd
014db5b135ce3753934d.pdf>.

Bear, Shirley. (2007). Culturing politics and politicizing culture. In Joyce
Green. (Ed.). *Making Space for Indigenous Feminism* (pp. 199–215). Black
Point, Halifax: Fernwood Publishing.

Belcourt, Billy-Ray and Lindsay Nixon. (2018, May 23). What do we mean by
queer Indigenous ethics? *Canadian Art*. Black Point Nova Scotia. <https://
canadianart.ca/features/what-do-we-mean-by-queerindigenousethics/>.

Belich, James. (1996). *Making Peoples: A History of the New Zealanders, from
Polynesian Settlement to the End of the Nineteenth Century*. Auckland:
Penguin Random House New Zealand Limited.

Bell, Diane. (1983). *Daughters of the Dreaming*. Melbourne: McPhee Gribble;
Sydney: Allen & Unwin.

Bell, Diane. (1985). Topsy Nelson: Teacher, philosopher and friend. In Diane
Barwick, Isobel White and Betty Meehan. (Eds.). *Fighters and Singers*
(pp. 1–18). Sydney: Allen & Unwin.

Bell, Diane and Pam Ditton. (1980). *Law: The Old and the New, Aboriginal
Women in Central Australia Speak Out*. Canberra: Aboriginal History for
the Central Australian Aboriginal Legal Aid Service.

Bell, Diane and Topsy Napurrula Nelson. (1989). Speaking about rape is
everyone's business. *Womens Studies International Forum*, 12, 403–416.

Bell, Diane and Renate Klein. (1996). Beware: Radical feminists speak, read,
write, organise, enjoy life, and never forget. In Diane Bell and Renate
Klein. (Eds.). *Radically Speaking: Feminism Reclaimed* (pp. xvii–xxx).
North Melbourne: Spinifex Press.

Bell, Roberta and Rick McConnell. (2016, July 27). Edmonton kids sold as
sex workers, as teen prostitution becomes more common. *CBC News*.
<http://www.cbc.ca/news/canada/edmonton/edmonton-kids-sold-as-sex-
workers-as-teen-prostitution-becomes-more-common-1.3698129>.

Bellrichard, Chantelle. (2020, December 9). AFN resolution calling for
probe into gender-based discrimination sparks heated debate. *CBC News*.
<https://www.cbc.ca/news/indigenous/afn-gender-discrimination-probe-
resolution-1.5835295>.

Benedet, Janine. (2013). Marital rape, polygamy, and prostitution: Trading
sex equality for agency and choice? *Review of Constitutional Studies/Revue
d'etudes constitutionnelles*, 18(2), 161–188.

Benedet, Janine. (2018, May 10). Professor Janine Benedet (Professor of
Law, Peter A. Allard School of Law, University of British Columbia, as an
Individual) at the Justice and Human Rights Committee. Open Parliament,

Government of Canada. <https://openparliament.ca/committees/justice/42-1/97/professor-janine-benedet-1/only/>.

Benoit, Cecilia, Renay Maurice, Gillian Abel, Michaela Smith, Mikael Jansson, Priscilla Healey, and Douglas Magnuson. (2020). 'I dodged the stigma bullet': Canadian sex workers' situated responses to occupational stigma. *Culture, Health* and *Sexuality*, 22(1), 81–95. <https://doi.org/10.1080/13691058.2019.1576226>.

Bindel, Julie. (2017, October 11). Why prostitution should never be legalized. *The Guardian*. <https://www.theguardian.com/commentisfree/2017/oct/11/prostitution-legalised-sex-trade-pimps-women>.

Bindel, Julie. (2019/2017). *The Pimping of Prostitution: Abolishing the Sex Work Myth*. London: Palgrave Macmillan; Mission Beach: Spinifex Press.

Blaney, Fay. (1996). Backing out of hell. In Brenda Lea Brown. (Ed.). *Bringing It Home: Women Talk about Feminism in Their Lives* (pp. 19–33). Vancouver: Arsenal Pulp Press.

Bolger, Audrey. (1990). *Aboriginal Women and Violence: A Report for the Criminology Research Council and the Northern Territory Commissioner of Police*. Darwin: ANU North Australia Research Unit.

Bourgeois, Robyn. (2018a). Generations of genocide: The historical and sociological context of missing and murdered Indigenous women and girls. In Kim Anderson, Maria Campbell and Christi Belcourt. (Eds.). *Keetsahnak/Our Missing and Murdered Indigenous Sisters* (pp. 65–88). Edmonton: University of Alberta Press.

Bourgeois, Robyn. (2018b). Race, space, and prostitution: The making of settler colonial Canada. *Canadian Journal of Women and the Law*, 30(3), 371–397.

Bowles, Gloria and Renate Klein. (Eds.). (1983). *Theories of Women's Studies*. London: Routledge & Kegan Paul.

Brennan, Shannon. (2011). *Violent Victimization of Aboriginal Women in the Canadian Provinces, 2009*. Statistics Canada. <http://www.statcan.gc.ca/pub/85-002-x/2011001/article/11439-eng.pdf>.

British Columbia Representative for Children and Youth. (2016). *Too Many Victims: Sexualized Violence in the Lives of Children and Youth in Care*. <https://www.rcybc.ca/sites/default/files/documents/pdf/reports_publications/rcy_toomanyvictimsfinal.pdf>.

Brodsky, Gwen. (2016). Indian act sex discrimination: Enough inquiry already, just fix it. *Canadian Journal of Women and the Law*, 28(2), 314–320.

Brownmiller, Susan. (1973). Speaking out on prostitution. In Anne Koedt, Ellen Levine, and Anita Rapone. (Eds.). *Radical Feminism* (pp. 72–77). New York: Quadrangle/New York Times Book Co.

Brunton, Cheryl, Lisa Fitzgerald, Catherine Healy and Gillian Abel. (Eds.). (2010). *Taking the Crime Out of Sex Work: New Zealand Sex Workers' Fight for Decriminalisation*. Bristol: Policy Press.

Burns, Madeline. (2020). Reclaiming Indigenous sexual being: Sovereignty and decolonization through sexuality. *The Arbutus Review*, 11(1), 28-38.

Butler, Judith. (2006). *Gender Trouble: Feminism and the Subversion of Identity* (Ser. Routledge classics). New York: Routledge.

Canadian Femicide Observatory for Justice and Accountability. (2018). *106 Women and Girls Killed by Violence: Eight-Month Report by the Canadian Femicide Observatory for Justice and Accountability*. Canadian Femicide Observatory. <https://femicideincanada.ca/sites/default/files/2018-09/CFOJA%20FINAL%20REPORT%20ENG%20V3.pdf>.

Carleton, Sean. (2021). 'I don't need any more education': Senator Lynn Beyak, residential school denialism, and attacks on truth and reconciliation in Canada. *Settler Colonial Studies*. DOI: 10.1080/2201473X.2021.1935574.

Carlson, Kathryn Blaze. (2015, May 15). More than a tragic headline: Cindy Gladue dreamt of a happy life. *The Globe and Mail.* <https://beta.theglobeandmail.com/news/national/the-death-and-life-of-cindy-gladue/article24455472/>.

Carter, Sarah. (1997). *Capturing Women: The Manipulation of Cultural Imagery in Canada's Prairie West*. Montréal: McGill-Queen's University Press.

Carter, Vednita and Evelina Giobbe. (1999). Duet: Prostitution, racism and feminist discourse. *Hastings Women's Law Journal,* 10(1), 37–57.

CBC News. (2010, October 14). 'Micro-brothels' used to hold child sex workers. *CBC News.* <https://www.cbc.ca/news/canada/manitoba/micro-brothels-used-to-hold-child-sex-workers-1.879994>.

CBC News. (2018, March 8). 'We need to do something': Stepping Stone seeks to help youth in sex trade. *CBC News.* <https://www.cbc.ca/news/canada/nova-scotia/we-need-to-do-something-stepping-stone-seeks-to-help-youth-in-sex-trade-1.4567707>.

Clarke, Annette and Ravida Din and National Film Board of Canada (Montréal). (2013). *Buying Sex.* National Film Board of Canada.

Cler-Cunningham, Leonard and Christine Christensen. (2001). *Violence against Women in Vancouver's Street Level Sex Trade and the Police*

Response. Vancouver: PACE Society. <http://www.pace-society.org/library/sex-trade-and-police-response.pdf>.

Cole, Anna M. (2000). *The Glorified Flower: Race, Gender and Assimilation in Australia 1937–1977.* A thesis submitted for the degree of Doctorate of Philosophy, University of Technology, Sydney.

Comack, Elizabeth. (2018). Corporate colonialism and the "crimes of the powerful" committed against the Indigenous peoples of Canada. *Critical Criminology,* 26(1), 455–471.

Conseil du statut de la femme. (2002). *La Prostitution: Profession ou Exploitation? Une Réflexion à Poursuivre.* <https://www.csf.gouv.qc.ca/wp-content/uploads/resume-etude-la-prostitution-profession-ou-exploitation.pdf>.

Coy, Maddy, Josephine Wakeling and Maria Garner. (2011). Selling sex sells: Representations of prostitution and the sex industry in sexualised popular culture as symbolic violence. *Women's Studies International Forum,* 34(5), 441–448. <https://doi.org/10.1016/j.wsif.2011.05.008>.

Coy, Maddy, Cherry Smiley and Meagan Tyler. (2019). Challenging the "prostitution problem": Dissenting voices, sex buyers, and the myth of neutrality in prostitution research. *Archives of Sexual Behavior: The Official Publication of the International Academy of Sex Research,* 48(7), 1931–1935. <https://doi.org/10.1007/s10508-018-1381-6>.

Crenshaw, Kimberlé. (1991). Mapping the margins: intersectionality, identity politics, and violence against women of color. *Stanford Law Review,* 43(6), 1241–1299.

Crago, Anna-Louise, Chris Bruckert, Melissa Braschel and Kate Shannon. (2021). Sex workers' access to police assistance in safety emergencies and means of escape from situations of violence and confinement under an "end demand" criminalization model: A five city study in Canada. *Social Sciences,* 10(1), 1–13. <https://doi.org/10.3390/socsci10010013>.

Daly, Mary. (1985). *Beyond God the Father: Toward a Philosophy of Women's Liberation.* Boston: Beacon Press.

Davis, Megan. (2017). Deploying and disputing Aboriginal feminism in Australia. In Joyce Green. (Ed.). *Making Space for Indigenous Feminism* (2nd Ed., pp. 146–165). Halifax: Fernwood Publishing.

de Beauvoir, Simone. (2011). *The Second Sex* (Constance Borde and Sheila Malovany-Chevallier, Trans.). New York: Vintage.

De Leeuw, Sarah. (2016). Tender grounds: Intimate visceral violence and British Columbia's colonial geographies. *Political Geography,* 52, 14–23.

Doe, Jane. (2013). Are feminists leaving women behind? The casting of sexually assaulted and sex-working women. In Emily van der Meulen, Elya M. Durisin and Victoria Love. (Eds.). *Selling Sex: Experience, Advocacy, and Research on Sex Work in Canada* (pp. 181–197). Vancouver: University of British Columbia Press.

Donne, Thomas Edward. (1927). *The Māori—Past and Present*. London: Seeley Service & Co. Limited.

Driskill, Qwo-Li. (Ed.). (2011). *Queer Indigenous Studies: Critical Interventions in Theory, Politics, and Literature*. Tucson: University of Arizona Press.

Du Plessis, Rosemary and Phillida Bunkle. (1993). *Feminist Voices: Women's Studies Texts for Aotearoa/New Zealand*. Auckland: Oxford University Press.

Dworkin, Andrea. (1974). *Woman Hating*. New York: Penguin Books.

Dworkin, Andrea. (1993). Prostitution and male supremacy. *Michigan Journal of Gender and Law*, 1(1), 1–12.

Dworkin, Andrea. (1996). Dworkin on Dworkin. In Diane Bell and Renate Klein. (Eds.). *Radically Speaking: Feminism Reclaimed* (pp. 203–217). North Melbourne: Spinifex Press.

Dworkin, Andrea. (1997). Women in the public domain: sexual harassment and date rape. In A. Dworkin. (Ed.). *Life and Death: Unapologetic Writings on the Continuing War against Women* (pp. 196–216). New York: Free Press.

Eberts, Mary. (2017). Being an Indigenous woman is a "high-risk lifestyle." In Joyce Green. (Ed.). *Making Space for Indigenous Feminism* (2nd Ed., pp. 69–93). Halifax: Fernwood Publishing.

EPCAT Child Alert. (2018). *Sexual Exploitation of Children in New Zealand*. <https://uprdoc.ohchr.org/uprweb/downloadfile.aspx?filename= 5966&file=EnglishTranslation>.

EPCAT. (n.d.). *Stop Sex Trafficking of Children and Young People*. <https:// www.ecpat.org/wp-content/uploads/2016/04/Factsheet_New%20Zealand. pdf>.

Farley, Melissa. (2006). Prostitution, trafficking, and cultural amnesia: What we must not know in order to keep the business of sexual exploitation running smoothly. *Yale Journal of Law and Feminism*, 18, 109–144.

Farley, Melissa. (2009). Theory versus reality: Commentary on four articles about trafficking for prostitution. *Women's Studies International Forum*, 32(4), 311–315. <https://doi.org/10.1016/j.wsif.2009.07.001>.

Farley, Melissa, Ann Cotton, Jacqueline Lynne, Sybille Zumbeck, Frida Spiwak, Maria E. Reyes, Dinorah Alvarez and Ufuk Sezgin. (2003).

Prostitution and trafficking in nine countries: An update on violence and posttraumatic stress disorder. *Journal of Trauma Practice*, 2(3/4), 33–74.

Farley, Melissa, Ann Cotton, Jacqueline Lynne, Sybille Zumbeck, Frida Spiwak, Maria E. Reyes, Dinorah Alvarez, and Ufuk Sezgin. (2004). Prostitution and trafficking in nine countries. *Journal of Trauma Practice*, 2(3–4), 33–74. <https://doi.org/10.1300/J189v02n03_03>.

Farley, Melissa, Jacqueline Lynne and Ann J. Cotton. (2005). Prostitution in Vancouver: Violence and the colonization of First Nations women. *Transcultural Psychiatry*, 42(2), 242–271.

Farley, Melissa, Julie Bindel and Jacqueline M. Golding. (2009). *Men Who Buy Sex: Who They Buy and What They Know*. Eaves and Prostitution Research Action. <https://documentation.lastradainternational.org/lsidocs/Mensex. pdf>.

Feith, Jesse. (2016, June 8). Montréal Grand Prix: Local teens recruited to work in sex trade, experts say. *Montréal Gazette*. <http://montrealgazette. com/news/montreal-grand-prix-local-teens-recruited-to-work-in-sex-trade-experts-say>.

Ferguson, Michaele L. (2010). Choice feminism and the fear of politics. *Symposium: Women's Choices and the Future of Feminism*, 8(1), 247–253.

Frye, Marilyn. (1983). *The Politics of Reality: Essays in Feminist Theory*. Freedom, CA: Crossing Press.

Gauthier, Jennifer L. (2010). Dismantling the master's house: The feminist fourth cinema documentaries of Alanis Obomsawin and Loretta Todd. *Post Script*, 29(3), 27–43.

Gordon, Linda. (1979). The struggle for reproductive freedom: Three stages of feminism. In Zillah R. Eisenstein. (Ed.). *Capitalist Patriarchy and the Case for Socialist Feminism* (pp. 107–136). New York: New York Monthly Review Press.

Gorkoff, Kelly and Jane Runner. (2003). Introduction: Children and youth exploited through prostitution. In Kelly Gorkoff and Jane Runner. (Eds.). *Being Heard: The Experiences of Young Women in Prostitution* (pp. 12–27). Black Point, Halifax: Fernwood Publishing.

Graca, Marta, Manuela Goncalves and Antonio Martins. (2018). Action research with street-based sex workers and an outreach team: A co-authored case study. *Action Research*, 16(3), 251–279. <https://doi.org/10.1177/ 1476750316685877>.

Graham, Erin. (2014). More than condoms and sandwiches: A feminist investigation of the contradictory promises of harm reduction approaches to prostitution [Unpublished doctoral dissertation]. Vancouver: University of British Columbia.

Green, Rayna. (1975). The Pocahontas perplex: The image of Indian women in American culture. *The Massachusetts Review,* 16(4), 698–714.

Green, Joyce. (Ed.). (2007). *Making Space for Indigenous Feminism.* Black Point, Halifax: Fernwood Publishing.

Green, Joyce. (Ed.). (2017). *Making Space for Indigenous Feminism* (2nd Ed.). Halifax: Fernwood Publishing.

Greer, Germaine. (2008). *On Rage.* Carlton: Melbourne University Press.

Grey, Sam. (2004). Decolonising feminism: Aboriginal women and the global 'sisterhood'. *Enweyin* 8, 9–22.

Hanisch, Carol. (2000). The personal is political. In Barbara A. Crow. (Ed.). *Radical Feminism: A Documentary Reader* (pp. 113–116). New York: New York University Press.

Hawthorne, Susan. (1994). A History of the Contemporary Women's Movement (pp. 92–97). In Susan Hawthorne and Renate Klein. (Eds.). *Australia for Women: Travel and Culture.* Melbourne: Spinifex Press.

Healy, Catherine, Ahi Wi-Hongi and Chanel Hati. (2017). It's work, it's working: The integration of sex workers and sex work in Aotearoa/New Zealand. *Women's Studies Journal,* 31(2), 50–60.

Hargreaves, Allison. (2017). *Violence against Indigenous Women: Literature, Activism, Resistance.* Waterloo, Ontario: Wilfrid Laurier University Press.

Henne, Kurt and David Moseley. (2005). Child sex workers. *Human Rights,* 32(1), 14–21.

Hill Collins, Patricia. (1985). Learning from the outsider within: The sociological significance of black feminist thought. *Social Problems,* 33(6), S14–S32.

Hill Collins, Patricia. (1990). *Black Feminist Thought: Knowledge, Consciousness, and the Politics of Empowerment.* New York: Routledge.

hooks, bell. (1986). Sisterhood: political solidarity between women. *Feminist Review,* 23(1), 125–138. <https://doi.org/10.1057/fr.1986.25>.

House, Tina. (2016, February 22). Families outraged over serial killer Pickton's memoir. *APTN National News.* <https://www.aptnnews.ca/national-news/families-outraged-over-serial-killer-picktons-memoir/>.

House, Tina. (2021, May 31). 'It was horrid': Survivor tells APTN News about loss and fear at Kamloops residential school. *APTN National News.* <https://www.aptnnews.ca/national-news/it-was-horrid-survivor-tells-aptn-news-about-loss-and-fear-at-kamloops-residential-school/>.

Howe, Adrian. (2009). Addressing child sexual assault in Australian Aboriginal communities—The politics of white voice. *Australian Feminist Law Journal*, 30(1), 41–61.

Huggins, Jackie. (1998). *Sister Girl: The Writings of Aboriginal Activist and Historian Jackie Huggins*. St Lucia: University of Queensland Press.

Huggins, Jackie, Jo Willmot, Isabel Tarrago, Kathy Willetts, Liz Bond, Liz, Lillian Holt, Eleanor Bourke, Maryann Bin-Salik, Pat Fowell, Joann Schmider, Valerie Craigie and Linda Mcbride-Levi. (1991). Letter to the editor. *Women's Studies International Forum*, 14(5), 506–507.

Huhndorf, Shari M. and Cheryl Suzack. (2011). Indigenous feminism: Theorizing the issues. In Cheryl Suzack, Shari M. Huhndorf, Jeanne Perreault and Jean Barman. (Eds.). *Indigenous Women and Feminism: Politics, Activism, Culture* (pp. 1–20). Vancouver: University of British Columbia Press.

Hunt, Sarah and Cindy Holmes. (2015). Everyday decolonization: Living a decolonizing queer politics. *Journal of Lesbian Studies*, 19(2), 154–72. <https://doi.org/10.1080/10894160.2015.970975>.

Hunter, Rosemary. (1996). Deconstructing the subjects of feminism: The essentialism debate in feminist theory and practice. *Australian Feminist Law Journal*, 6, 135–163.

Huntley, Audrey. (2015). Details. *10th Annual Strawberry Ceremony for Missing and Murdered Indigenous Women and Girls*. <https://www.facebook.com/events/703866506400035/?active_tab=discussion>.

Huncar, Andrea. (2016a, March 4). Edmonton-area First Nation chief charged with sexual assault. *CBC News*. Retrieved from <http://www.cbc.ca/news/canada/edmonton/edmonton-area-first-nation-chief-charged-with-sexual-assault-1.3476757>.

Huncar, Andrea. (2016b, September 14). Election results quashed at Alexander First Nation reserve. *CBC News*. Retrieved from <http://www.cbc.ca/news/canada/edmonton/alexander-first-nation-reserve-election-1.4288977>.

Hunt, Sarah. (2013). Decolonizing sex work: Developing an intersectional Indigenous approach. In Emily van der Meulen, Elya M. Durisin and Victoria Love. (Eds.). *Selling Sex: Experience, Advocacy, and Research on Sex Work in Canada* (pp. 82–100). Vancouver: University of British Columbia Press.

Innes, Robert Alexander. (2015). Moose on the loose: Indigenous men, violence, and the colonial excuse. *Aboriginal Policy Studies*, 4(1), 46–56.

Iseke, Judy M. (2011). Indigenous digital storytelling in video: Witnessing with Alma Desjarlais. *Equity and Excellence in Education,* 44(3), 311–329. <https://doi.org/10.1080/10665684.2011.591685>.

It's called garbage can, not garbage cannot [Digital image]. (2018). <https://www.reddit.com/r/PacificCrestTrail/comments/a2si6s/its_called_garbage_can_not_garbage_cannot/>.

Jagger, Alison. (2004). Feminist politics and epistemology: The standpoint of women. In Sandra Harding. (Ed.). *The Feminist Standpoint Theory Reader: Intellectual and Political Controversies* (pp. 55–66). Abingdon: Routledge.

Jeffreys, Sheila. (1997). *The Idea of Prostitution.* North Melbourne: Spinifex Press.

Jeffreys, Sheila. (2003). The legalization of prostitution: A failed social experiment. <https://www.antiprostitutie.ro/docs/Legalisation.of.Prostitution.a.failed.social.experiment.pdf>.

Jeffreys, Sheila. (2003). *Unpacking Queer Politics: A Lesbian Feminist Perspective.* Cambridge: Polity Press.

Jeffreys, Sheila. (2014). *Gender Hurts: A Feminist Analysis of the Politics of Transgenderism.* London: Routledge.

Jiwani, Yasmin and Mary Lynn Young. (2006). Missing and murdered women: Reproducing marginality in news discourse. *Canadian Journal of Communications Special Issue on Sexuality,* 31(4), 895–917.

Jones, Adam. (2015). For a gender-inclusive inquiry into murdered and missing Aboriginal Canadians. *Change.org.* <https://www.change.org/p/first-nations-and-government-of-canada-for-a-gender-inclusive-inquiry-into-murdered-and-missing-aboriginal-canadians>.

Justice Canada. (2016). Gender identity and gender expression. <https://www.canada.ca/en/department-justice/news/2016/05/gender-identity-and-gender-expression.html>.

Kaye, Julie. (2017). *Responding to Human Trafficking: Dispossession, Colonial Violence, and Resistance among Indigenous and Racialized Women.* Toronto: University of Toronto Press.

KAIROS Canada. (n.d.). *Timeline.* KAIROS Canada. <https://www.kairoscanada.org/missing-murdered-indigenous-women-girls/inquiry-timeline>.

Kingsley, Cherry and Marian Krawczyk. (2000). *Sacred Lives: Canadian Aboriginal Children and Youth Speak Out about Sexual Exploitation.* Vancouver B.C.: Save the Children Canada.

Klein, Renate. (1983). How to do what we want to do: Thoughts about feminist methodology. In Gloria Bowles and Renate Duelli Klein. (Eds.). *Theories of Women's Studies.* London: Routledge & Kegan Paul.

Knickerbocker, Madeline Rose. (2020). Making matriarchs at Coqualeetza: Sto:lo women's politics and histories across generations. In Sarah Nickel and Amanda Fehr. (Eds.). In *Good Relation: History, Gender, and Kinship in Indigenous Feminisms* (pp. 25–47). Winnipeg: University of Manitoba Press.

Koshan, Jennifer. (2010). *The Legal Treatment of Marital Rape and Women's Equality: An Analysis of the Canadian Experience.* The Equality Effect. <http://theequalityeffect.org/pdfs/maritalrapecanadexperience.pdf>.

Kovach, Margaret. (2010). *Indigenous Methodologies: Characteristics, Conversations, and Contexts.* Toronto: University of Toronto Press.

Krüsi, Andrea, Jill Chettiar, Amelia Ridgway, Janice Abbott, Steffanie A. Strathdee and Kate Shannon. (2012). Negotiating safety and sexual risk reduction with clients in unsanctioned safer indoor sex work environments: a qualitative study. *American Journal of Public Health,* 102(6), 1154–1159.

Kubik, Wendee and Carrie Bourassa. (2016). Stolen sisters: The politics, policies, and travesty of missing and murdered women in Canada. In Dawn Memee Lavell-Harvard and Jennifer Brant. (Eds.). *Forever Loved: Exposing the Hidden Crisis of Missing and Murdered Indigenous Women and Girls in Canada* (pp. 17–33). Toronto: Demeter Press.

Kuokkanen, Rauna. (2015). Gendered violence and politics in indigenous communities. *International Feminist Journal of Politics,* 17(2), 271–288.

Laidlaw, Leon. (2017). 'Playing two people': Exploring Trans Women's Experiences in Sex Work. [Unpublished doctoral dissertation]. Ottawa: University of Ottawa.

Lajimodiere, Denise K. (2013). American indian females and stereotypes: warriors, leaders, healers, feminists; not drudges, princesses, prostitutes. *Multicultural Perspectives,* 15(2), 104–109. <https://doi.org/10.1080/1521 0960.2013.781391>.

Lakeman, Lee. (2005). *Obsession, with Intent: Violence Against Women.* Montréal: Black Rose Books.

Lavell-Harvard, Dawn Memee, and Jennifer Brant. (Eds.). (2016). *Forever Loved: Exposing the Hidden Crisis of Missing and Murdered Indigenous Women and Girls in Canada.* Toronto: Demeter Press.

LaRocque, Emma. (1994). *Violence in Aboriginal Communities*. Health Canada. <https://publications.gc.ca/collections/Collection/H72-21-100-1994E.pdf>.

LaRocque, Emma. (1999). Native writers resisting colonizing practices in Canadian historiography and literature [Unpublished doctoral dissertation]. Winnipeg: University of Manitoba.

LaRocque, Emma. (2017). Métis and feminist: Contemplations on feminism, human rights, culture and decolonization. In Joyce Green. (Ed.). *Making Space for Indigenous Feminism* (2nd Ed., pp. 122–145). Halifax: Fernwood Publishing.

Leigh, Carol. (1997). Inventing sex work. In Jill Nagle. (Ed.). *Whores and Other Feminists* (pp. 223–231). London: Routledge.

Lederer, Laura. (Ed.). (1982). *Take Back the Night: Women on Pornography*. New York: Bantam.

Lerner, Gerda. (1986). *The Creation of Patriarchy*. Oxford: Oxford University Press.

Lewis, Jacqueline, Eleanor Maticka-Tyndale, Frances Shaver and Heather Schramm. (2005). Managing risk and safety on the job: The experiences of Canadian sex workers. *Journal of Psychology* and *Human Sexuality*, 17(1/2), 147–167.

Lorde, Audre. (1984). The master's tools will never dismantle the master's house. In Audre Lorde. (Ed.). *Sister Outsider: Essays and Speeches* (pp. 110–114). Freedom, CA: Crossing Press.

Lorde, Audre. (2019). *Sister Outsider*. London: Penguin Classics.

Lyons, Gracie. (1988). *Constructive Criticism: A Handbook*. Berkeley, CA: Wingbow Press.

Mahmoudi, Hoda. (2019). Freedom and the Iranian women's movement. *Contexts*, 18(3), 14–19. <https://doi.org/10.1177/1536504219864953>.

Malone, Kelly. (2017, September 21). Wab Kinew allegations turning into 'witch hunt,' Senator Murray Sinclar says. *CBC News*. Retrieved from <http://www.cbc.ca/news/canada/manitoba/murray-sinclair-wab-kinew-1.4300130>.

Maracle, Lee. (1996). *I Am Woman: A Native Perspective on Sociology and Feminism*. Vancouver: Press Gang Publishers.

Martin, Carol Muree and Harsha Walia. (2019). *Red Women Rising: Indigenous Women Survivors in Vancouver's Downtown Eastside*. Downtown Eastside Women's Centre. <https://dewc.ca/wp-content/uploads/2019/03/MMIW-Report-Final-March-10-WEB.pdf>.

Marwaha, Seema. (2017, January 29). 'Anyone can be a victim': Canadian high school girls being lured into sex trade. *CBC News*. <https://www.cbc.ca/news/canada/toronto/human-sex-trafficking-domestic-1.3956214>.

Maryuama, Hiroshi. (Ed.). (2022). *Decolonizing Futures: Collaborations for New Indigenous Horizons*. Uppsala: Hugo Valentin Centre.

Mathieson, Ane, Easton Branam and Anya Noble. (2016). Prostitution policy: Legalization, decriminalization and the Nordic model. *Seattle Journal for Social Justice*, 14(2), 367–428.

Mawani, Renisa. (2002). "The iniquitous practice of women": Prostitution and the making of white spaces in British Columbia, 1898–1905. In Cynthia Levine-Rasky. (Ed.). *Working Through Whiteness: International Perspectives* (pp. 43–68). Albany: State University of New York Press.

Maxwell, Krista. (2014). Historicizing historical trauma theory: Troubling the trans-generational transmission paradigm. *Transcultural Psychiatry*, 51(3), 407–435.

McClintock, Anne. (1992). Screwing the system: Sexwork, race, and the law. *Boundary 2*, 19(2), 70–95.

McIntyre, Sheila, Christine Lesley Boyle, Lee Lakeman and Elizabeth Sheehy. (2000). Tracking and resisting backlash against equality gains in sexual offence law. *Canadian Woman Studies*, 20, 72–84.

McIvor, Sharon Donna. (2004). Aboriginal women unmasked: Using equality litigation to advance women's rights. *Canadian Journal of Women* and *the Law*, 16(1), 106–136.

McIvor, Sharon Donna and Teresa Nahanee. (1998). Aboriginal women: Invisible victims of violence. In Kevin Bonnycastle and George S. Rigakos. (Eds.). *Unsettling Truths: Battered Women, Policy, Politics, and Contemporary Research in Canada* (pp. 63–69). Vancouver: Collective Press.

Mies, Maria. (1983). Toward a methodology for feminist research. In Gloria Bowles and Renate Klein. (Eds.). *Theories of Women's Studies*. London: Routledge & Kegan Paul.

Mies, Maria, Veronika Bennholdt-Thomsen and Claudia von Werlhof. (1988). *Women: The Last Colony*. London: Zed Books.

Mikaere, Annie. (1994). Māori women: Caught in the contradictions of a colonised reality. *Waikato Law Review, 2*. <https://www.waikato.ac.nz/law/research/waikato_law_review/pubs/volume_2_1994/7>.

Miriam, Kathy. (2005). Stopping the traffic in women: Power, agency and abolition in feminist debates over sex-trafficking. *Journal of Social Philosophy*, 36(1), 1–17.

Missing Justice. (2016). Annual Montréal Memorial March to Honour the Lives of Missing and Murdered Women/Marche commemorative annuel en hommage aux femmes disparue. <https://www.facebook.com/events/m%C3%A9tro-st-laurent-st-laurent-and-de-maisonneuve/annual-montreal-memorial-march-to-honour-the-lives-of-missing-and-murdered-women/923717884350650/>.

Monture-Angus, Patricia. (1999). Considering colonialism and oppression: Aboriginal women, justice and the "theory" of decolonization. *Native Studies Review,* 12(1), 63–94. <http://iportal.usask.ca/docs/Native_studies_review/v12/issue1/pp63-94.pdf>.

Moreton-Robinson, Aileen. (2003). Tiddas talkin' up to the white woman: When Huggins et al. took on Bell. In Michele Grossman. (Ed.). *Blacklines: Contemporary Critical Writing by Indigenous Australians.* Carlton: Melbourne University Press.

Morgan, Robin. (1970). Introduction: The woman's revolution. In Robin Morgan. (Ed.). *Sisterhood is Powerful: An Anthology of Writings from the Women's Liberation Movement* (pp. xiii-xl). New York: Random House.

Morgan, Robin. (1977). *Going Too Far: The Personal Chronicle of a Feminist.* New York: Random House.

Morgan, Robin. (1989). *The Demon Lover.* New York: W. W. Norton.

Morgan, Robin. (2000). On women as a colonized people. In Barbara A. Crow. (Ed.). *Radical Feminism: A Documentary Reader* (pp. 471–472). New York: New York University Press.

Nadal, Kevin, Vivian H. Vargas, Vanessa Meterko, Sahran Hamit and Kathryn Mclean. (2012). Transgender female sex workers in New York city: Personal perspectives, gender identity development, and psychological processes. In Michele Antoinette Paludi. (Ed.). *Managing Diversity in Today's Workplace: Strategies for Employees and Employers, Volume 1: Gender, Race, Sexual Orientation, Ethnicity, and Power* (pp. 123–153). Santa Barbara: Praeger.

Nagle, Jill. (1997). Introduction. In Jill Nagle. (Ed.). *Whores and Other Feminists* (pp. 1–18). London: Routledge.

Naples, Nancy. A. (2003). *Feminism and Method: Ethnography, Discourse Analysis, and Activist Research.* London: Routledge.

Nash, Catherine Jean. (2011). Trans experiences in lesbian and queer space. *Canadian Geographer/Le Géographe Canadien,* 55(2).

National Inquiry into Missing and Murdered Indigenous Women and Girls. (2017). *Our Women and Girls are Sacred: Interim Report of the National Inquiry into Missing and Murdered Indigenous Women and*

Girls. The National Inquiry. <https://www.mmiwg-ffada.ca/wp-content/uploads/2018/03/ni-mmiwg-interim-report.pdf>.

National Inquiry into Missing and Murdered Indigenous Women and Girls. (2018a). *The Mandate of the National Inquiry.* Our mandate, our mission, our vision. <https://www.mmiwg-ffada.ca/mandate/>.

National Inquiry into Missing and Murdered Indigenous Women and Girls. (2018b). *Lexicon of Terminology.* The National Inquiry. <http://www.mmiwg-ffada.ca/wp-content/uploads/2018/05/lexicon-of-terminology.pdf>.

National Inquiry into Missing and Murdered Indigenous Women and Girls. (2019). *Lexicon of Terminology.* The National Inquiry. <https://www.mmiwg-ffada.ca/wp-content/uploads/2019/06/MMIWG_Lexicon_FINAL_ENFR.pdf>.

National Inquiry into Missing and Murdered Indigenous Women and Girls. (2019a). *Reclaiming Power and Place: The Final Report of the National Inquiry into Missing and Murdered Indigenous Women and Girls, Volume 1a.* The National Inquiry. <https://www.mmiwg-ffada.ca/wp-content/uploads/2019/06/Final_Report_Vol_1a-1.pdf>.

National Inquiry into Missing and Murdered Indigenous Women and Girls. (2019b). *Reclaiming Power and Place: The Final Report of the National Inquiry into Missing and Murdered Indigenous Women and Girls, Volume 1b.* The National Inquiry. <https://www.mmiwg-ffada.ca/wp-content/uploads/2019/06/Final_Report_Vol_1b.pdf>.

Nelson, Topsy Napurrula. (1991). Letter to the Editor. *Women's Studies International Forum,* 14 (5), 507.

Newshub. (2017, September 13). Prostitute's collective questions report on child sex trafficking in NZ. *Newshub.* <https://www.newshub.co.nz/home/new-zealand/2017/09/prostitutes-collective-questions-report-on-child-sex-trafficking-in-nz.html>.

New Zealand Prostitutes' Collective (n.d., a). *History.* Aotearoa New Zealand Sex Workers' Collective. <https://www.nzpc.org.nz/History>.

New Zealand Prostitutes' Collective (n.d., b). *NZPC | Aotearoa New Zealand Sex Workers' Collective.* Aotearoa New Zealand Sex Workers' Collective. <https://www.nzpc.org.nz/About-NZPC>.'

Nickel, Sarah A. (2017). 'I am not a women's libber although sometimes I sound like one': Indigenous feminism and politicized motherhood. *American Indian Quarterly,* 41(4), 299–335.

Nickel, Sarah and Amanda Fehr. (Eds.). (2020). In *Good Relation: History, Gender, and Kinship in Indigenous Feminisms.* Winnipeg: University of Manitoba Press.

Norma, Caroline, and Melinda Tankard Reist. (2016). (Eds.). *Prostitution Narratives: Stories of Survival in the Sex Trade.* North Melbourne: Spinifex Press.

Nussbaum, Martha. (1998). 'Whether from reason or prejudice': Taking money for bodily services. *Journal of Legal Studies,* 27(2), 693–723.

Oppal, Wally. (2012). *Forsaken: The Report of the Missing Women Commission of Inquiry, Executive Summary.* <https://missingwomen.library.uvic.ca/wp-content/uploads/2010/10/Forsaken-ES-web-RGB.pdf>.

Orchard, Treena, Katherine Salter, Mary Bunch and Cecilia Benoit. (2021). Money, agency, and self-care among cisgender and trans people in sex work. *Social Sciences,* 10(6). <https://doi.org/10.3390/socsci10010006>.

Ortner, Sherry B. (1972). Is female to male as nature is to culture? *Feminist Studies,* 1(2), 5–31.

Ouellette, Grace Josephine Mildred Wuttunee. (2002). *The Fourth World: An Indigenous Perspective on Feminism and Aboriginal Women's Activism.* (Basics from Fernwood Publishing). Halifax: Fernwood Publishing.

Palmater, Pamela. (2016). Shining light on the dark places: Addressing police racism and sexualized violence against Indigenous women and girls in the National Inquiry. *Canadian Journal of Women and the Law,* 28(2), 253–284.

Pateman, Carole. (1988). *The Sexual Contract.* Redwood City, CA: Stanford University Press.

Pateman, Carole. (1999). What's wrong with prostitution? *Women's Studies Quarterly,* 27(1–2), 53–64.

Payne, Sharon. (1990). Aboriginal women and the criminal justice system. *Aboriginal Law Bulletin,* 2(46), 9–11.

R. v. Anwar and Harvey. (2018). *Evidence of Ms. Smiley.* Ontario Court.

Raymond, Janice G. (2013). *Not a Choice, Not a Job: Exposing the Myths about Prostitution and the Global Sex Trade.* North Melbourne: Spinifex Press.

Raymond, Janice G. (2018). Gatekeeping decriminalization of prostitution: The ubiquitous influence of the New Zealand Prostitutes' Collective. *Dignity,* 3(2), DOI: 10.23860/dignity.2018.03.02.06.

Razack, Sherene. (2015). *Dying from Improvement: Inquests and Inquiries into Indigenous Deaths in Custody.* Toronto: University of Toronto Press.

Razack, Sherene. (2016). Gendering disposability. *Canadian Journal of Women and the Law,* 28(2), 285–307. <https://doi.org/10.3138/cjwl.28.2.285>.

Redstockings Collective (2000). Redstockings manifesto. In Barbara A. Crow. (Ed.). *Radical Feminism: A Documentary Reader.* New York: New York University Press.

Rich, Adrienne. (1980). Compulsory heterosexuality and lesbian existence. *Signs,* 5(4), 631–660.

Rowland, Robyn. (1991). Correspondence, Anthropological Forum, 6:3, 429–435. DOI: 10.1080/00664677.1991.9967422.

Rowland, Robyn and Renate Klein. (1996). Radical feminism: History, politics, action. In Diane Bell and Renate Klein. (Eds.). *Radically Speaking: Feminism Reclaimed* (pp. 9–36). North Melbourne: Spinifex Press.

Royal Canadian Mounted Police. (2014). *Missing and Murdered Aboriginal Women: A National Operational Overview.* <https://www.rcmp-grc.gc.ca/wam/media/460/original/0cbd8968a049aa0b44d343e76b4a9478.pdf>.

Royal Canadian Mounted Police. (2015). *Missing and Murdered Aboriginal Women: 2015 Update to the National Operational Overview.* <https://www.rcmp-grc.gc.ca/wam/media/455/original/c3561a284cfbb9c244bef57750941439.pdf>.

Royal Commission on Aboriginal Peoples. (1993). *The Path to Healing: Report of the National Round Table on Aboriginal Health and Social Issues.* Royal Commission on Aboriginal Peoples.

Royal Commission on Aboriginal Peoples. (1996). *Report of the Royal Commission on Aboriginal Peoples.* Royal Commission on Aboriginal Peoples. <https://data2.archives.ca/e/e448/e011188230-01.pdf>.

Rubenson, Birgitta, Le Thi Hanh, Bengt Höjer and Eva Johansson. (2005). Young sex-workers in Ho Chi Minh City telling their life stories. *Childhood,* 12(3), 391–411.

Rubin, Gayle. (2012). *Deviations: A Gayle Rubin Reader.* Durham, North Carolina: Duke University Press.

Russell, Diana. E. H. and Nicole van de Ven. (1976). *The Proceedings of the International Tribunal on Crimes Against Women.* Brussels: Les Femmes Publishing.

Russell, Diana E. H. (1980). A feminist perspective on pornography. <https://www.dianarussell.com>.

Russell, Diana. E. H. and Jill Radford. (1992). *Femicide: The Politics of Woman Killing.* New York: Twayne.

Russell, Diana E. H. and Roberta A. Harmes. (2001). *Femicide in Global Perspective* (Athene Series). New York: Teachers College Press.

Russell, Diana E. H. (2012). *Defining Femicide*. <https://www.femicidein canada.ca/sites/default/files/2017-12/RUSSELL%20%282012%29%20 DEFINING%20FEMICIDE.pdf>.

Russell, Jennie and Wallis Snowdon. (2021, February 20). Bradley Barton found guilty of manslaughter in death of Cindy Gladue. *CBC News*. <https://www.cbc.ca/news/canada/edmonton/bradley-barton-guilty-1.5921392>.

Saphira, Miriam and Pam Oliver. (2002). A review of literature on child prostitution. *Social Policy Journal of New Zealand Te Puna Whakaaro* (19). <https://www.msd.govt.nz/about-msd-and-our-work/publications-resources/journals-and-magazines/social-policy-journal/spj19/review-literature-child-prostitution19-pages141-163.html>.

Schechter, Susan. (1982). *Women and Male Violence: The Visions and Struggles of the Battered Women's Movement*. Boston: South End Press.

Schwarzerbach, Sibyl. (2006). Contractarians and feminists debate prostitution. In Jessica Spector. (Ed.). *Prostitution and Pornography: Philosophical Debates about the Sex Industry* (pp. 209–239). Redwood City, CA: Stanford University Press.

Sheehy, Elizabeth A. (2014). *Defending Battered Women on Trial: Lessons from the Transcripts* (Law and society series). Vancouver: University of British Columbia Press.

Shum, David. (2016, July 5). Girl, 16, threatened with knives, pellet gun to work in sex trade: Toronto police. *Global News*. <http://globalnews.ca/news/2803681/girl-16-threatened-with-knives-pellet-gun-to-work-in-sex-trade-toronto-police/>.

Shoji, Masahiro and Kenmei Tsubota. (2021). Sexual exploitation of trafficked children: Survey evidence from child sex workers in Bangladesh. *Journal of Comparative Economics*. <https://doi.org/10.1016/j.jce.2021.06.001>.

Silman, Janet. (1987). *Enough Is Enough: Aboriginal Women Speak Out*. Toronto: Women's Press.

Simpson, Audra. (2016). The state is a man: Theresa Spence, Loretta Saunders and the gender of settler sovereignty. *Theory* and *Event*, 19(4), 1.

Simpson, Leanne Betasamosake. (2017). *As We Have Always Done: Indigenous Freedom through Radical Resistance*. Minneapolis: University of Minnesota Press.

Sinha, Maire. (2013). Measure violence against women: Statistical trends. *Statistics Canada*. <https://www150.statcan.gc.ca/n1/pub/85-002-x/2013001/article/11766-eng.pdf>.

Smiley, Cherry. (2023). Madonnas, Whores, Squaws, and Other Lies about Indigenous Women in Canada. *Womynifesto: Decolonizing Feminist Essays.* Forthcoming.

Smith, Barbara. (1982). Racism and women's studies. In Akasha (Gloria T.) Hull, Patricia Bell Scott, and Barbara Smith. *All the Women Are White, All the Blacks Are Men, but Some of Us Are Brave: Black Women's Studies.* New York: Feminist Press.

Smith, Linda Tuhiwai. (2012). *Decolonizing Methodologies: Research and Indigenous Peoples.* London: Zed Books.

Smith, Molly and Juno Mac. (2018). *Revolting Prostitutes: The Fight for Sex Workers' Rights.* London: Verso.

Spender, Dale. (1980). *Man Made Language.* London: Pandora Press.

Starblanket, Gina. (2018). Complex accountabilities: deconstructing "the community" and engaging indigenous feminist research methods. *American Indian Culture and Research Journal,* 42(4), 1–20. <https://doi.org/10.17953/aicrj.42.4.starblanket>.

Stark, Christine and Carol Hodgson. (2003). Sister oppressions: A comparison of wife battering and prostitution. In Melissa Farley. (Ed.). *Prostitution, Trafficking, and Traumatic Stress* (pp. 17–32). Binghamton, New York: The Haworth Maltreatment & Trauma Press.

Statistics Canada. (2021). *A Statistical Portrait of Canada's Diverse LGBTQ2+ Communities.* Statistics Canada. <https://www150.statcan.gc.ca/n1/daily-quotidien/210615/dq210615a-eng.htm>.

Stoler, Ann L. (1989). Making empire respectable: the politics of race and sexual morality in 20th-century colonial cultures. *American Ethnologist,* 16(4), 634–660.

Stote, Karen. (2015). *An Act of Genocide: Colonialism and the Sterilization of Aboriginal Women.* Black Point, Halifax: Fernwood Publishing.

Stringer, Rebecca. (2012). Impractical reconciliation: Reading the intervention through the Huggins-Bell debate. *Australia Feminist Studies,* 27(71), 19–36.

Suzack, Cheryl, Shari M. Huhndorf, Jeanne Perreault and Jean Barman (Eds.). *Indigenous Women and Feminism. Politics, Activism, Culture.* Vancouver: University of British Columbia Press.

TallBear, Kim. (2014). Standing with and speaking as faith: A feminist-indigenous approach to inquiry [Research note]. *Journal of Research Practice,* 10(2), Article N17. Retrieved from <http://jrp.icaap.org/index.php/jrp/article/view/405/371>.

Tankard Reist, Melinda. (2022). *"He Chose Porn over Me": Women Harmed by Men Who Use Porn*. Mission Beach: Spinifex Press.

Thorburn, Natalie and Irene de Haan. (2014). Children and survival sex: A social work agenda. *Aotearoa New Zealand Social Work*, 26(4), 14–21.

Thorburn, Natalie. (2016a). Consent, coercion and autonomy: Underage sex work in Aotearoa New Zealand. *Aotearoa New Zealand Social Work*, 28(1), 34–42. <https://doi.org/10.11157/anzswj-vol28iss1id114>.

Thorburn, Natalie. (2016b). Surviving shame: Adolescent sex workers' experiences of accessing and avoiding helping services. *New Zealand Journal of Counselling*, 35(2), 14–26.

Thorburn, Natalie. (2017). Practitioner knowledge and responsiveness to victims of sex trafficking in Aotearoa/New Zealand. *Women's Studies Journal*, 31(2), 77–96.

Thorburn, Natalie. (2018). You Can't See It if You're Not Looking: Sex Trafficking in Aotearoa New Zealand [Unpublished doctoral dissertation]. University of Auckland.

Thorburn, Natalie. (2019). Researching underage sex work: Dynamic risk, responding sensitively, and protecting participants and researchers. In Pranee Liamputtong. (Ed.). *Handbook of Research Methods in Health Social Sciences* (pp. 2111–2126). Singapore: Springer.

Todd, Douglas. (2017, February 9). Douglas Todd: Inquiry into missing Indigenous women garbles issue of men and boys (Update). *Vancouver Sun*. <https://vancouversun.com/opinion/columnists/missing-indigenous-womens-inquiry-adds-men-and-boys>.

Toronto Sun. (2017, August 30). Xeni Gwet'in First Nation Chief Roger William charged with sexual offence involving minor in B.C. *Toronto Sun*. Retrieved from <http://www.torontosun.com/2017/08/30/xeni-gwetin-first-nation-chief-roger-william-charged-with-sexual-offence-involving-minor-in-bc>.

Truth and Reconciliation Commission. (2015). *Truth and Reconciliation Commission: Calls to Action*. Truth and Reconciliation Commission of Canada. <https://publications.gc.ca/collections/collection_2015/trc/IR4-8-2015-eng.pdf>.

Tunney, Catharine. (2020, November 18). RCMP tolerates 'misogynistic, racist, and homophobic attitudes': former Supreme Court justice. *CBC News*. <https://www.cbc.ca/news/politics/rcmp-merlo-davidson-final-report-1.5807022>.

US State Department. (2019). *Trafficking in Persons Report.* <https://www.state.gov/wp-content/uploads/2019/06/2019-Trafficking-in-Persons-Report.pdf>.

US State Department. (2021). 2021 Trafficking in Persons Report: New Zealand. <https://www.state.gov/reports/2021-trafficking-in-persons-report/new-zealand/>.

Valaskakis, Gail. (2005). Sacajawea and her sisters: Images and native women. In Gail Guthrie Valaskakis. (Ed.). *Indian Country: Essays on Contemporary Native Culture* (pp. 125–150). Waterloo, Ontario: Wilfred Laurier University Press.

van der Meulen, Emily, Elya M. Durisin and Victoria Love. (2013). Introduction. In Emily van der Meulen, Elya M. Durisin and Victoria Love. (Eds.). *Selling Sex: Experience, Advocacy, and Research on Sex Work in Canada* (pp. 1–25). Vancouver: University of British Columbia Press.

Vowel, Chelsea. (2016). *Indigenous Writes: A Guide to First Nations, Métis and Inuit Issues in Canada* (The debwe series). Somerville, Massachusetts: HighWater Press.

Walking With Our Sisters Collective. (2017). The Project. *Walking With Our Sisters.* <http://walkingwithoursisters.ca/about/the-project/>

Ware, Cellestine. (2000). The relationship of black women to the women's liberation movement. In Barbara A. Crow. (Ed.). *Radical Feminism: A Documentary Reader* (pp. 98–112). New York: New York University Press.

Waters, Kristin. (1996). (Re)turning to the modern: Radical feminism and the post-modern turn. In Diane Bell and Renate Klein. (Eds.). *Radically Speaking: Feminism Reclaimed* (pp. 280–296). North Melbourne: Spinifex Press.

Weitzer, Ronald. (2005). Flawed theory and method in studies of prostitution. *Violence Against Women,* 11(7), 934–49.

Whisnant, Rebecca and Christine Stark. (2004). *Not for Sale: Feminists Resisting Prostitution and Pornography.* North Melbourne: Spinifex Press.

Whisnant, Rebecca. (2015). Not your father's Playboy, not your mother's feminist movement: Feminism in porn culture. In Miranda Kiraly and Meagan Tyler. (Eds.). *Freedom Fallacy: The Limits of Liberal Feminism* (pp. 3–16). Brisbane: Connor Court Publishing.

Wheeler, Marika. (2016, October 11). Former Atikamekw police chief gets 6 years for sexual assault. *CBC News.* Retrieved from <http://www.cbc.ca/news/canada/montreal/atikamekw-wemotaci-jean-paul-néashish-sentenced-1.3800495>.

Wilton, Caren and Madeleine Slavick. (2018). *My Body, My Business: New Zealand Sex Workers in an Era of Change*. Dunedin: Otago University Press.

Women's Studies Online. (n.d.) *Women's Studies Online*. <https://www.wmstonline.com>.

Yee, Jessica. (Ed.). (2011). *Feminism for Real: Deconstructing the Academic Industrial Complex of Feminism*. (Our Schools/Our Selves book series, 4th v). Ottawa: Canadian Centre for Policy Alternatives.

Youthline. (n.d.) *Running to America in High Heeled Shoes; Youth Sex Workers in South Auckland: Telling Their Stories*. <https://www.youthline.co.nz/uploads/2/9/8/1/29818351/running-to-america-in-high-heeled-shoes.pdf>.

Zaman. (2020, December 9). Abstracts for chapters of new book *Decolonizing Futures*. Centre for Environment and Minority Policy Studies (CEMiPoS). <https://cemipos.org/book-abstracts/>.

Other books by Spinifex Press

Trauma Trails, Recreating Song Lines: The Transgenerational Effects of Trauma in Indigenous Australia
Judy Atkinson

Shortlisted, Australian Educational Award
Trauma Trails moves beyond the rhetoric of victimhood, and provides inspiration for anyone concerned about Indigenous and non-Indigenous communities today. Beginning with issues of colonial dispossession, Judy Atkinson deals sensitively with trauma caused by abuse, alcoholism and drug dependency; she points towards change and healing through didirri: listening, telling stories and sharing.

I recommend this complex, well-composed and emotionally satisfying book …
—Craig San Roque, *Aboriginal History*

ISBN: 9781876756222

Prostitution Narratives: Stories of Survival in the Sex Trade
Caroline Norma and Melinda Tankard Reist (Eds.)

For too long the global sex industry and its vested interests have dominated the prostitution debate repeating the same old line that sex work is just like any job. In large sections of the media, academia, public policy, Government and the law, the sex industry has had its way. Little is said of the damage, violation, suffering, and torment of prostitution on the body and the mind, nor of the deaths, suicides and murders that are routine in the sex industry.

Prostitution Narratives refutes the lies and debunks the myths spread by the industry through the lived experiences of women who have survived prostitution.

How precious the voices of women! Those trying to end male violence against women are confirmed by this truth-telling.
—Lee Lakeman, feminist activist, front line anti-violence worker at the Vancouver Rape Relief and Women's Shelter, Canada

ISBN: 9781742199863

Body Shell Girl: A Memoir
Rose Hunter

Body Shell Girl is a memoir in verse about the first two years of a decade that Rose Hunter spent in the sex industry in Canada. When Rose walked into a massage parlour in Toronto in 1997, she was looking for a temporary fix to pay rent and avoid having to go back to her home country of Australia.

Naively believing she could do only what was required of her, without trauma or side effects and leave the industry on her own terms, she was shattered by what unfolded.

Shimmering, relentless and candid. You didn't expect to find yourself here and neither did she; the author takes you deftly through hell with an unexpected tenderness.
  —Simone Watson, from Latji Latji Country in Victoria,
    Director, Nordic Model Australia Coalition (NorMAC)

ISBN: 9781925950502

Vortex: The Crisis of Patriarchy
Susan Hawthorne

In this enlightening yet devastating book, Susan Hawthorne writes with clarity and incisiveness on how patriarchy is wreaking destruction on the planet and on communities. The twin mantras of globalisation and growth expounded by the neoliberalism that has hijacked the planet are revealed in all their shabby deception. So too, the appropriation and commodification of women's bodies and of land rendering them homeless in their own bodies and on their own land.

This is the book that we have been waiting for!
  —Alison Laurie, academic and long time New Zealand feminist
    and lesbian activist

ISBN: 9781925950168

If you would like to know more about
Spinifex Press, write to us for a free catalogue, visit our
website or email us for further information
on how to subscribe to our monthly newsletter.

Spinifex Press
PO Box 105
Mission Beach QLD 4852
Australia

www.spinifexpress.com.au
women@spinifexpress.com.au